Stepped Out
of the
Womb

A memoir of a journey to the land where the sun falls

To My Friend at
Messenger Public Library

11/29/2011

Stepped Out of the

Womb

of the

A memoir of a journey to the land where the sun falls

THAVISOUK PHRASAVATH

*Academy Award and Film Independent Spirit Award Nominee.
2010 Creative Arts Primetime EMMY Award Winning Filmmaker;
Member of WGAW (Writers Guild of America West)*

LAO CENTURY
MEDIA

DEDICATED TO

Those who are refugees, immigrants and asylum seekers.

My mother, father, brothers and sisters
My wife Moukdavone V. Phrasavath and
my most precious daughter Ahmeeta O. Phrasavath

CONTENTS

Acknowledgments

This book was written to honor my parent, grandparents and great-grandparents. They are my life's heroes and the core of my inspiration that helped me overcome all of the obstacles and hardships in my life. I am very fortunate to be able to inherit their most precious and insightful knowledge, wisdom and philosophy of life, the world and the universe. I have become who I am today, as a human, and as an artist, because of them. I owe a debt of gratitude to all of them. I hope that their thousand years of knowledge, wisdom and philosophy, with some of my own personal life experiences, will be a small token that will contribute to better humanity and the human conditions. Hopefully, there will be someone, somewhere out there who will find my words provoking for their own inspiration and will not be afraid to open their heart and share their heritage and philosophy with others.

I cannot conclude this acknowledgment without expressing most of my gratitude to my beloved mother, Orady Phrasavath, and my father, Santi Phrasavath, and the love of my life, Moukdavone V. Phrasavath. I also express gratitude to my most precious daughter, Ahmeeta O. Phrasavath, and all of my beloved brothers and sisters who are always there for me through thick and thin, through happiness and misery, through my failures and my glorious times. Also, thank you from the bottom of my heart to all my friends from around the country and around the world—you know who you are.

Also, I would like to extend my special thanks to all of my English as a Second Language Program teachers at Martin Luther King Jr. High School.
They were the root and foundation of my English language. Thank you.

About the Author

Thavisouk Phrasavath is an Academy Award (Oscar) and Film Independent Spirit Award nominated filmmaker. As well as being one of the creators, writer, co-director, a narrator and a subject of the 2010 Creative Arts Primetime EMMY Award winner for Exceptional Merit in Nonfiction Filmmaking—The Betrayal (Nerakhoon). He is also the first Laotian American writer to be a member of WGAW (Writers Guild of America, West) in 2008.

Thavisouk (Thavi) Phrasavath is a former electrical engineer, painter and community activist turned filmmaker. In the early 1980s through the mid-1990s Phrasavath was extremely active within the Laotian community and other Asian-American communities. Phrasavath was officially elected to be an Area Policy Board member in Brooklyn, New York. He also served as the primary liaison for Laotian residents in the greater New York City area. He founded the Laotian Gang Prevention for Youth program and the Laotian Family Crisis Intervention program. Thavisouk was also a Lao culture consultant and advisor.

In the past 25 years Phrasavath's film work has extended from production assistant to writing, editing and directing—music video, public service announcements, documentaries and dramatic films.

Film work Awards:

2008 Academy Award Nominee
2008 Film Independent Spirit Award Nominee
2008 Cinema Eyes Honor Award Nominee
2008 Full Frame Spectrum Award Winner
2008 Sundance International Grand Jury Award Nominee
2008 Ann Arbor Film Festival Grand Jury Award Winner
2008 Cinereach Award /Human Rights Watch International Film
 Festival Winner
2008 Fresno Independent Filmmaker Audience Award Winner
2008 Kodak Audience Award Winner
 (Minnesota International Film Festival)
2008 Best Emerging Filmmaker Award
 (Minnesota International Film Festival)
2010 Creative Arts Primetime EMMY Award Winner for Exceptional
 Merit in Nonfiction Filmmaking.

Stepped Out of the Womb

Womb

of the

A memoir of a journey to the land where the sun falls

Introduction to the Story

As I was laying in my bed quietly trying to gather my guts and strength, I was anxious, and frustrated over the abnormally slow ticking of the clocks. It felt like I was staring straight into frozen time.

Again, it was April 14, 1977.

When the minute hand of the clock was 15 minutes away from midnight, I knew my time was about to arrive. I was well prepared, because I knew if I failed to make it this time there would be no other time. The only other option was possible imprisonment or punishment for sins I had never committed.

Finally the moment arrived. Before I left, I ran to mother's room and I said to her, "Mom I have to go; I have to go now." She reached out to grab my wrist, pulled me close to her chest and held me tightly, not letting go. She was breaking down with rivers of tears as she told me:

"Be safe my son, you must remember your mother, your father, your grandmother and grandfather."

As my anxiety took over, I broke free from her arms of love and comfort. I hurried away.

The night was dark and mysterious; the echo of calling crickets resounded, giving me chills deep into my flesh. It was an almost unbearable feeling of loneliness. I felt like my mind was struggling through a magnetic storm. The more I pushed myself forward, the more I felt resistance pulling me back with an equal magnitude. My heart began to tremble. My soul felt as if it were burning with fire from hell, bursting with an uncontrollable blaze.

I kept holding my pride with my stubborn attitude. I kept walking forward, however. I had no intention of going back this time. My one and only goal was to make it to Thailand. At that moment it was not necessary to think about everything that would come afterward.

Through thick woods I crawled and ran. Through thick woods I ran and crawled. Step after step my bare feet slid through the wet dew and sharp saw weed. Bit by bit I slid through the shadow of darkness. Now I was a lost child with a heavy heart, leaving with a hundred troubles, stumbling through a thousand fears. Here I go! Crawling through sharp reeds following the sound of the river. All of a sudden I felt a welcoming longing for death; it calmed my nerves and comforted my flesh. The death, the longing death was so close and near that I could feel its presence. I went through a moment of transcendence, and was totally dazed by it.

When I got down to the edge of the Mekong it seemed to be getting even darker. I could clearly hear the voices of the Pathet Lao soldiers who were drinking, chatting and singing a few hundred feet away. I crawled through the mud and reeds down to the water. I took a moment to rest and hide under a puddle of mud. I grabbed a handful of it, put it on my head and prayed to Mae Toranee, the godmother of the earth, to protect me on my journey. I closed my eyes, and held my breath and talked to her as if she were there accompanying me.

I slowly stepped into the water. Then I said, "This could be my last minute, or this could be my continuance. If I am going to die this second, I am still going to die any way." So I took off my clothes and blew up the plastic bags to float me across the river.

I said, "Let's leave it up to the nature of the world. Now I am going—no matter what. I will gladly die in this water and be food for the fish." It was cool and peaceful. I was drifting along with the current of the Mekong River. Slowly, slowly I was going and going, further away from home. I stepped out of the womb, which bore my birth, buried my umbilical cord, comforted me with love, and gave me identity. Slowly, slowly I drifted away into the darkness—then nothing else.

1

Childhood and War

I was born on March 14, 1964 in Thakhek, Khammouane province, Laos, now known as PDR Lao (People of Democratic Republic of Lao). I was the third child and the first son in the family. When I was born my dad was overjoyed, because he had been waiting for this moment for a long while. He named me Thavisouk Phrasavath. Thavi means multiple or increase. Souk means peace or happiness. My last name, Phrasavath, means God of happiness. When I was growing up, my friends and family called me Souk.

Talking about names, I think my parents were one of the most innovative couples when it came to the names of their children. Laotians have a traditional belief that how they name a child is what they want that child to grow up to be. I came from a family of ten brothers and sisters, four boys and six girls. All of our names are unique, poetic and rhyme together. In Laos almost every family names their children to rhyme with each other and each name must have a special meaning, that is why when you look at most Laotian names they are long and complicated to pronounce. For example, if you want your child to grow up to be bright person with a radiating spirit, the Lao parent will name his/her son or daughter with the word "Seng" in front of it. It doesn't matter if the baby is boy or girl. For example, a name like Sengphet means "the radiating light (spark) of diamond.'

As for me, Thavisouk, I did live up to my name. My childhood in Laos was preciously happy, but odd. Lao was the society and community where people were brutally honest and straightforward. As a child I wasn't appreciated, maybe because I was skinny and pale with crooked teeth. I was

3

kind of confused growing up. I couldn't comprehend the full social circumference of where I was growing up. Everywhere I went people made comments about my teeth. Kids always made fun of me on the street and in school. After a long period of time the image of my teeth became the mirror that reflected in the back of my consciousness. I was not a social child; I couldn't deal with the kids and adults who ridiculed me. I had very few selective friends who didn't make a big deal out of my teeth. I grew up with a lot of psychological pain; I was too young to understand what this bullying was all about. All I really knew was I had to be tough and not take abuse from other kids or adults.

This led to a lot of fights when I was a kid. Almost every day I came home from school with a bloody nose, scratches on my face, black eyes or a split lip. Too often there were suspension notes or termination letters from school. When I got home either my mom or oldest sister would beat me as punishment for getting myself into trouble, regardless if I was right or wrong. For any trouble I got into at school or on the street, I got into twice as much at home.

I failed almost every class. I got stuck in third grade for three years. Every time I brought home a report book I was afraid to show my dad or my oldest sister because they would assume that I was doing nothing in school but causing trouble. I remember once I brought home a report book for my father to sign; he just looked at it and he said, "I can't sign my name in your report book. My signature is worth much more than this." I didn't understand why he said that. He didn't say it in a mean way, he was simply refusing to sign my report book. I knew my childhood failure was an embarrassment to him because he was a school teacher before he went to military officer school and became a professional soldier. After that I learned how to forge my father's signature. I became so good at it that he couldn't even tell. I was growing up as an outcast. I felt it was the only way to maintain my happiness. Of course, I wasn't clearly realizing this. To avoid all the troubles in the city I went to my grandparent's village where I ended up spending a lot of time with them out in their rice paddy and tobacco field. There I was introduced to Lao oral history, Lao mythical stories, Lao legendary heroes and folklore.

I was growing up in the middle of a civil war in Laos. When I was a child I didn't understand many details about the war, such as who was really fighting who, and why Laotians were fighting each other.

The few things that I knew at that time were that Laos had three political factions or parties: the Left wing, the Right wing and the Neutralists. Each of these parties were led by different princes. They were mutually hostile toward each other and were rivals contending for ascendancy to the throne.

Prince Souvanna Phoumma was the Neutral party leader and Prime Minister.

Prince Boun Oum Na Champassak was the Right wing political leader who favored democracy and the west. Prince Souphanouvong was the Left wing political leader, the pro-Communist. He was known as Lao Isara, meaning "Free Lao." This group was fighting to free Laos from foreign oppression and influence including the French, who were allied with the North Vietnamese and were fighting the Americans during the American involvement in Laos. Prince Souphanouvong was also known as the Red Prince.

Of these three princes, two were half-brothers, and the other, Prince Boun Oum Na Champassak, was their cousin from the south. This was how much I knew about my country's history during my childhood in Laos. As little as it was and as inaccurate as it is, I didn't get this information in school. My father and grandfather gave me bits and pieces as to why Laos was in a civil war, and I pieced it together, drawing my own conclusions from a child's perspective.

Laos was unlike America where you can get a book and read about your history or any history. We didn't have that luxury like here in America where there are libraries in every neighborhood and town. We were lucky if we had one elementary school in our village or town. I grew up knowing almost nothing about my political history. This subject was not something that we were allowed to be exposed to. Governmental or political activities were only for elite members of government or political party members to talk about. Political and government business was not meant for ordinary people to know, to talk about or to understand. During the time I was growing up, many people who lived on the farms and plantations or in the mountains and jungle knew only the name of their country: Prarasa Anachak Lao, or the old names Anachak Lanxang Homkhoa. (The Vast Kingdom of Lao) or Kingdom of a Million Elephants Under the white Parasol.

From what my grandfather told me, he said:

"The reason why the old name of our country was called Prarasa Anachak Lao was simply Laos used to be very large kingdom, sixteen provinces of Thailand today, used to be part of Phrarasa Anachuck Lao, until our land was divided during the French and British imperialism and colonialism. In the old time the Mekong River used to flow through the heart of the land, not on the edge of it, as we all could see the description in one part of Master Sila Viravong's poem in the first grade textbook"

Pathet koi Zarn Zue mouang Lao
Louang Khouang nho sood tar rio arn
Narm Khong parn Ri pa tarng karng......

My country named Lao
Its length and width stretch beyond our readable sight
Mekong River flows through the center of its heart.

Over 50 percent of the Lowland Lao, who inhabited along the Mekong valley, is where most of us still have many close relatives, living on the west side of the Mekong River, which is now known as Lao-Isan or Thai-Isan. I still have many relatives living there.

Even though Laos was a kingdom at the time, not many people knew the king's real name, had ever seen him or heard his voice. In my thirteen and a half years of living there, I never saw the king, never heard his voice, and never knew if he ever left his palace to help the ordinary people in his kingdom. I never knew his full name. When I was a child all I knew about the Lao king was from the picture that I saw on our paper currency.

When I was young, I had many questions regarding the war and displacement in the country. My family was moving from town to town, city to city depending on wherever my father's military assignment was. When we moved we didn't necessarily live on his military base; we just moved to live in the same city or province so he could have easier access to us. Once in a while for a special occasion I would have a chance to go with my mother to visit him in his military base at the frontline. I clearly remember my dad was always leaving home on missions regardless of where our family resided. He would go from one province to the next. He was always going somewhere. I wondered where he went and exactly what his job was.

When I was a child my father was my warrior. A child always thinks his father is the best man, and that he is better than anybody else. I had so much respect and honor for him; he was my everything—my role model, my protector and my hero. I was very blessed that I had parents and grandparents who paid attention to my needs and planted a seed of goodness within me. They taught me to love myself, to be proud to be who I am, and to respect and honor our national heroes who sacrificed their lives and blood for our country. They also made sure that I understood the meaning of being born Lao and to love Laos. I was reminded of our history and the division that was brought upon us by the colonizer, conqueror and invader, which brought many divisions and in-fighting among the various factions of Lao government and society. They exploited our weaknesses by creating disunity among our people, who were uneducated and blind to the bigger picture and the importance of our unity as a people and nation.

Under such a suppressive policy and strategy they sabotaged, undermined, controlled, enslaved and robbed us for a long time. We were treated as unimportant and dehumanized by the various contending powers throughout our history, up to the point that it seeped into our culture and numbed our mentality (mind set). Things no longer mattered and, as a result (Borpen nhang!), this has become a part of our character and culture and acts as a numbness in our history.

Siam (Thailand) exploits the incoherent of Lao leadership and unity. The French exploit royal rivalry as a result a royal family feud. The Americans exploit ethnic enmity and division. Despite the misfortune of our history, we were very fortunate as people and as a country to maintain our moral high ground and find peace and harmony in our land. We have maintained our diverse ethnicities by preserving our culture, tradition, and the bond of our nation. We respect one another as brothers, sisters and family.

When I was 8 years old, I spent most of my time away from my family. I stayed with my grandparents and helped them on the farm during my school break. The longer I stayed with them, the more I enjoyed learning about myself and about my own parents through my grandparents. My grandparents were the kind of people who always gave their honest opinion, and they tried as hard as they could to answer my questions - regardless of what those questions might be.

Both of my grandparents were like ancient oral historians. They introduced me to old-world wisdom in many areas including life, humanity, peace and harmony, cosmology, geology, plants and trees. Ancient Lao wisdom is phenomenal, even though Laos was considered one of the poorest countries in the world by economic and industrial standards. Because of this, many Laotians feel embarrassed that they have been citizens of Laos, or even that they are descendants of someone from Laos. It is true that Laos doesn't have a great economy or great industrial development like many other countries in the modern world.

Laos may not be rich, financially, but to me it is still one of the richest countries in cultural heritage, natural resources and spirituality. We are fundamentally prosperous and wealthy as a people and as a culture. The ancient Laotian civilization still contributes by nourishing the intellect and spirituality of the people of the region up to this very day.

Lao literature, music, art and philosophy continue to be part of our day-to-day life, resulting in a colorful culture, practical rituals and unique traditions.

Despite deficiencies in their educational systems, Laotians still manage to endure hardship and overcome obstacles to maintain their culture and pass on the legacies and wisdom from their past forefathers to the youth of our generation. Through their dedication and determination all Laotians today manage to protect and maintain a high cultural value and spiritual quality. Laotian's morality is highly humane and our wisdom is universal.

Just spending time with my grandparents was extraordinary, hearing their folklore, seeing the way they planted rice, watching them treat the soil and observing them dealing with birth and death in the community.

Occasionally, while I was living with my grandparents I was blessed with the opportunity to witness how my grandparents, relatives and their fellow villagers used their sacred songs and dances, and their chanting prayer ritual to tune themselves into a trance-like state of being before channeling their soul and spirit into communication with the spirit of their ancestor or spirit of the sky. This was done to heal the sickness and to forecast weather so they would know when and when not to plant, and to foresee their crop even before the harvest season arrived. Tuning their innermost-self, their intuition and spirituality to synchronize with all of their surroundings seemed simplest but sacred.

My childhood world was so pure, and innocently simple. I'll never forget the Mekong River bank—the golden sand beach on the night of the full moon at the end of harvest season. As part of our leisure season my grandfather would go out and hunt during the day for wild bird, rabbit, squir-

8

rel, boar and chicken. At night my grandparents would take me and my nearby cousins for campfire fishing at the beach by the Mekong River. My grandfather would sink his fish nest and bamboo fish trap baited termites to attract many kinds of fish. Every two or three hours throughout the night he would break away from our circle around the fire pit to collect the fish from the nest and trapper. Whenever grandpapa went out to the nest and trap we would get very anxious with excitement—each of us would prepare our own unique red hot wood charcoal as a platform where we would lay the fish to cook. Of all my cousins, I was the one who was most particular about crafting the platform. Grandmother would nudge her red yam into the hot ashes around the center of the fire pit to get the most flavor out of it. After grandpapa emptied his traps he would come back with a bamboo bucket full of all kinds of fish. Each of us would jump in and grab the biggest fish we could grab, sprinkle it with a little salt then throw it to our red-hot charcoal platform while they were still jumping. The meat was so tender, like warm butter. It smelled of paradise and tasted like heaven. Under the luminous full moon we were nourishing our body with the freshest fish given to us by our mother river, the Mekong. Throughout the night my grandmomma would provide food for thought for our young minds. By reciting her favorite poem or proverb as her introduction, our excitement and interest were provoked. Then grand momma would gracefully launch her prophecies like The Journey to the Land Where the Sun Falls, or City of Phraleusy. Then she would follow with mythical stories and legends, like Khounloo Nang Oua (the Laotian version of Romeo and Juliet); Toad King, Phadaeng Nang Ai; Kon bang bot (People who live in parallel world), or Mouang Lablae (City of Lablae—the city in a different dimension where all the enlightened spirits of our ancestors reside).

Toward the end of the night after grandmomma finished delivering her myths and legends, and our stomachs were close to bursting, grandpapa would carry on sharing and transferring his ancient cosmology wisdom to us. In the circle of around the diffuse fire pit with the fading full moon before dawn; while the edge of the other side of heaven and constellations of a million stars still sprinkle and flicker, grandpapa would use his pointer finger connecting each star into our earthly picture of a dipper, an elephant and. ….. in the heaven. We were fascinated when we managed to see shapes and pictures as he was connecting the dots and lines in the constellation. Grandpapa liked to emphasize the North Star so we would have a directional reference. He would say:

"If any one of you ever got lost anywhere at night—you must search for the North Star. Whenever you see it, your front is your North, your back is your South, your right is your East and your left is your West".

For some unknown reason before he would end his thoughts and words, he would take a few seconds and just stare blankly at the constellation. It seemed to be a special gesture as though he had some kind of spiritual connection to the sky and constellations. Then, he would softly deliver his conclusion with *"That's where it all began."*

According to my grandparents, our human physical descendants are chemically related to a very comparable element that created the cosmos and the constellations.

He said, "The name of our people and country, LAO, was derived from the word "DAO." The difference between the letter L and D in front was just a mispronunciation by people of a different region who spoke with a different accent. DAO means star in Lao".

My grandpapa in particular truly believed that his meditative consciousness is the **THING** that is out of our earthliness that he experienced daily, and it resonated within his internal being by some bio-chemical reaction. My grandpapa called this **THING** "Prang Chit;" my personal interpretation—power or energy of internal extrasensory perception. He was also very definite with his **THING** and his very own internal universe is co-referential with all of our worldly living—animal, tree, rock, soil, water, air and sky; and as well as celestial, constellation of distance star and heavenly universe.

My grandparents were very confident that the philosophy of their origin was not earthly but rather originated from elsewhere far above. They referred to this people as "Khon mouang thung." My personal interpretation is "people of the upper city (world)." They also insisted that they were the descendants of a parallel dimensional voyager and their souls were on a mission to challenge evil and demons in different forms, different realms and in different incarnations. They believed they were in the process of their journey to their soul-enlightened realm.

I was considered lucky to be able to be exposed to such wisdom and to live my early childhood in rich tradition and culture. I witnessed many rituals, healing ceremonies; and I experienced living life close to the spiritual realm of my ancestors. I was well prepared for life from very early on.

While these good things were happening in my life, the war in Laos was escalating. Every day I would see the Royal Lao Army infantry with their armored vehicles, artillery, ammunition and complete combat gear roaming the streets, rice fields and edge of the jungle searching for their Pathet Lao enemy.

In the sky I would see T-28 bombers. The F4-Phantoms flew over the roof of my house on the way to their bombing target. In the distance, deep in the mountains and jungles, I would see the B-52's emptying cluster bombs from their belly. It looked like drops of the monsoon rain.

The sound of explosions roared and echoed through the air like thunder, and the shock waves that rumbled through the ground would make our house shake, as if earthquakes were nearby. Almost every morning when I walked to school I would see wounded soldiers crying in pain on stretchers—surrounded by body bags—lying on the field in front of the army hospital. The army funeral home went hardly a day without being in service. Everyday when I was sitting in my classroom, I had a very hard time concentrating because the sound of war in the background was awfully noisy. There was always some interruption—either the sound of machine guns nearby or gigantic bombs exploding in the distant jungle. Every day and night the sound of war was like the sound of a gigantic wok of popcorn in the making. Towns and cities were flooded with ethnic minority refugees from distant villages who were escaping the bombing rage and the takeover by the Pathet Lao Communists.

In the dry season of 1972 my hometown, Thakhek, was also under attack by the Pathet Lao and Vietcong. The night of the attack we were blessed because my father had just gotten back from a long mission, and he was at home with us. In the middle of the night battalions of Royal Lao soldiers who were guarding the city, roamed our town. Unfortunately, they couldn't barricade against the strong forces of their opposition; the Pathet Lao and Vietcong were forcing their way inside the heart of our town and entering almost every neighborhood. Wherever they were running, we could hear the pack of neighborhood dogs barking and howling in their path. We heard their footsteps and heard them calling out to each other. They strictly stayed close to the residential area to avoid being detected by the American-supplied AC-47 aircraft, filled with gathering-type machine guns and illumination flares, sometimes called "Puff the Magic Dragon" or "Spooky" of the Royal Lao Army Air support.

The flares turned our town into broad daylight. The AC-47 Spooky's were popping the "magic dragon" with 6,000 rounds per minute all night to rescue the town from being taken over by the Pathet Lao (PL) and Vietcong (VC). I was actually enjoying watching the stream of bullets and flares from the planes; to me it was almost like Chinese New Year. There was the excitement of light from flares, sounds of machine guns, and bomb explosions.

My father was up all night along with two other soldiers who were our house guards. Three of them together were guarding our house with their lives. My father was standing in one of the upper floor bedrooms with the lights off by the partial opened window with a loaded M-16 aiming outside and another loaded pistol in the holster around his waist. His hands were on the trigger of his M-16 at all times, waiting to see if any stranger or presumed enemy would dare to approach our residence. One of the house guard soldiers was guarding the back door of the house, and the other was standing next to my family, which was packed together like fish in the fish trap—all except me. I was right by father's side upstairs like a little soldier. I was so fascinated by the whole event; I felt like I was hunting wild boar with my father. His military experience and skill impressed me. I observed his every move and tried to mimic him — every movement he made was cautiously calculated and meticulously meditated. There was something about his eyes that branded the most remarkable memory in my mind. I could see his pupils catching the reflection of the flares while he sorted out shade and movement in the dark shadows underneath the trees and behind the bushes around the house. He was like a predator strategizing to trap his prey. He was beyond an ordinary soldier; that night he was a warrior. No one in our family could fall asleep. We stayed up until the dawn was rising and the sounds of soldiers' footsteps began to fade. Then, finally, we heard the sound of whistling and a few rounds from the AK-47. This was a signal by the Pathet Lao and Vietcong superiors for their troops to withdraw from town, and then they dispersed into the dense forest and mysterious jungle.

"The whole act was a test of the Royal Lao Army's strength by the Pathet Lao and Vietcong," my father said to my mother the next morning. "That's why they didn't shoot at us?" my mother asked. "Yes, that is the reason," he replied. Then he stated, "They just wanted to see how much force they need to be able to penetrate and cut this country in half if they want to.

They are also checking on how conscious we are about their presence in this province. I don't think it is going to be safe for our family to continue to stay in Thakhek. Maybe we should split our family into different groups just in case."

The war was getting so intense that my father felt there was a direct threat to our family. To prevent all of us from being wiped out at once—if there is a worst-case scenario—my father usually divided our family into two groups. One group stayed home inside the city of Thakhek, another group was sent to my grandparent's village of Nhangnam, ten kilometers away from Thakhek. Sometimes the family was sent as far away as Savannakhet, my father's hometown. Depending on the situation and the condition of the war, I was part of the second group that was usually sent away to live with my grandparents.

After the night of the invasion, my father did not hesitate to act upon his instincts. This time he divided the family into two groups. I was sent to my grandparent's village.

At the village, almost every night thereafter, we ate dinner then prepared our needs. We took water, pillows, blankets, mosquito nets and gasoline lamps into our homemade underground bomb shelter. Some villages were being attacked by the PL, and then the Royal Lao Air Force would shell the surrounding village with AC-47 Spooky Gunships which were capable of 6000 rounds per minute. At night they were shooting from such a high altitude they couldn't really see anything. So many times they ended up shooting at water buffalos, cows, houses, and villagers. Many lost their lives and their villages were burned to the ground—either way, we were the victims of war—we might be killed by the enemy or by friendly fire.

Seen through the eyes of an adult, war could be brutal and scary, but through the eyes of a child, war could be terrifying or terrifically fascinating. As for me at that time, growing up with war, and as the son of a soldier—for whom I had so much admiration —war was more fascination and fantasy than fear.

Even though it was very dangerous and scary, every time I heard the sound of airplanes circling around the area, I would beg my grandfather to take a peak at the sky from the bomb shelter's door. Most of the time he would say yes.

It was so fascinating as a child to see the AC-47 Spooky puffing its magic dragon with 6,000 rounds per minute. All I could see was the stream of light, beautiful light flying down from across the dark sky with the accompanying flares and sounds like a mad giant elephant screaming from heaven. It was awesomely fascinating. After the night of shelling, I would wake up very early. Before I went to school I would run around on my grandparents' tobacco plantation and rice field searching for parachutes that carried the flares. The flares had the magnitude of two million candlepower, so they would turn the night almost into day before they puffed the magic dragon on everything.

This fascinating and intense lifestyle went on from the time I was born until I was 8 years old. Within that eight year period Laos managed to earn the title of the most bombed country in the world: 177 sorties per day, 7 days per week for 8 years. Almost 3 million tons of bombs were dropped. This was more than all the bombs that were dropped during World War I and II added together. Though this sounds horrifying, during the time when I was growing up, I must have been immune to it. I was like all other Laotian children who were born during the war. We were the children of war, the war was our life, the war became us; the war was our first true history lesson that we learned by living it; the war became our way of life and way of death.

The status of the war was constantly fluctuating. When the affairs of war cooled off, my mother went to my grandparent's village to pick us up and bring us back to Thakhek. It was about four months since the first Pathet Lao and Vietcong invasion, and the intensity of the war had relaxed a bit in the city, so, I came home trying to move on with my life.

Growing up in a military family, my displacement was constant, from province to province, city to city, town to town, and often between my grandparent's village and my hometown Thakhek. My displacement was dependent on the status of the war. Whenever the war cooled down I would have a chance to be with my siblings and briefly live a normal life.

In Thakhek, I would often see the white man come to my house to talk to my dad. Most of these white men spoke Lao very well. They always brought their big dog, who they would tie to the mango tree in front of my house. My dad would open his favorite bottle of whiskey to welcome them, and my mom, my older sister and some neighbors would cook and serve them. Most of the time when they were drinking my father would call me into the room to pay my respects to his friends. My dad would teach me how to salute like a little soldier, then I would bow my head in the Lao tradition of paying respect. When I was in the room, I would often see a big map lying on the table in front of them while they were talking and drinking whiskey. They would mark the map in grease pencil with the letters X and O, so when I was a kid I thought that's how the white men played tic tac toe.

Usually, a few days after this kind of special occasion, my father would be away on long mission. Sometimes he would be away for six to eight months, and usually none of us knew where he went or what he was doing.

A few months after returning from my grandparent's village, while my father was away on the mission, it was unexpected quiet and peaceful one afternoon while the whole town was falling asleep after lunch. All of a sudden the ground of the town was shaken from the loud explosion. My second older sister, Mok, and I were helping my great aunt Keo planting the flowers on her garden a few blocks away from our house. We were curious about an explosion but didn't really pay much attention to it—because we were very familiar with the sound of machine guns and bomb explosions all the time. But this one in particular sounded much closer than usual. I could feel the shock wave run through my feet. My great aunt Keo was trying to comfort us with her assuring words. Very calmly and collectively she said:

"Don't worry—that is our Royal Lao Military artillery exercise." As soon as she finished her sentences, came another louder explosion. This one was really close; it felt like it was just about six or seven hundred meters away. A moment later, that was followed by a strange sound in the distance— somewhere at the flesh market place. It was a sound like a group of bees flying out from their nest. it seemed like a million of them at once. The sound was so unusual and strange. As we came to realize, this wasn't the sound of bees, but the scream of fear and terror from the bomb that had just exploded. Our city was once again being attacked. This time it was in broad daylight; the Pathet Lao rockets were bombarding the city. People in the whole city were running everywhere; every path, every road and street were filled with streams of crowds. Some were frantically running backward and forward without knowing where they are going. Some were frantically crying out in desperation for help. Some ran around in circles, some were dazed and pacing, some were glazed over with horror and lost within fear. Some were hysterical and out of their minds from the sudden shock. My sister Mok and I were trying to get home. We ran and ran within a distant of few

hundred feet, but it seemed like a feet turned to miles. Through the crowd and chaos of our neighborhood street we finally arrived at the house. My mother and the rest of my brothers and sisters were ready to run out of the house and join the crowd on the street. The crowd was moving toward the Mekong River edge to seek shelter or find the escape route. With frustration, my mother was shouting at my older sister Mok and me because she didn't know where we were while she was panicking, wondering what to do, where to go, and where were the rest of her children.

"We have to leave the house and follow the crowd now!" she shouted. All of my little brothers and sisters were holding each other's hands–connecting like a chain rushing out of the house to join the crowd on the street and move with the flow or current. Mok and I were carrying the bag full of baby towels and cloths, medicine and blankets. The bomb explosions were surrounding us; I could smell the gunpowder from the rocket and the fumes of burning houses. We forced our way to the crowd. We were half way to the river edge when all of a sudden my mother shouted out, "Did you take your baby brother and sister's thermos with you?" to my oldest sister Chayphet, who was leading the battalion of my young brothers and sisters. Chayphet was quickly checking her bag—"No," she shouted in reply to my mother. My mother was immediately plunged into another state of panic. She commanded that Mok run back to the house and bring the thermos, the one that she filled with hot water earlier. That was the essential need. Without that we couldn't make milk for our little brother and sister because they were all fed by condensed milk. My sister Mok was scared and she asked me to go with her, so I did. To get back to the house we had to rush against the flow of the crowd. As we tried to make our way through the crowd, my sister's shouting registered in my ear: "Look up at the sky. Look up at the sky."

I saw the rocket was coming right toward us. My whole heart and soul went completely numb. Within some hundred meters away, here comes this lady. She was riding on her bicycle, peddling through the thick crowd and chaos. As my eyes were fixed upon her slow moving figure, I saw the bomb hit her on her back. Her body and bicycle were dispersed into dust and blew away like powder. Her life was just like a breath of wind. Right after that moment, pure horror took over me. I couldn't remember much of anything in detail. I was internally numb. All I could remember after that was that Mok and I managed to get back to the house, grabbed the hot water thermos and rushed out, running after the rest of my family. We met up with them at the river edge, right before they were about to board the rescue boat. My family escaped to Nakhon Phanom, Thailand safely. The city of Thakhek was in chaos and bloody on that day. It was abandoned within a few hours after the rocket attack landed in a residential area. A few days after that terrible day my family returned to our home. Though things seemed to get back to normal, the scene of the aftermath from the attack was a scar in my neighborhood. Two of my neighbors' houses were burned down to the ground, one of my best friend's sisters was killed, and my other friend lost his older brother by flying debris from an explosion. The wall on the first floor of my house cracked from the ground all the way up to the ceiling from the shock wave of the explosions. As horrific as it was, it seemed normal for me because my childhood's world was surrounded by death and dying. Death and dying were very normal things.

Right after that very intense, life-threatening situation, my father returned home. He took a day off from his mission so he could rescue us. This time my father went to extremes; he moved my entire family to his hometown of Savannakhet where the war was also very intense, but not near the city area. We stayed in a rented house near our aunts, uncles and many cousins, some of whom I never had met before. At Savannakhet our life was not much different than in Thakhek. Everywhere we went the sign of war was written in bloodstains all over the land. It didn't matter where we moved; the war seemed to follow us everywhere. When we were living in Savannakhet our rental house was close to the airport. It was terribly noisy place, but it was rather fascinating to live there. My father had moved us away from the intensity of war in Thakhek with the hope that Savannakhet was a safer place to be at the time, but it seemed to me that it was closer to the core of the war.

Every day during my lunch break, I would rush home, quickly eat my lunch and then hang out with my classmate who lived a few houses away. He would take us to the airport where all the action took place. There, we would watch helicopters, the single engine T-28 bombers, and the AC-47 Spooky. Sometimes we sat there for hour at the edge of the fence just staring at the planes parked in the parking lot, dreaming that someday I would grow up to be a pilot and fly a T-28 bomber, fighting the war alongside my warrior father.

Most of the time when we were watching the airport activities there was something fascinating to see, pilots with their fancy G-force suits, wounded soldiers with their limbs blown off, body bags being dragged out from helicopters, airmen loading ammunition on to the planes, or pilots training for crash and rescue. There were many different kinds of planes taking off and landing during the day and through out the night—from practicing and training pilots to those flying in and out from their bombing missions. AC-47 Spookys were constantly taking off and landing from their night missions from different provinces around the country.

We were living there until early 1973, which, now that I look back on it, was right after the Paris Accord of January 27, 1973, when the cease-fire agreement was signed by North Vietnam, South Vietnam and the United States of America, granting the immediate withdrawal of U.S. troops out of South Vietnam. The U.S. withdrawing their troops out of South Vietnam meant the U.S. would also withdraw their funding from the Royal Lao Army.

As for the Lao people, that meant it was up to the Lao government to determine the destiny of their political future. Under the terms of the Paris Accord (1/27/1973) the North Vietnamese who were considered to be invaders by the Laotians, were not required to move their forces out of Laos.

Therefore, the war against the spread of Communism and the invasion continued in Laos, but the pace of the war was much calmer without the further commitment of support from the U.S. superpower. When the U.S. signed the cease-fire agreement with North and South Vietnam, meaning the Vietnam War would soon come to an end, Laos was no longer needed. This meant, in this moment of calmness, that we were able to sneak back to Thakhek to try and resume our normal way of life. My father, as usual, was still away on his mysterious military missions.

2

Ending of the Lao Civil War

Later in the same year after we moved back to Thakhek (late 1973) my father came home from his long mission. He seemed to be a changed man, there was something about his attitude toward his confidence. As young as I was, I managed to detect a vibe from my parents—especially my father, because I had a special connection with him. Up to this very day I still remember what he said to me:

"I will be home for a while because very soon this bloody war will be ended."

And, of course, I asked him the usual question:

"Dad, which side is winning?"

I'll never forget the moment before he answered my question; he hesitated slightly and didn't seem confident in his answers.

"Of course we are winning! We have to win this war! We got great help from the super power; of course we will win."

Right after the Paris Accords of January 27, 1973, the cease-fire agreement was signed by North Vietnam, South Vietnam and the United States of America. This granted the immediate withdrawal of U.S. troops out of South Vietnam. Most of the Royal Lao Army and Lao SGU military officers and soldiers, who fought the U.S. covert war and Lao civil war, didn't know that the Americans would also withdraw their financial support and other war support such as Air America, Raven and USAID.

As for my father, I knew he knew and saw very clearly what was going on, but he was living deeply in internal denial, and refusing to believe that the U.S. would let down the freedom fighters who wholeheartedly believed in western democracy. He thought the

U. S wouldn't bring down the spirit and ideology of anti-Communism in Southeast Asia. My father, especially, was very hopeful that the U.S. would continue to support the Royal Lao Government, carry on the fight against the spread of the Red Aggression, especially the North Vietnamese on Laotian soil.

In the meantime, the war in Laos was much calmer than it used to be— when the sound of bomb explosions popped like popcorn, the Royal Lao Army troops were roaming the streets, and the T-28, F-4 Phantom, B-52 and AC-47 Spooky night missions conger our day and night sky. Those chaotic began to fade away in the day as well as in the night

It was a hopeful time for my family, but as far as progress of the Royal Lao Government toward a peaceful solution to the civil war, Laos had also signed the cease-fire treaty between the Right wing and the Left wing governments, but no one really knew for sure how the Lao planned to determine their own political future. I was very sure my father knew what was happening every step of the way, but I believe he got caught up in his own convictions. Even though there was nothing definite concerning anything at the time, I didn't think that even the Right wing government knew what the Left wing intended to do.

All the ordinary people knew was that the war between royal brothers would soon come to an end, and we would have a coalition government. That was why we began to see the representative of Lao Issara (Pathet Lao) soldiers moving into the city. Everybody called them "The Brother." At the time, I had no idea why people called them that. I was too young and I wasn't smart enough to put two and two together. During this time, occasionally my father still left home on a mission, but not for long or as often as he did in the past. He was still fully part of the Royal Lao Army, and the Royal Lao Army was still the Royal Lao Army as usual.

At this time, the "The Brother" introduced us to new kinds of music. This type of music did not deal with the issues of romance, social commentary or lovesickness that we usually heard all the time on the Prarasa Anachak Lao Radio. Their music dealt with the issues of Nationalism, Capitalism, Lao ethnicities, Lao heritage and Lao ordinary life in general. Every time I listened to their music I felt peace, and I felt important. I felt like I was part of something and had a better understanding of what was going on in the country politically. As young as I was, that was the first time that I was introduced to Lao politics. Even though all of this was just part of their propaganda, what did I know—I was only 9 years old.

I was overwhelmed by fantasies: fantasies that the war would soon end, that there would be no more Lao killing Lao, that there would be peace and development, that poverty and the struggle of the people would soon end. It was also the first time that I ever felt there was hope; there was a dream; there was peace; there was harmony; there was a solution to conflict; and there would be a time soon to come that my father wouldn't have to ever leave home ever again. All of these thoughts and feelings filled my heart and soul. I believed at that time that all of the ordinary people were very much feeling the same as I was. I didn't think most of the Lao people knew much detail as to reason why we were feeling good about the big things to come. I was longing for some big things to happen.

I didn't exactly know what the coalition government was doing during the period from 1973 to December 2, 1975. All I knew at the time was that I was dreaming; I was longing for something that I knew nothing about. I was in a daze most of the time, and I didn't quite know what to make out of it. I was very confused.

My heart and soul were filled with hope and dreams, but every day I began to see there were serious student demonstrations against the Royal Lao Government. Most of the time I would cut my class and join the march along with the demonstrators. I was in the third grade, but all the demonstrators were high school students. When I was marching with the demonstrators I would just read all the slogans on their signs and banners, and listen to the songs they were singing. I would pay very close attention to all the lyrics of the songs, slogans on the signs and the cartoon characterizations of political leaders, ministers and some important government officers. To this day I still remember it very clearly.

Most of the slogans opposed the Royal Lao Government, also known as the Viengchanh (Vientiane) government. At that time they called themselves the Righteous Wing government which was led by Prince Boun Oum Na Champassak, and demonstrators labeled him as a thief and capitalist America's tool.

Other political leaders who were marked by the demonstrators were Phoui Sananikone, the Defense Minister and Souvanna Phouma, the Prime Minister of the Royal Lao Government. In the caricatures they would draw the Prime Minister, Souvanna Phouma, with two heads as an equivalent to the Lao popular saying "Nok Sorng Houa," Bird with Two Heads. They called him the "Bird with Two heads," because he was neutral, as if he were friends with both the Left and Right Wing parties.

For the defense minister of the Lao military they would draw his character with two big monster eyes as if he were greedy; and the cartoon character of Prince Boun Oum Na Champassak was drawn with a big stomach symbolizing his corruption by taking all of the U.S. military and developmental financial aid to the Laos. They also wrote a song for the Defense Minister, Phoui Sananikone. All the student demonstrators sang this song when they were marching:

> Phoui Big eyes
> The leader of the traitors
> Phoui was the man with the face of Buddha and the heart of a demon.
> Phoui was evil that is why we people must punish him.
> Punish him Mr. Phoui big eyes
> Punish him Mr. Phoui big eyes.

This was the kind of song that the students used all over the country. I still remember, even today, a few of the many slogans that they used:

> "Ugly American Go home"
> "American bloody face capitalist"
> "Boun Oum and Phoui are traitors who sold the country"

All of these slogans, cartoon characters and song lyrics were political. They sounded very mean and harsh every time the students raised their signs and screamed at the top of their lungs with anger and hatred. One day my dad was at home and he saw a young group of student demonstrators. Some of these students were the sons and daughter of his own friend in the neighborhood and mostly were students from the countryside, the farmers. They burned the U.S. flag and ripped a Three Headed Elephant Flag on the street. My dad was very upset, but he couldn't say much except "They all took the communist bait." He would just shake his head with a look of antipathy in his eyes. I didn't really understand why he would say that nor did I make much sense out of what demonstrators did on the street. A few days after this I overheard him and mom having a very serious discussion about the family's safety. My father begged my mother to leave the country.

He said, *"We must leave the country now, I foresee that danger is coming toward our family."*

My mother was very upset to hear this from him, and she angrily replied,

"Why do we have to leave? The country is still a country, the king still a king. This is the place where I was born and this is the place where I am going to die. I am not going anywhere; if you want to go—go ahead and leave us here at home."

Every day after I came home from observing all the action on the street I would turn on the radio and listen to all The Brother's songs; and I would switch back to a hopeful state of mind again. This kind of confusion and limbo dragged on for almost two years, then the demonstrations were much more relaxed. Every time there were demonstrations on the street, the focus shifted from anti-American sentiment and anger against other foreign nations, who were American allies during the war, to focusing closer on the issues of peace, ending the war, unity, and the well being of the people.

There was one song called "Peace Is Coming." This song, I believed, was magically sent for some kind of peace and serenity, and it soon became the song that led to the end of the civil war and helped the Pathet Lao take over in a peaceful manner in comparison to the take over in South Vietnam and Cambodia. Lao was considered to be physically non violent, using psychological tricks and twists instead. From the Lao point of view, at that time we were introduced to the idea of peace, harmony and nationalism. This was the kind of ideology that had not quite been introduced so freely or properly before. We bought into these ideas of nationalism. For me, that was a joyful moment; through all of these songs I became a believer. I believed what I heard. I believed that whenever peace would come, it would be the end of all the Lao struggles. Just like what they wrote in one of their songs, "Peace Is Coming," there was a lyric that made everyone become more or less a believer.

In the song PEACE IS COMING:

Peace is coming
It will be like the magic jar of water that will pour to bless all surfaces of our motherland

With all our support and prayer
May our Lao land fill with peace and walk toward development

and civilization.

Now is the time that we Lao will be bright and shine
Everyone's goal and hope is for improving our life and building our land.

All the enemy now is behind our peaceful treaty
All sides will honor the word and their promise
As what they all had signed on the treaty.......

When I heard all of these words, I was so proud and so hopeful that my country soon would be definitely at peace. We were sick of war, so all of the Lao population was eager and longing for peace and harmony. We would all march along behind whomever or whichever political party could provide and fulfill these hopes and dreams.

This hunger for peace, and longing for the moment of transition, was drawn out for almost two years from 1973 to 1975. During these years the internal transformation between the coalition government was very slow. We didn't necessarily notice the changes; all that I can clearly remember was I began to see more and more of the "The Brother" present inside the city, not just seeing them walking with their boom-boxes and pre-historic Hip Hop hairdos and bicycling around town with their red Chinese bicycles. But we began to see that more and more of the old office buildings in our town were turned into their headquarters, where their families lived commune style. At the same time, they began to try to inspire us and ensure us that they had come in peace.

They would show black and white documentary films about the history of their revolution and their war against capitalism and western ideology, which they said was conquering our homeland and conducting war against the people of peace. All of their films were basically aimed to inspire us to hate the foreigners and invaders—mainly the United States of America. The more people had an opportunity to see the films, the more they would spread rumors all over town. Through their songs and through the Lao student demonstrations and hear say, the rumor was that if all the Pathet Lao would come out of the jungle and join forces with the Viengchanh (Vientiane) government, they would bring peace and development to our country.

The more I saw their films and the more I sang their songs, the more

I trusted them and accepted them for who they said they were. It was very easy to like them because they were Lao like me and everybody else. Though some of them were from an ethnic minority, I never had any problem with that. This is why everyone's hopes and dreams kept building more and more as the days passed. It was one of the most hopeful moments in Lao history.

3

During the Lao Revolution

It was the early morning of December 2, 1975, a day I will never forget because it was the day that changed my life forever.

It was about 6 o'clock in the morning. As I was trying to wake up, I heard a very hard knock on the old wooden door of my house. As my mother was rushing to open the door she made me jump out of my bed. I was running after her to see if anything had just happened. There was my great aunt, Keo, who lived a few blocks away from us. She was one of my favorite great aunts as I was growing up. I remembered her as a news anchor for our neighborhood. She was usually the first person who delivered any news. As she was rushing into our house with such extreme excitement, I was curious to know what had just happened. While my mother was trying to clear a place for her to sit, I took the opportunity to ask her,

"What has just happened, great aunty Keo?"

Great Aunty Keo answered, "You kids, all of you must get ready today. There will be a parade, the biggest parade of your lifetime that you should not miss. If you do, you will regret it for the rest of your life.

She was overexcited. Parade! Parade!

What parade? I asked

"The peace parade for our liberation; we just got liberated," Great Aunty Keo said.

As soon as she said the word "liberated" I immediately began to make sense out of what had happened in the past two years. Prior to December 2, 1975 Laos was under a tidal wave of change, as I remembered that every day there was a student demonstration criticizing the Viengchanh's (Vientiane)

Government for being corrupt and selling their country to the capitalist superpower, the United States of America, and the West. I was too young to understand what this was all about. All I knew at the time was, deep in my heart, I was full of hope, peace and joy, and my head was full of dreams and great expectations.

December 2, 1975 was the day that the Pathet Lao Regime marched and paraded their militant (revolutionary) armed forces in, and rolled their tanks, heavy artillery and armor vehicles into our town; the day that changed Lao history.

To me as a child it was the most beautiful moment; the day that the Pathet Lao took over the country. Everything seemed to be perfect in that particular moment. It was like my dream had come true. My heart was full of joy and fascination, observing the takeover in full and up close. All the Pathet Lao infantry men and women were marching in formation followed by slow moving tanks and military armored vehicles with guns and rockets. At the very end of the parade there were military cargo trucks, pick up trucks and old jeeps. There was an old tank with a full load of civilians, and soldiers were pacing and interacting with the crowd.

Citizens and Pathet Lao soldiers were standing arm in arm on top of the tanks and in the trucks, cheering and singing the most popular song of the time, "Peace is Coming," while the peace parade was slowly rolling into town. The police of the Viengchanh (Vientiane) government were blowing their whistles and yelling out safety instructions to the spectators with their bullhorns to pave the way for the parade. Both sides of the main street were packed with people, people of all kinds and all backgrounds, all genders, all generations and every possible walk of life I imagined that all were there together; the strength of a bonding unity was beyond my description.

Most of the kids my age, along with my schoolmates and neighborhood friends, were climbing the trees alongside the main street so we could have a great view and observe everything that went on that day. After the marching and parading passed us at one spot we would climb down and run after the tanks, trucks and marching crowd to advance to the next spot and climb another tree. There we would wait for the parade to pass so we could have another look at the same marching and parading.

We were repeating the same pattern numerous times until I was exhausted from climbing the trees. Then, one of my neighbors and I decided to just follow the crowd up and down and around the town. Everywhere I went I could hear the sounds of music. On every corner I turned, people were singing and dancing. The Lao traditional circle dancing with Mor-lum Lao formed on every street corner and every old, official, government building courtyard. People were drinking everywhere. I could smell the perfume of Laotian rice wine in the atmosphere throughout the whole city. Through the loud bullhorn speakers on the top of the trucks the Pathet Lao Revolutionary soldiers weren't hesitant to freely express their nationalistic statements to the crowds and spectators:

"We are the free Lao today—we fought to free our motherland from the oppression of French colonialism and imperialism. We liberated our land from the bloody American capitalism and their invasion. We have been waiting for 30 years for this day. Long live our liberation—long live our revolution—long live my brothers, sisters and comrades—long live..."

All the spectators and crowds were applauding and yelling out cheers of agreement and support. All day long my friend and I were singing one song after another. We repeated "Peace is Coming" about a thousand times. There was another song that we were repeatedly singing backwards and forwards, backwards and forwards like a broken record. That song was Nok Santi Pharb (Bird of Peace). I was so overwhelmed by joy and fascination, I convinced my friends to skip lunch so I could continue observing the event in more detail.

December 2, 1975 was the day that came and wasn't meant to go away. It was very peaceful to see it through my innocent child's eyes. Right after they took over, within the first two months, there would be a free outdoor movie almost every night showing in different neighborhoods in our town. Most of the movies that they showed were black and white documentaries; more or less the same kind of film that they were showing before the takeover, except they related to a very specific subject about development, union work, and adult education. At the time, I was a little too young; I didn't have the maturity to analyze what I was watching. All I saw was a free movie. Great! Let's watch and have fun. I was disregarding the content that embedded Marxism, Leninism, Mao Zedong and Ho Chi Minh ideology within the images and narration. Besides showing outdoor movies almost every night, during the day groups of government workers worked very hard hanging loud speakers on the trees and on the roof tops and electrical poles along the side of every street in town.

Every morning they would turn on the loudspeakers at 5 or 6 a.m., blasting with revolutionary songs and music, government news and public service announcements. At first, I thought it was kind of cool. I didn't have to turn on my own radio, I just listened to music through their loudspeakers. It wasn't very long, however, before I started getting annoyed. As the loudspeakers were annoying me, I began to ask myself a question, "Why does everything else seem strange?" At first, most of the stores in town, which were mostly run by Chinese-Lao and Vietnamese-Lao, would not open on time. Then one by one they would close out their stores. If they were open, there was hardly anything on the shelves. In the morning, fresh markets, were usually made up of at least 20 percent Thai merchants and vendors from the city of Nakhon Phanom (Thailand) who came across the Mekong River to Thakhek (Laos) every morning to sell their goods and seafood.

Because Laos was a landlocked country. We didn't have access to the sea or ocean, so the Thai had been making big profits from Laotian seafood cravings for centuries. All of a sudden they stopped coming to Laos to sell their goods and I began to wonder why everything changed so suddenly.

New rules and regulations regarding how everyone should dress and style their hair were imposed. Any young man or teenager who had long hair and wore jeans or pants with bell-bottoms would get stopped by the Pathet Lao police at gunpoint, and the Pathet Lao police would give them a military crew cut or shave half their head to intimidate and humiliate them publicly. Women and young ladies were banned from wearing miniskirts and bell-bottom jeans. Their hair had to be in a topknot - like the old-fashioned Lao.

Listening to Thai radio or watching Thai TV programs was banned. Bars and nightclubs were commanded to close down. We were not allowed to listen freely to foreign music. Everything was beginning to be regulated.

As young as I was at the time I was in sympathy with what my older sister had to deal with. She was in a rough spot because Laos had been on the verge of western influence. The Lao hippy was everywhere. Most of the guys and girls in my older sister's generation were just beginning to get deep into adapting the hippie culture and western lifestyle. Most of the teenagers and young adults in my hometown, including myself, were more or less beginning to look like and transform into the mirror image of the western rock star—men with long hair, bell-bottoms and high heeled boots.

For the girls, instead of wearing their old traditional Siin or Sarong with

29

a topknot hairdo, they were in knee high boots, high-heeled shoes, mini-skirts, pants and bell-bottom jeans. They had let their traditional topknot hairdos loose, and some had shoulder length hair.

Western rock and roll and psychedelic rock were just being introduced. I still remember listening to Carlos Santana, The Who, KISS, Creedence Clearwater Revival, Jimi Hendrix and some French music like Christophe "Aline."

Lao at the time was politically and culturally free and westernized. There were suddenly so many rules and regulations that kept popping up to interfere with our lives. The Pathet Lao took away from us, one by one, the freedom of expression that we used to have. A curfew was set in my hometown; no one was allowed to leave the house or walk the streets after 9 p.m. except in serious cases of medical emergencies. For every new rule and regulation that they forced in to our lives they had excuses and reasons. This was part of their lip service just to keep things calm and in good order before they took complete control over all aspects of people's lives.

These drastic changes took place within the first two months into the revolution. These bits and pieces of change were so subtle, it didn't just shock me, it dazed me with disbelief just like I was watching a magician performing his tricks and deception.

One day I was walking home from school and I heard a public announcement over the loudspeaker. I still remember word by word what they announced on that fateful day:

"We would like to set up meetings with all the former Royal Lao Government military officers, soldiers, colonels and generals. To strengthen our nation's security and prosperity we need to work and collaborate together as a family, as in unity we are all brothers..."

As I was listening to the public announcement I began to get curious about what kind of meeting they were referring to, but I just kept this question in a corner of my mind, and told myself not to worry about it. It been two months since the takeover—dad was still at home; he had no plans of going away on any missions. That fateful day was just like every other day; I was lost in my deep thoughts and daydreams. I was just leisurely pacing the streets, dragging myself home, before I had to deal with my usual boring life.

When I was about to arrive at the gate of my house I saw my father being guarded by a group of soldiers, and I knew for sure that they were

Pathet Lao. My father was unarmed, and they were all armed with their AK-47 automatic assault rifles. My father looked at me and I looked at him; I could see the hopelessness deep within his eyes. As I was observing, I was memorizing the moment as it was occurring. My knees were shaking and weakened by the fear that had just suddenly overtaken me. My father gave me a very dry smile as a substitute for his internal words, "don't worry," but I could tell the fear that was embedded in that little glimpse of his dry smile. The soldiers deposited him in the back seat of their jeep, and then they just drove him away. The only thing that I could see was the dirt that came up from the road.

Right after they took my father away I came to the realization that the country was closing all its doors to the rest of the world. Cities now became deserted, all private businesses and entrepreneurships were banned or shut down; everything was coming to a halt. The next big thing was that they changed the currency. Each family had a limit on how much you could exchange. It didn't matter how much money you had either at home or in the bank. No one was allowed to exceed the set limit. People were beginning to wonder what they would do with the rest of their money. They didn't know if there would be any value to it or not.

By the third day of the currency exchange, people found out for sure that all of their paper money and bank notes would no longer have any value. So many people very upset, angry and disappointed. Some people in my town just went insane, some were piling up all their money, pouring gasoline on it and lighting the match. There was one merchant in our town who took his disappointment to an extreme—he jumped out the window with a sack of his money in hand. One of my aunts—my mom's older sister—didn't know what to do with all her paper money. She decided to make a mattress out of it, and she slept on that mattress with her broken heart until the day she died.

Right after the crazy, messy changing of currency, the new government was pounding us with all kinds of new policies such as land reform, labor unions and a new social order.

For the land reforms, landowners and property owners, who owned a lot of land or if they also rented extra houses or living space, were ordered by the local authority or central government to give up part of their land. Their extra luxury living space was to be shared or distributed to other people who didn't have a place to live.

31

For the labor unions, the mobile labor-force was established, but in a more or less reverse direction from our prosperity as a country and as a people. We were backtracking to the old laborious, backbreaking agricultural and labor ways. The whole country became a state of union labor. I remember at a very young age I was sent away to a rural area rice farm where I had to work with the rice farming labor union. I had to learn how to plow the rice paddy with water buffalo and prepare the soil for planting rice depending on the week or the day.

Some days I was assigned to a food gathering team, to gather the food supply for all the laborers. This meant gathering food by doing anything and using every possible way to get it. We would be out in the deep jungle and forest searching for edible wild vegetation and hunting wild animals. I remember being in the dense forest and deep jungle walking barefoot for miles searching for wild mushrooms, bamboo shoots, crickets, grasshoppers, jungle red ant eggs, creek mussels and snails. I hunted birds, wild squirrel and rabbit with a slingshot and built traps on the wild hens' and water monitor lizards' trails. At night after the monsoon rainstorms we would be out in the open fields and rice paddies with homemade bottle lamps to catch frogs, rice paddy crabs, snakeheads and cat fish climbing out from the creeks and rivers to find ponds to lay their new eggs.

Living the rural life, I had been taught a great deal of survival skills like how to pick edible mushrooms, hunt wild animals, grow rice and make my own sandals from busted car tires. I knew how to make wooden shoes, nesting fish traps, baskets from bamboo and bottle lamps. I was also developing a habit of smoking tobacco. Every time I went out in the jungle with the elders, they would roll tobacco on a dried banana leaf for me to smoke. They said it was *"To keep all bloodsucking insects like mosquitoes and leeches away."* Ever since then I have been a tobacco smoker.

At the farming labor union I was treated like, and carried the full tasks and responsibilities of, an adult laborer. Every day I had to put up with 12 to 14 hours of intense heat, humidity and monsoon storms—far away from civilization—no electricity, no water well, no toilet or water closet. I was working on the rice farm with villagers whom I had never met before. It was my first time living a communal life style. The only benefit that I got from such hard labor was rice grain at the end of the harvest season. It was just about enough to feed 1 or 2 out of the 11 people in my family. The labor union work was random in arrangement. No one really knew where he or she would be assigned. It depended on your neighborhood group leader or the head of the village authority.

At that time everything was measured by your family biography. Anyone who was mistrusted was interrogated by the local authorities or was just imprisoned. Anyone who opposed the new rule secretly disappeared either by day or by night. People began to hide their past identity, such as their formal education, their former work position or rank, as well as their former employer. For the new social order this was one of the very hardest things to handle. For all the people, especially the elderly, the respected and the former elite educated city people, it was almost inconceivable to deal with because the old Lao social order was patriarchal. The new social order reform took place and it caused major upset in Lao culture and traditional values. In the old Lao patriarchal system, the order of authority went according to the rank of age, seniority and status.

Under the Pathet Lao regime the uneducated rural peasants, many of them were very young, didn't have the proper education or experience in leadership or management skills to carry their appointed official government positions. Their qualifications were very much based upon their trustworthiness and their devotion to the revolutionary army. He or she was just a trusted community member who resided in the liberated zone prior to December 2, 1975. These were now our new community leaders, high ranking government officials who handled government business, educational or political duties, as well as operating, managing, making big decisions and governing our new way of life and future.

These were the principles that set the early state of the Lao revolution in backward gear and plunged Laos into turmoil and unproductiveness. It was a dark era that affected our history and our life. These bits and pieces are what I remember from my childhood, and up to this day I believe these were some of the reasons that many Laotians tried to escape from Laos right after December 2, 1975.

I don't believe that any one of us who fled Laos to seek a new life and liberty would have been willing to take the enormous risk of losing their life escaping across the Mekong to Thailand and going through hell on earth (the Thai refugee camp) if our lives at that time had not been so desperate.

Every time I needed to buy a little bag of sugar or one can of condensed milk for my baby brothers and sisters, I had to wait on line for 2 to 3 hours.

Many times when it was my turn to buy, the government store would just run out of stock. Then, I would have to wait for another day or two. Sometimes my little brothers and sisters went without milk for days. My mother had to boil the sticky rice and mash it up with raw sugarcane juice so she could use that as a milk substitute. Many times my baby brothers and sisters got stomach viruses and diarrhea from it. Sometimes their condition was so bad we had to take them to the hospital. There was not much the hospital could do, because there were only a few nurses and doctors. Also, there was no medicine in the hospitals or in the pharmacies.

Laos completely closed its door. There was no communication with the western world, only with their Communist ally nation. There was no exporting and no importing of goods into the country. The hospitals ran out of medicine, the government merchandise stores were out of stock; there were cars but there was no gasoline. That was a time of extreme desperation. It was every man for himself. Survival was the name of the game; people would do anything to stay alive.

It was extra hard for my family. My mom became a single mother after they took my father away. At this time most of my siblings were still very young. Out of 10 siblings—only two of my older sisters and myself were old enough to help out. There was not much I could do to help my family, however, besides working in the labor union to earn the rice grains and stand in line to buy government merchandise.

Despite the complications and government regulations to prevent entrepreneurship and the ideology of capitalism there were some odd loopholes within their strict rules and regulations. Some legal permits were given to people who were willing to share their full profit margins of their entrepreneurship with the local authorities. As long as a person could come up with their own capital for their entrepreneurships, they could have their own businesses.

Luckily, one of my older sisters, Mok, got a permit to make and sell her coconut yucca desserts in the fresh market. There she earned a small income. This was just enough to buy some small portions of extra food and supplies on a day-to-day basis. My mother on the other hand was risking everything, including her own life, to sell items in the underground world and black market. My mother did almost everything to supplement money or food to feed our mouths and fill our empty stomachs.

During that period my mother went through hell and back at least a thousand times. She went through so much to survive and to keep all of us alive. Even though it was only a few years of terrible hardship, it sucked so much life out of her. Since surviving that dark period, my mother's physical health has never fully recovered. Besides overwork and heavy lifting, she had also given birth to ten children and raised all of them more or less on her own. She became both mother and father to us. Her uterus literally collapsed and she suffered severely from that for many years, until she had a hysterectomy after we made it to America.

In spite of what was going on in the country, my family and I still tried to go on with our life and free our minds from all the trouble and fear surrounding us. We were always taught to love our homeland, the land where we were born and the land we would willing to die for without asking questions. We loved our country unconditionally and our duty was to protect, preserve and sacrifice with our sweat and blood for it.

While I was growing up under the revolution and Communist rule I could not just close my eyes and ignore what was really happening in my surroundings. Besides being mentally pounded with Marxism, Leninism, Mao Zedong and Ho Chi Minh ideology, there were so many other things that I heard and saw that were unforgettable and un-erasable.

The following are two of the most terrifying moments that I encountered; they will be with me forever.

My first encounter:

One morning I went fishing with my grandfather in the Mekong.

It was very early and the river was so foggy I could hardly see my grandfather a few meters in front of me. While we were fishing, I spotted something very strange out of the corner of my eye. I pointed it out to my grandfather. Out of curiosity we paddled our boat to get a closer look at the strange looking object. As we were getting closer I could see the nervousness in my grandfather's face, but he was acting very calm and composed. I got a feeling that this was not something good. Finally our boat was a few meters away from this strange object that was floating in the muddy river on this foggy day.

Soon, we realized that it was the body of a man facing downwards. Half of his body was just emerging from the water and there was a bullet hole in the back of his head. His hands were tied behind his back. The rope was tied like a chain connected to six other dead bodies—a woman and five children. All of them had their hands tied behind their backs; some had bullet holes in them and some did not.

The children were just tied up to drown along with their executed parents who had attempted to escape across the Mekong River. It could have been a case of robbery, rape or being killed by either Thai border police or Pathet Lao soldier. Possibly the family was robbed and killed by underground boatmen who they hired to help them escape. Most people, when they escaped, would take everything they had, their most valuable treasures—gold, silver, money and their whole inheritance. They took whatever they could in hopes of building a new life somewhere else. Those were my grandfather's assumptions of what might possibly have happened to that family in particular.

My second encounter:

One afternoon, a group of my classmate, and I were playing in front of the schoolyard. All of a sudden I saw a group of kids and people in the neighborhood rushing to join the crowd on the street. I didn't know what was going on. Out of curiosity I decided to join the crowd. A moment later I managed to push my way through to the heart of the crowd. I saw a man who was pale and skinny like a skeleton. Both of his arms were tied behind his back, and they had hung a sign around his neck that said " Traitor." His neck was also tied with rope like a dog on a leash.

People were shouting at him with slogans like:

"Traitor! Traitor!"

"The Traitor of the people will be condemned to hell"

The man was so unhealthy I couldn't really tell how old he was. I guessed he must have been in his thirties. I was just marching along with the crowd, which soon became a parade. We finally arrived at the town soccer field where they had a public stage for government bands and performing arts. When we walked in we were the last group of people to arrive at the soccer field. The field was already full of people and the stage was already set up. Almost everyone in the entire town was there. It was like a special town meeting, which by rule every family must have at least one person attend. I still didn't have a clue what was going on, but I felt a little bit strange about whatever it was. I asked myself, "If it is a town meeting, why did they bring the prisoner here?"

The field was very crowded, and there were no seats left on the benches so I ran to the front where I could sit on the grass. Finally one of my friends and I found a space to squeeze in—right in front of the whole crowd. As I was trying to get myself comfortable and ready for a special surprise event I looked up on the stage right in front of me. There was a group of soldiers taking the prisoner up on the stage. A few moments after that one of the soldiers walked up to the microphone, which was to the front and center of the stage. Over the microphone the soldier welcomed everybody who was attending the special event.

"To all my beloved and highly respected brothers, sisters and all good Comrades. I would like to welcome you all. Your sincere attendance is highly recognized and highly appreciated by our Central Committee and party. Thank you. Thank you to all of you, my dear comrades, brothers and sisters..."

After the first soldier finished his welcome speech he walked off the stage and shortly thereafter another soldier came up on the stage and made a special announcement. He said, "The reason that you all were invited to come here today is to support us and to witness the justification of the one who dared to betray us ..."

When I heard his voice I immediately felt chills run through my spine.

The way he delivered that brief statement was just like some demon spirit possessed him. Without knowing what was going to happen my heart was already raging and my knees were starting to tremble. I felt like some evil spirit possessed me. It was one of those unexplainable phenomenons.

After he finished delivering his chilling statement to the crowd, all of a sudden, three other soldiers were dragging the prisoner onto the center stage. At gunpoint the prisoner came up to the microphone. He tried to lift his face and raise both of his arms, but his wrists were tied. The prisoner was about to read his confession statement. He tried to clear his dry throat before he attempted to deliver his first word.

It was so painful to watch as the prisoner tried word by word to get through the confession in front of the crowd. He said:

"My dear brothers, sisters and comrades, every act that I committed was against the will of the people of the liberation and against the policy of the government of the people, and I admit that I deserve the extreme punishment."

The prisoner was so pale I could see the reflection of sunlight bouncing off the skin on his face. He was so weak he could hardly finish reading the confession written on a small wrinkled piece of paper. While the prisoner was reading the confession to everyone—men, women and some young children who had come with their mothers—we were all dead silent.

I could see the chill and confusion that was written on everyone's face.

As soon as the prisoner finished his confession he stood there, frozen in front of the microphone. Within a brief moment there was another group of three soldiers who almost magically appeared from the back of the stage and walked up toward the center stage where the prisoner was standing. As soon as the soldiers were a few meters away from the prisoner, one of them called out his order commanding the prisoner to kneel down on his knees.

The prisoner did what he had been told. Then the soldier took out a black piece of cloth from his pants pocket and tied it around the prisoner's eyes. As soon as he finished wrapping the black cloth, the other two soldiers rapidly took out their pistols and shot him in the back of the head. Pop! Pop!

The prisoner collapsed forward falling on his face as fast as the blast of the pistol. Right after the prisoner was face down flat on the floor, the soldiers flipped his corpse over and picked up his body by his feet and head because both of his arms were still tied together. Then they just threw his corpse into a coffin that was just a few feet away from where he had been executed.

All of a sudden, lightning, thunderstorms and heavy rain appeared from nowhere. It was like the spirit of the dead prisoner was possessed by furious demons. That was a most bizarre thing; people on the entire soccer field were panicked and eager to leave. All of a sudden, I saw the crowd begin to disperse to avoid the heavy rain, thunder and lightning. A few people were walking with their heads down and they appeared confused, but most of them just ran. One of my best friends, who was a few years older than me, grabbed me by the wrist and dragged me in a panic out of the chaotic crowd.

While I was being dragged through the panicked crowd there was a woman who must have been 7 or 8 months pregnant. She had fainted and was lying down on the ground. I remember I jumped over her; I almost stepped on her stomach. After my friend and I managed to break away from the chaos of the crowd and the most heavy rain, thunderstorms and lightning, we ran out of the soccer field. We both just kept running. We ran and we ran, without looking back, until we got to my house. Both of us were very shaken by what we had just witnessed, so that day we decided to cut our afternoon class. We just hung out in my house and played marbles all afternoon.

Right after that first public execution in my town, day and night there were people trying to escape the country. Almost every night I would hear the sound of machine guns at the riverbank. Whenever I heard these sounds I always said a prayer for the safety of the escapee.

Almost a year prior to the public execution, I was already beginning to try to find a way to escape. I had attempted to escape once before. Four friends and I pretended that we were going fishing along the Mekong River. When it was starting to get dark we went to a cemetery and hid out and waited for night. We were then going to steal a fishing boat from the local fishermen or cut down a banana tree and use it as our float. That was our plan. We decided to hide in the cemetery, because that was the only place where nobody dared to go at night. Everyone including the soldiers was scared of ghosts and spirits.

It was unfortunate, because for some unknown reason on that night, the Pathet Lao border guard squadron decided to have a special patrol in the nearby area. It was rather odd that on the night that we were attempting to escape, a small group of daredevil soldiers decided to go into the cemetery where we were hiding. They were only a few hundred feet away from where we were hiding. We decided not to make any move on that night. It was too dangerous and too scary for us to try to go farther with our plan. Besides being afraid that the soldiers would shoot us, we also were terrified of the ghosts. In fact, we were more scared of the ghosts then the border guards. We assumed everything that moved and every sound we heard were ghosts.

Throughout the night we stayed awake and held each other like a pack of wolves. That night we made a promise to each other that when we returned home, we would live our lives quietly, and no one would breathe a word about our failed attempt. After that close encounter with death I came to my own reality. If I tried to escape with a bunch of friends, I was definitely not going to make it. If I dared to attempt to escape the same way again, I might get arrested and imprisoned, or shot and killed at the riverbank.

We were just a bunch of crazy kids in the neighborhood who wanted to get out of town without knowing what we were going to do even if we made it to the other side of the Mekong River. To beat all the odds I made up my mind that if I wanted to make it to Thailand alive, I would have to go alone. The moment I made up my mind with this definite decision, I kept all my plans secretly to myself. I hoped and prayed that sooner or later there would be some window of opportunity for me to escape. While I was waiting for my chance, the political pressure was getting extremely intense. Laos was at the peak of its internal revolution.

Two years after my father was taken away, we had no idea what had happened to him. Since the day they took him away, there was no way of knowing where he could possibly be. I heard rumors that all the former military commanders, colonels and generals, who had been taken away at the same time as my father, had been executed. After hearing that rumor I lost my hope. Furthermore, unexpected pressure from the local authorities was heating up on my family. In school and around the neighborhood people were calling me the son of the traitor. In the local market, where my mother was secretly attempting to conduct her underground business, people were calling her a bloody faced capitalist.

At home, a couple of times without any warning, the local authorities were sending the Pathet Lao soldiers to come and search our house. They were searching for photos and documents that were written in any foreign language to be used as evidence against us. We were lucky, because before my father was taken away, he told me that if anything were ever to happen to him, I should put all the photos and documents away in a safe place where no one could find them or destroy them. A few weeks after my father was taken away, in the middle of the night, I snuck out to bury all the documents and old photographs from my family in the woods near my back yard. As much as I wanted to burn all the documents and photographs, I couldn't, because I was afraid people would see the fire. After my house was searched my family was harassed and labeled as untrustworthy citizens of the people of liberation.

After being harassed and labeled as untrustworthy citizen of the people of liberation, and after seeing what happened on stage at the town's soccer field on that bad afternoon, there was nothing left for me to look forward to except the time that they would come to take my whole family or me away.

Almost every night I would hear the cargo trucks rumble into town to take people away. A few of our neighbors were taken away in the middle of the night. They were the families of former Royal Lao Army Soldiers, like us. Night and day I was afraid for my life, until one day my worst nightmare came true. I was secretly taken into local police custody for questioning. The Pathet Lao police officer asked me many questions regarding my father's past. I was only 12 years old; I couldn't possibly answer any of their questions. Their questions was:

"Do you know what your father did during the war?"

"Who were his friends and his associates?"

"Did your mother receive any letter from anyone?"

"Did anyone come to your house and talk to your mother about your father?"

After they asked me these unanswerable questions, they would just release me. Before they let me go, however they would threaten me with very harsh words like:

"If you dare to tell anyone anything regarding this matter, we will bring you back here again."

After I was released, I was frightened for my life, which led me to no other option than I must escape as soon as possible. Deep in my heart, though, I felt there was another thing coming.

Note to readers:

I want to clarify this section of the story.

Whatever happened in Laos 36 years ago should not concern the present government, which is trying to do the right things. By telling this story it is not my intention to jeopardize the good will for peace, harmony and progression for the future of the Lao people in Lao PDR. I am telling my story for the benefit of Lao-Americans and all Laotians abroad to have a better understanding of why we had to leave our beloved homeland. I personally understand in every revolution things need to be restructured, so the government can keep things in the right order. But it doesn't mean all things were done in the right way. It was a trial and error period in Lao history. Whatever happened to my family and things that I experienced at that very critical time were a shock. We had to learn to adjust and adapt to the new order, new rule, and regulations that I never experienced prior to 1975. Again, my true intention is to tell what really happened to me and my family at the time of the revolution. My purpose is to clarify and help the young Laotian who left the country too young to remember anything, then grew up confused, without knowing why we Laotians had to leave our beloved homeland and live in a foreign land. When these youths are asked by a stranger, what was the reason that their parent had to escape, they don't have a clear explanation of why they are out of the womb of their motherland. After reading this book, their answer should not be just "...

because my parent took me here," or "I don't know," or "we want to have a better life and better job, nice car, refrigerator, radio and big flat screen TV etc...."

They must have a better answer than that. Their answer should be, "something very traumatic did happen in our country; having to do with US foreign policy versus the ideology of people who seek freedom and liberty." It is like everyone else in the United States. We are just commoners who had almost nothing to do with anything political, except being victims of war. That's why, for anyone to understand the true history, we have to learn how to look at the history from more than one point of view, from as many views as possible. The same for anyone who dares to tell history; that person has to dare to tell the truth. History without the truth is the best way to blind a generation to come.

It is very complicated in our Laotian community—many young Laotians have grown up in America not having the privilege of access or expose to their true history. One of the few ways to access their true history is through their own parents, who lived through that period of history. But it is part of our culture that we like to keep things to ourselves, especially when something that traumatic happens to us.

To make wrong things right, we humans sometimes don't do the right things. We can see this when history repeats itself. Many times in order to make wrong things right, we end up doing wrong things over and over again.

As a filmmaker/writer it is very hard not to get tangled with political issue. It is very unfortunate in our lives that there is no way to avoid politics, because everything in our life is political, even buying a pack of cigarettes. In filmmaking it is unavoidable not to get tangled in the edges of political issues. It is just like being dropped in the middle of the Atlantic Ocean—either you are a Democrat or Republican; either you are Socialist or Communist; either you know how to swim or you don't. You will end up drowning anyway. There is no escape

4

Escaping to Thailand

A few days before the Lao New Year of 1977.

I made an urgent visit to my grandparents in their village that was 10 kilometers away from the city of Thakhek where I lived. When I got to my grandparents village I told them that I had to escape soon, hopefully by the Lao New Year.

As soon as I told them that I had already made up my mind to escape, my grandfather went downstairs and grabbed a chicken and boiling hot water for a de-feathering process to prepare for a Baci ceremony.

My grandmother went around the village and secretly told her sisters, a brother and several other respected elderly whom she could trust, and asked them to attend.

After my grandfather finished plucking the feathers from the chicken, he chopped off both feet and tied them together with lemongrass leaves. He then boiled them in the pot along with the rest of the chicken. This is known as "Kai Khwan," Chicken for Guardian Spirit.

One by one my great aunts and great uncles quietly arrived and got ready for the secret get together, and performed the sacred ceremony. The Baci ceremony is a very important part of Lao culture, especially for a person who is about to go on a long journey or is attempting to accomplish any objective where there are dangers involved.

In addition to my Baci ceremony, my grandparents also prepared to perform the chicken feet ceremony especially for me.

The chicken feet ceremony was an ancient Laotian ritual performed by Lowland Lao. This is not part of our Theravada Buddhism rituals or beliefs, but rather an ancient Lao Animism ritual, which was one of the ancient Lao religions before the influence of Buddhism in the 13th century. For centuries before the time our Lao ancestors practiced Animism, the chicken feet prediction was one of their often-performed rituals to predict a safe journey for travelers.

After the chicken and the chicken feet were finished boiling, my grandparents began the Baci ceremony where all my most respected elders—my great aunt, great uncle, aunt and uncle - were taking their places on the floor around a hand-net bamboo table which displayed a variety of foods, fruit, flowers, candles, money, rice whiskey or wine. Included also was Baci strings, the boiled chicken feet, which my grandfather put on a plate with five pairs of candles and five pairs of white flowers. This is called "Karn Har." Karn Har is a symbol of our respect for our first five holy precepts of our Theravada Buddhism. Each pair of flowers that accompanies a pair of candles is the representation of our body, soul, emotion, and commitment to faith and age.

My great aunts, all of the elderly I respected, and my great uncle (who was a shaman) were there to conduct the Baci ceremony. He lit a candle, then softly and quietly recited a blessing and a prayer, while everyone reached their hand out to touch the offering table. Within a brief moment, his blessing and prayer would elevate and transcend to a higher spiritual stage of his shamanism to call upon our 32-guardian spirits and demand all of them to return to our body. We believe that our soul consists of 32 guardian spirits, which occasionally wander elsewhere to another realm away from our soul and body due to external and internal discord or unhappiness. After he finished reciting the prayer and blessing, which called back our wandering spirits, he tied the Baci string on my wrist to symbolize knotting all of my scattered and wandering guardian spirits together, back where they belonged, deep in the core of my soul. As he was giving me his blessing upon my upcoming dangerous journey to the unknown, both of my elbows were held by all my elderly relatives in a gesture of support and encouragement gathering my body, soul and spirit into one. Then, one by one, they tied the Baci string on my wrist as they wished me the courage of our heavenly sky, strength of the sun at noon, and the spirit of our ancestors to protect me and guide me upon my journey to a safe place. Right after the Baci ceremony was over, my grandparents began the chicken feet prediction ritual.

Before all the respected elders would interpret the chicken feet, my grandfather would raise the plate above his forehead and send a silent prayer to the holy spirit of our ancestors and the universe. After he finished saying the prayer he would pass the plate around to be interpreted. Each elder would look at the chicken feet, to see how close or how wide the claws were separated from each other. If they were spread wide open it meant my journey would be wide open with safety and protection. If the chicken claws gap was narrow and close to each other, then I would have a very narrow chance to escape and my journey would be unsafe. My chicken feet were spread wide open—signifying that my journey would be wide open, and that it was safe to go.

That chicken feet prediction ritual did indeed boost my self-confidence and assured my faith that my journey would be safe.

Finally, the window of opportunity that I had been waiting for arrived, and I whould definitely make my escape.

April 14, 1977 was Lao New Year's Day—people, soldiers, government officers, everyone was busy preparing for the celebration. The first evening and throughout the first night of a New Year everyone lays low and relaxes, tries to forget about all their troubles by getting drunk all day and all night.

According to Lao New Year tradition, we celebrated the New Year for three days. I knew my widest window of opportunity was the first night of the New Year. I knew for sure that later during the first night all the soldiers who were guarding the border would lay low and hopefully, by 2 or 3 a.m., would either be asleep or drunk. This was my clear window of escape. On that day, all day, I walked around the river bank just to check and try to memorize exactly where the border guards were, so I would know exactly where I could get down to the river. Even though I had done this a hundred times in the past few months, I still had to make sure that I did my final inspection.

After I did my routine check I went looking for plastic bags, I went to the market and looked for the lady who sold rice. I asked her if I could buy a few of her clear, thick, very strong plastic bags. She didn't charge me. She gave me three of them because she was my older sister's former classmate. I was very pleased with her generosity for giving me my floating devices to freedom free of charge. I said to myself, this is a very good sign, then I went back to my house. My mother and my two older sisters were preparing food for a celebration. They offered some to me, but I couldn't eat. I felt full without eating anything.

I was walking and pacing around the house, holding, kissing and playing with my younger brothers and sisters. At the same time, I was trying to memorize them. I was photographing them with my mind's eyes so I could feel them and see them in my heart and mind when I left. I did that all afternoon. The evening of the first day of the New Year had finally come, and our family was celebrating quietly. We hardly had anything on the table, but Mom still tried to keep the spirit of New Year's up regardless of how sad our family condition was. As for me, the plan was set and my mind was determined.

Dead or alive, my heart was ready to face my worst fear. I gave myself no other choice but to face it like a man. I was trying to bully myself because I was very nervous. I said to myself, "Hey! If a few younger friends of mine managed to escape in broad daylight right in front of the border guard headquarters, than why can't I do this on my own?" The clock was starting to tick. I had a few hours left before midnight. I went back to my room. I sat there staring at the wall and ceiling. I was totally dazed. I felt like the spirit of the journey possessed me. The closer to the time, the more I felt like this was my destiny. This was my calling and I must go through with it. I didn't necessarily ask why I felt this way. I just took it with faith and trust. I trusted the wisdom of the universe and that our inventor somewhere out there would guide me through this. I really believed in that kind of supernatural phenomenon. My mind was spinning and wandering around in my head a million times as I was staring at the wall and ceiling of my room.

I was so distracted. I kept hearing my inner voice telling me,

"You must compose yourself. You must compose yourself."

As I was laying in my bed quietly trying to gather my guts and strength, I was anxious and frustrated over the abnormally slow ticking of the clocks. It felt like I was staring straight into frozen time.

Again, it was April 14, 1977.

When the minute hand of the clock was 15 minutes away from midnight, I knew my time was about to arrive. I was well prepared, because I knew if I failed to make it this time there would be no other time. The only other option was possible imprisonment or punishment for sins I had never committed.

Finally the moment arrived. Before I left, I ran to Mother's room and I said to her, "Mom I have to go; I have to go now." She reached out to grab my wrist, pulled me close to her chest and held me tightly not letting go. She was breaking down with rivers of tears as she told me:

"Be safe my son, you must remember your mother, your father, your grandmother and grandfather."

As my anxiety took over, I broke free from her arms of love and comfort. I hurried away.

The night was dark and mysterious; the echo of calling crickets resounded giving me chills deep into my flesh. It was an almost unbearable feeling of loneliness. I felt like my mind was struggling through a magnetic storm. The more I pushed myself forward, the more I felt resistance pulling me back with an equal magnitude. My heart began to tremble. My soul felt as if it were burning with fire from hell, bursting with an uncontrollable blaze.

I kept holding my pride with my stubborn attitude. I kept walking forward, however. I had no intention of going back this time. My one and only goal was to make it to Thailand. At that moment it was not necessary to think about everything that would come afterward.

Through thick woods I crawled and ran. Through thick woods I ran and crawled. Step after step my bare feet slid through the wet dew and sharp saw weed. Bit by bit I slid through the shadow of darkness. Now I was a lost child with a heavy heart, leaving with a hundred troubles, stumbling through a thousand fears. Here I go! Crawling through sharp reeds following the sound of the river. All of a sudden I felt a welcoming longing for death; it calmed my nerves and comforted my flesh. The death, the longing for death was so close and near that I could felt its presence. I went through a moment of transcendence, and was totally dazed by it.

When I got down to the edge of the Mekong it seemed to be getting even darker. I could clearly hear the voices of the Pathet Lao soldiers who were drinking, chatting and singing a few hundred feet away. I crawled through the mud and reeds down to the water. I took a moment to rest and hide under a puddle of mud. I grabbed a handful of it, put it on my head and prayed to Mae Toranee, the godmother of the earth, to protect me on my journey. I closed my eyes, and held my breath and talked to her as if she were there accompanying me.

I slowly stepped into the water. Then I said, "This could be my last minute, or this could be my continuance. If I am going to die this second, I am still going to die anyway." So I took off my clothes and blew up the plastic bags to float me across the river.

I said, "Let's leave it up to the nature of the world. Now I am going, no matter what. I will gladly die in this water and be food for the fish. It was cool and peaceful. I was drifting along with the current of the Mekong River. Slowly, slowly I was going and going, further away from home. I stepped out of the womb, which bore my birth, buried my umbilical cord which had comforted me with love, and gave me identity. Slowly, slowly I drifted away in to the darkness—then nothing else.

Two and the half hours later my feet touched Thai soil. I was very exhausted. My arms were sore, my legs were numb, and my hands and feet were cold. I needed a moment to rest my body so I lay down on my back on the sand. As I took the privilege to do that, a thousand thoughts and questions ran through my mind.

I realized the critical moments that I had experienced, the moments of transformation from life to death and back from death to life. The specific question that I had for myself was, "Now that I made it to the other side of the river and I am in a different country, now what?"

The sun was rising; the majestic Mekong River was once again reflecting and radiating life, beauty, hope and protection for thousands of escapees. As I was mesmerized by the beauty and compassion of this mother river that breathed life and soul into generation after generation of the Lao, I was a little sad to realize that this could be the last time that I would be able to swim in the comfort of this mother river ever again. While I was caught up with my bittersweet moment, lying on the sand, I heard the sound of footsteps. It was an old women who must been in her 70th year. She was there to water her tobacco plants, and she was shocked when she first saw me. I think she might have thought that she had just found a dead body washed up on her shore. I could see the surprise in her eyes; she was quite nervous when she discovered me. When she realized that I was alive, I could see signs of relief in her face.

She asked me, *"What are you doing here so early?"*

"I just got here from the other side of the river," I replied.

Without hesitation I immediately asked for her help, "Would you please help me locate my great uncle? I believe that he lives not too far from here."

Old lady:

"What is your great uncle's name?"

"His name is great uncle Deng. Do you know him?" I replied.

Old lady:

"There are so many Dengs around; I am not sure which one might be the right one. Do you know the name of his village?"

"Yes, my grandparents told me that he lives in Thakhor." I replied

Old lady:

"The best way to find him is to go to his village and ask for him."

I was quite young and the old lady took sympathy on me. I could hear it in her tone of voice. She was very kind and generous. To reassure my trust in her, she told me that she had been seeing a lot of escapees in her tobacco plants lately. She then told me the story about this particular family that she rescued a few months before I got there. She said, "I found a family of three in my tobacco plants. When I found them, their 2-year-old daughter was very sick with a high fever, the mother was seven months pregnant and the father had a bullet wound in his arm from the border guards' machine guns.

"They got here with a tire tube. After I found them I had to report them to the Thai authorities right away because they all needed immediate medical attention. I took them to the head of the town and the police came to take them. I never heard anything about that family ever again. I assume that they got to the refugee camp safely."

Compared to many others, my escape was considered easy, smooth and blessed with a lot of luck. Right after she watered her tobacco plants she took me to her house. She was a widow and all her children lived in a nearby village. She was alone in the house. She gave me some of her grandchildren's clothes to wear, then she gave me food and water before she took me to find my great uncle that same morning. She took me to Thakhor Village where I found my great uncle whom I had never met before. All I knew was his name. He was a poor farmer. He lived in a tiny hut with his wife and a few grandchildren who helped him on his farm. The lady turned me over to him.

I stayed with my great uncle, helping him with his farm work for two months. He suggested that I go to work in Bangkok as most of my distant cousins had. There was not much more he could do to help me.

I was young and had never had any particular plans or any clue about what I was going to do when I got to Thailand. All I knew was I would escape and stay there to be free and safe from persecution. I would then wait there until my mother and the rest of my brothers and sisters got their chance to escape.

Since my father had been taken away, my mother was secretly searching for a way to escape the country. She tried to bribe people, but no one would take a chance because we had such a large family. Besides the large size of the family, there was another problem. Between 1975 and 1978 Laos was at the peak of its revolution. It was the most dangerous and intense time to make any escape attempt. This was why I couldn't wait and had to take the chance to escape first and also to escape alone.

My great uncle took me to a little used clothing store in his town and bought me a student uniform. Then he took me to a local barbershop for a Thai student crew cut so I could pass as an elementary school student. He bought me a one-way bus ticket to Bangkok and gave me 500 Bahts and information on how to get to my distant cousin, whom I hadn't known even existed.

To get to Bangkok, the capital of Thailand, there are two checkpoints where the Thai police stopped every bus and car. The police would come up to the bus and do random checks for a Thai ID. If you didn't have it, you would be fined or the police would take you into custody and do further investigations. The Thai authorities were very rigorous, because the tension within the Thai Communist insurgency was high.

My great uncle told me that whenever you got to the checkpoints you must pretend that you are asleep. If, by chance you are asked, all you have to do is tell them that you are an elementary student going to visit relatives in Bangkok. He also emphasized that I must respond to the police in Thai, not Lao-Isan dialect, which was the same language that I spoke everyday in Laos. The Isan dialect and Lao are the same language. I promised him that I would respond to the Thai police in Thai. I knew how to speak and read Thai since I was a very young child. I learned how to speak it by watching Thai TV and listening to Thai radio, and how to read it from Thai comic books. I was very confident that there would be no problem for me. I was very fortunate on my way to Bangkok. The bus was stopped twice at the checkpoint. At the first one, the police were walking around and asking people questions. One was harassing a middle-aged man who sat two seats in front of me. The reason that he was being harassed was because he was of Thai-Vietnamese descent. The Thai were very strict with their ethnic minorities at the time, especially people of Vietnamese descent. It had something to do with Communist Vietnam.

I was safe. At the first checkpoint police looked at me and walked by. I remained calm and was thinking all good thoughts to block out the fear, the nervousness and the image of the worst possible thing that could happen. About four hours later the bus arrived at the second checkpoint. At the second checkpoint the Thai police were much meaner than at the first. This policeman didn't do random checking like at the first checkpoint. He checked and questioned everybody on the bus. I was very nervous, but I had to remain calm and just wait for my turn. All I had to do was make sure that I correctly pronounced the name that was embroidered on the student shirt that I got from the used clothing store, and I had to calmly speak Thai.

The policeman with a mustache and was mean looking. His voice was as harsh as his face. Before he asked for my ID he just stared at my face with his mean look than he called me Ai Noo – which means little rat. (Little rat is a very commonly used expression for a little guy or a young person; it is not an insulting term).

"Where are you going?" he asked.

"Bangkok!" I said.

"Go back to sleep little rat!" he replied.

"Yes sir," I said. I was so painfully relieved. I was thinking to myself, someone is watching over me. I got to Bangkok the next morning at about 8 a.m.

Bangkok is a really big city in comparison to Thakhek, the city that I came from. At the time, Bangkok was on the verge of transformation from a big city to a modern city. The construction of skyscrapers was happening all over the city and the Transit System was being modified, and reconstructed at almost every street and avenue. I was so fascinated to see for the first time a modern city at its birth. I came from a town with a population of about two hundred thousand people, and here I was in a city of several million.

It was quite a scene, the size and complexity of the city didn't really intimidate me; I was immediately intimidated by the attitude of the big city people. Most of people seemed very hyper and rather mean. When I got off the bus and tried to follow the instructions that my great uncle gave me, it was confusing. I began to ask people at the bus station for directions on how to get to my distant cousin's place at Kong Teuiy, which is an administrative division of the Bangkok capitol. Most of the people I asked were kind of rude and not helpful. Even though I asked them in Thai, I was speaking it with a slight Lao-Isan accent. Back in Laos I had heard about the Thai reputation regarding how much they looked down on the Lao-Isan ethnic minority in Thailand.

That is why, when I asked for directions, they assumed an antagonist attitude. This didn't stop me from asking more people. Finally, I asked the janitor who worked in the bus station. While I was asking him, he asked me if I came from Isan. I told him that I was Lao. He said that if you are Lao, when you tell that to the people from Isan, they will automatically assume that you are Lao-Isan, which politically means you are a Thai citizen. But being a Thai ethnic Isan is very different from being considered as pure Thai; we are not considered equal.

I was sad when I heard this. My grandfather always told me that in ancient history the Lao and Thai were brothers. If I came from a different continent I could understand that they may not like me because I would have come from a completely different race, different culture and different religion. Besides, between the Lao and the Thai, even our closest Cambodian cousins couldn't tell the difference. The janitor told me that he also lived in Kong Teuiy, and he promised that he would take me there if I could wait until he finished his shift.

So, I paced around the station, observing the big city lifestyle and taking notes on everything that was going on in that chaotic city. By the end of the first day I was mentally exhausted from the noise and the crowds. I was so glad when we were on a city bus heading to Kong Teuiy. I didn't know Kong Teuiy was one of the Bangkok slums. Most of the population that resided there were different Thai ethnic minorities, mostly Thai-Isan at the section where I stayed.

To me it was like a small Lao city within the heart of the Thai capitol, so much of a slum that I felt comfortable immediately. The janitor took me to the address where I was supposed to meet my distant cousin. When I got to his place he wasn't there. His best friend, who had shared the same hut, told me that he had moved to the southern province to work on a sugarcane plantation.

"You are more than welcome to stay here in your cousin's quarters," he said. I told him that I would be grateful to stay, and the janitor left. Before he left he told me if I ever needed help for other things just to go and see him. He gave me his contact information. So far I had been very blessed. On my first day in this chaotic and mean city, there was somebody with a kind heart who still gave, shared and helped. I believe the kindheartedness and generosity that I received from this stranger had something to do with his being of Lao descent. He was a man who carried Lao blood in his veins just like me.

I truly believed in that kind of karma because of the principles of my faith. I believe this kind of value exists in every essence of our blood and veins. That was why this man treated me the way he did; it was part of the sub-consciousness of the Lao. It didn't matter when or where this generosity occurred, it was part of our impulse and our life. This one principle always gave me reason to be proud that I was born Lao, and to be grateful for my culture's traditions and heritage. This was the amulet that protected me and helped me to see beyond Kong Teuiy.

In my personal opinion Kong Teuiy was the heart and soul of Bangkok poverty at that time. It was very hard to describe. It was a place where the bottom of the bottom of society lived. Each ostracized community had a little street or path. Each group of people had its own rules and leaders. It was all about utilizing animalism for any means to survive. Hunger and the decency of human respect were the main drivers for everything that went on within that society.

People were desperate; they were all living day-to-day, hand to mouth. Almost all of the kids my age were not in school. They were working as dishwashers, construction workers, day servants, landscaper assistant in the rich businessmen's homes, or street hustlers selling various goods. It was a hopeless place. In that place a dream was just a dream. Well, what else could I do at the time? This was my unexpected destiny. Good or bad I had no choice but to accept it. A few days after I got there, the friend of my distant cousin who had taken me in, helped me to connect with the job network. He took me to meet a man name Phod. Everyone in the territory called him "Loukphee-Phod" (Loukphee is a very popular nickname for a big, tough guy or big godbrother). He was in his mid-thirties, sleek looking, and smooth talking. He was calm and had a very persuasive personality. When I was introduced to him, he just threw his arm around my shoulder and tried to reassure me that I had been introduced to the right person. He told me he felt good about me, and he was willing to take care of my needs.

We talked for about 15 minutes; he was checking out my personality to see what I was made of. After this 15-minute sort of heart-to-heart conversation, he said, " I think you should join a group of kids your age, a special group, to be an assistant at jobs in landscaping around town. At night we might be able to hook you up with different groups if you are interested." I was really happy to hear that from him. He made me feel comfortable with him. I was ready for anything as long as I would have a place to sleep, food to eat and be safe.

He told me to get myself ready and be at his place by the next morning at 6 a.m. It was exactly 6 a.m. when I got to his place, and there was a pickup truck parked in front of his hut. There were already some kids sitting and waiting in the trunk of the pickup, so I hopped into the trunk and was ready for work. The driver drove us to a rich neighborhood in the Bangkok capitol, and dropped us off at a landscape site in front of an obnoxiously large and elegant house. I immediately drew my own personal assumption that whoever the owner of this place was, he must have been one of those big bosses of all the bosses.

I was greeted by one of the supervisors. He must have been in his late teens, and he was Thai Muslim. He gave me instructions on the work routine and my responsibilities. I was assigned to the yard paving and planting grass unit. That became my day job for two years while I was waiting for my mother and the rest of my family to escape. In our unit there must have been about 20 kids. They were all more or less my age, and mostly from Isan, so we were all Lao descendants. I developed some good, trusted friends.

The Bangkok climate was absolutely brutal. It was a minimum of 95 to 105 degrees F. There was 90 percent humidity every day almost all year round. Work was an average of 12 to 14 hours per day. There was a 20-minute lunch break. The pay was 35 Thai Baht per day ($1.05 per day in American dollars). It was so hot and so humid, the only way to keep ourselves cool while we were roasting in the sun was to cover our faces with cooling cream and with a piece of cloth that we would constantly soak with ice-water cover our heads. From our 35 Baht per day every one of us had to share 20 percent with our "Loukphee-Phod," big godbrother, who had given us the job connection.

Shortly after I started working I developed close friendships with a couple of other kids that worked in my unit. They invited me to stay with them so we could play Takraw and hang out after work on days when we got back before it was too dark. So, I moved in with them. We were a group of very young kids, who knew almost nothing about life; we were without parents and guidance. No one really cared or looked out for our interests. All the kids I was staying with were orphans. They really had no one to live for, except themselves. It was brutally harsh and depressing. They were all very good kids, but their circumstances gave them very little chance to make it in life.

When I first met them I immediately became good friends with them without really knowing anything about them. All I knew was that every day in our day job we had to endure 12 to 14 hours of hardship together. Not until I moved in to live with them did I realize that "Loukphee-Phod" didn't just give them their day job; he also had a night job for them as well, so they could have some extra cash to save.

None of them could really save anything though, because all of them were addicted to an abusive illegal substance. Despite the environment and circumstances that I had fallen deeply into, I always tried extra hard to maintain my inner peace and navigate along the surface of the current, and live through it. "Loukphee-Phod" did what he did. It was just simply all he knew. While I was there within his close circle, he offered me different options, but he never pushed or mandated me to do things that I didn't want to do. Regardless of how strong I was and how much I knew myself, the circumstances and environment were very unforgiving, and it was impossible for me to avoid or stay free from it.

The harder I tried, the more deeply I fell into it. I was part of that entity for almost two years. Even though I was at the bottom, I always stayed conscious of my influences and kept my little hopes and expectations alive. My hope was to save some money and soon be reunited with the rest of my family. Within that period of living under the radar, I continued to stay in contact with my great uncle who lived on the border.

Every month I would write my great-uncle a letter with my return address asking if he had heard any news about my family. Before I left his place to Bangkok I told him that whenever my mother managed to escape from Laos, she would be heading toward his place. He was the only close relative that we still had, and my grandparents had always stayed in contact with him, even before the Lao revolution.

My life in Bangkok's slums moved on. The longer I was there, the more I saw and the more I lost control. I kept losing my friends with whom I shared the place. Deep in my heart I knew it was time to escape again. I was desperately in need of some money to feed myself and was hoping for something extra so I could help my family and pay back my great uncle the money he had given me. This would be a token of my appreciation.

Here I was once again at the end of the time before I took off from the bottom of the underworld. I ended up diving deeper into the bottom of that underworld for the last time before I left it forever. I am very sure everyone understands what I mean. It is too difficult to talk about, too painful to even try to revisit those memories. To have a clearer view of what that underworld was like, I will give a short description of what Bangkok was like at the time when I was there. This is through my personal knowledge and details are from my personal observation.

Bangkok back in the late 1970s was more or less operating with underground outlaw bosses. Business was booming at the time, but the Thai people did not own most of these businesses. Most of the businesses were owned by those of Chinese, Thai-Chinese descent, westerners and some other foreign investors. The gap between prosperity and poverty was as large as the distance from the earth to the sky. Corruption and greed roamed the nation's capitol; it was a society where the biggest fish ate the bigger fish, the bigger fish ate the big fish, the big fish ate the small fish, the small fish ate the smallest fish and the smallest fish had to eat its own shit.

Just about the same time that I was planning to escape from the Bangkok slum, it was by luck that my mom managed to escape to Thailand. As soon as I got the news from my great uncle, I once again dressed up in that very same elementary student uniform that I had gotten from the used clothing store with my great uncle. I got a nice crew cut, got on the bus and returned to Nakhon Phanom. Before I left, I went to see "Loukphee-Phod" to tell him that I was going back to Isan for a visit with family and relatives. He was very drunk when I told him; that was his usual lifestyle. He was drunk from Friday through Sunday night, and when he drank, sometimes he would cry in front of all of us and sing a very sad, classic Thai country song. When he was drunk he would tell us how much he wished God could just give him one hour in his life to be with his parents so he could see what they looked like and get to know them at least for a brief moment.

He gave me 251 Baht from his wallet and a few coins from his pants pocket—"Here's money for your bus." I took it and headed to the bus station. The next morning I reached Nakhon Phanom. I then took another bus to Thakhor village to meet my mother and the rest of my family at my great uncle's little hut.

When I saw my mother, it was indescribable happiness for me. It was one of those moments that can only happen once in a lifetime. If you are lucky it might happen twice. Beside the happiness of seeing my mother, I had an additional surprise: my sister Mok came with her newlywed husband—Tou - the older brother of my best friend in the neighborhood. That moment of indescribable joy and surprise was shattered within a few minutes after our reunion, however because right after I saw my mother I realized that two of my sisters weren't there. For my mother to be able to escape from Lao to Thailand she had to sell all of her gold and silver jewelry, all of her valuable possessions including the inheritance that she had gotten from her parents. She sold all the things that she had and then secretly searched for underground fishermen, boatmen and smugglers to bribe so they could smuggle her out of the country.

After she found an underground boatman to bribe, she had to wait years before the boatman could find his own escape route. She considered it lucky that she only had to wait two and a half years. Many other people who were not as lucky would have to wait for three to four years, and their chance might never even come. The underground world was mostly a scheme of ripping off people when they were most vulnerable and desperate.

Although my mother seemed to be in luck regarding her waiting time, she also had misfortune. The day that the boatman came to take her and the rest of my family away, he told my mother that she had to leave with him within two to three hours. At that moment two of my sisters, my oldest sister, Chayphet, and my youngest sister, Keodouangchay, were at my grandparent's house 10 kilometers away.

Ten kilometers is quite far. There was no time for my mother to wait for my sisters to walk or ride their bicycles home. She had to make the extreme decision to leave my two sisters behind. Her thinking was to try and bring all her seven children to safety, and it was better to leave two behind than to lose them all.

This was a very unfortunate situation for our family but there was not much we could do about it except for life to go on. After a week of recuperating with our sadness in my great uncle's hut, he made a suggestion that we should report to the Thai authorities so they could legitimize our refugee status. Since we didn't know any better, we took his advice and moved on.

Deep in my heart, from my two years of experience living in Thailand, I knew that this was not the greatest idea. Hardly anything was considered legitimate with the Thai authorities. I had learned what we could use for bribes and which authority figure was corrupt, but there was not much I could do or that was in my mom's power do. We were simply too poor; we had nothing left. All the money that my mom had from selling all of her precious belongings had already gone to pay for bribing her way to get into Thailand. I couldn't save anything, because there was not much for me to save—except my own life.

Since we didn't have any money left to bribe our way to the refugee camp, we had no other option but to give ourselves up to the Thai authority and go through the Thai legal process.

5

Thai Refugee Camp Life

After my great uncle took us to the local police station in his town, the police took us to

their higher authorities who were located in the main city of Nakhon Phanom, in Nakhon Phanom Province, right across the river from my hometown of Thakhek. While we were sitting in the bed of their pickup truck, we seemed to be happy, we looked at each other and believed we were doing the right thing. Sooner or later, after the Thai legal process was over, we would all be in good hands.

We were a very faithful Buddhist family. When we were growing up, my mother always taught me how to pray, and here I was praying to Buddha. I could feel deep inside, however, that we had made the wrong move.

Surrendering ourselves to the police authorities was like signing your life away; they could do whatever they wanted. Our lives were in the palms of their hands. I had been hearing all of these crazy rumors about Thai pirates killing, raping and extorting the Vietnamese boat people. Crooked Thai police were raping and selling young Laotian, Vietnamese and Cambodian girls to the nightclubs and prostitution houses in Bangkok. Laotian, Vietnamese and Cambodian teenage boys were sold to the sugarcane plantations in the southern province of Thailand where they became slave workers. They had to work at gunpoint 14 hours per day, 7 days a week without pay. Many teenage boys who tried to escape were killed execution style. Some young Cambodian male refugees were taken by dishonest Thai police and sold to street gangs where their leg or arm would be cut off so they became disabled. They would then become a beggar—begging for sympathy and mercy money from society to feed their gang member. Also, in the refugee camp, corrupt Thai officers would take all the refugee benefits and foreign aid, and pocket it themselves. So many rumors went through my mind. I didn't know how truthful they were, but I knew in every myth and rumor there is always a grain of truth.

As all of these thoughts were present in my mind, I became more and more concerned about my family. As we were getting closer to the city, the more anxious I became. I wished that I could grab all 10 of my family members and hold them in my arms and just jump out of the pickup truck and run away.

Finally, we arrived at the police headquarters at Nakhon Phanom. A police sergeant greeted us. He must have been in his late thirties. He had a typical attitude. From the way he greeted us I could tell that he was biased. I could feel the intensity of his bias and revulsion radiating from him while we were sitting in his office. As he began to prepare the forms for us to write down our names, the first words that came out of his mouth were:

"What is so bad about communism?"

My mother nervously answered in a shaky voice:

"We are just refugees—escaping from the tyranny of communism to seek mercy in a prosperous place. My children were hungry, everything we had was taken away: properties, lands and liberty. We lived day to day without any hope of a better tomorrow. People were being persecuted and imprisoned for almost everything."

With a flash of anger in the pupils of his eyes and a chilling voice from his cold heart, he cut my mother off. "Alright, alright! I keep hearing the same story from all of you Lao-people.

It seemed like we were infuriating him just by being Lao. His fire of anger was just bursting from nowhere. He began to push my mother to give him each of our names. My mother became more frightened by his irritated attitude, and tried to compose her thoughts while she attempting to give our names to him accurately.

After my mother gave him my long complicated name, her voice became shakier as she realized there were six more names to give. Every time my mother gave him a name he gave my mother a weird look. When she came to one of my younger brother's name—Sethy, which literally mean "millionaire or rich man" - he couldn't help himself but laugh very hard as if

"Sethy" were made of laughing-soup. "Laughing-Soup" was named because when we made chicken soup we put in a lot of marijuana. Right after eating it, you were guaranteed to laugh all day long. Laughing-soup would make you laugh at everything, including the leaves falling from the trees. I had that once with my cousin when I was ten. I didn't get a good laugh out of it, but instead it was my first near death experience.

After having a good laugh, he finally finished writing down all of our names on the form. Then he panned his mean eyes around the room examining each of us. He then made a remark toward my mother just to humiliate her. He said sarcastically,

"Don't worry, I will take good care of you guys; all of you will be sent to the Rong Puck. Thailand welcomes you." In Thai, Rong Puck, in a word-to-word translation, means resting room, but the actual meaning of this slang word is "jail."

As soon as he finished delivering his welcome to Thailand, I could see big drops of sweat running down my mother's temple. I knew she was very frightened. I wished I could say something or do something to get us out of this situation. I knew what Thai jail would be like. When I was in Bangkok most of the friends who I was staying with were in and out of jail all the time. Every time they were in police custody at Rong Puck, they would tell me how brutally abusive the police were. After I realized that I was going to Rong Puck with my family I immediately felt chills run up my spine. How would all my little brothers and sisters be able to understand or know what to make out of this?

In Nakhon Phanom police custody there were two—approximately 10x12 meter rooms. One room was empty and three Thai prisoners, who had been there for some years waiting to be tried, already occupied the other room. The police prison guards opened the gate and pushed us in. We decided to walk toward the empty room. All three prisoners were playing a chess game and staring at us with a look of wonder in their eyes. I could hear their silent voices in the back of my eardrum,

"Why the fuck are women and children being put in this jail house?"

It was kind of weird and a most awkward moment. As soon as I finished hearing that silent voice one of the prisoners was nodding at us. It seemed like he accepted the fact that we would all be together for a while.

"Welcome to the hell hole."

There was nothing in the room except the toilet and a small standing shower without a door. Each one of us had a few pairs of clothing for a change. My mother told us to take out our oldest piece of clothing, one that was not our favorite, from the plastic grocery bag so we could use it as a cushion. We all did as we were told. The cement floor was very hard and very cold when you sat or laid down on it.

The Rong Puck was very hot and humid. There was only two or three small electric fans that they put in an approximately 2 by 3 foot window high up near the ceiling. This was their ventilation system. It was hot and humid, but this was no problem for us. We were born in Laos, which was located right on the earth's equator. Heat and humidity didn't frighten me at all. What frightened me were the mosquitoes and the hard cement floor. Even though we had just stepped into the jail cell, it was so hot and humid that I became very sleepy. I must have fallen asleep almost immediately after being put in that cell.

The next thing I remember was waking up to the sound of the prison guard's solid wood stick banging on the metal rods. He was screaming, ordering us to get ready for our food. I was very tired from not having slept since the reunion with my family and I was still thinking and wondering about my other two sisters whom my mother had left behind. Although the prison guard was waking me up in such a mean way, I was still quite happy, because I was hungry.

There was a ball of sticky rice the size of a tangerine wrapped in thin clear plastic with a small bowl of mixed vegetable beef soup. At least that was what they called it, but there were hardly any pieces of vegetable or beef in it. It was just clear liquid in a little bowl. It was as clear as a cat's tear, as my mother would say, but I wasn't complaining about the kind of food that they gave us. We appreciated every offer because we were prisoners in their country. Everything was dependent on their law and their mercy.

One thing that bothered me was how they handled the food they gave us. They gave the food to us with no compassion. The prison guards counted how many people were in each cell, and they just laid all our sticky rice balls and cat's tears soup on the cement floor and then called us to pick them up. It was as if we were their dogs or some other kind of domestic animal. In the Lao culture this was a very inappropriate manner. At least all the Thai prisoners who were locked up in the same cell with us acknowledged that we were just refugees, not criminals.

The Thai and the Lao were so closely blood related, that we shared the same culture and religion. The prison guards behaved in such a way, we found out, as a cultural gesture to insult us and to hurt our feelings. They knew all to well that was one of their secret weapons to break down our spirit. In the first five days that we were in the prison it was calm and quiet. The Thai prisoners were in their same routine, smoking cigarettes all day, and once every other hour they would argue over their chess game and talk shit to each other.

Since they were not physically threatening us, we just pretended to ignore them and whatever they were doing. There was nothing for us to do in jail. There was no TV, no books, newspapers, magazines to read, no pens or pencils and paper to write on. I was so bored and hopeless. My little brothers and sisters were so young they didn't even know that they were in jail. They were all very bored, but at least they had their brothers, sisters and imaginary friends to play house with.

As more days went by, the cigarette smoke and thick humidity were beginning to irritate my eyes and lungs. It began to have an effect on my breathing. I could feel my breathing becoming heavier and my eyes beginning to tear more, but there was nothing that I could do. All I could do all day was wipe the sweat off my face.

Late afternoon on the sixth day in the rat-cage after we were finishing our lunch, I was feeling so beaten down. All day long I was so depressed and hopeless. The best way for me to deal with it was just to sleep it off. I was lying on the hard cement floor without a mattress or any kind of cushion. My whole body was beginning to be sore. My back especially was beginning to feel numb from the coolness of the hard cement floor.

I was about ready to take my depressing nap when all of a sudden I heard the call to attention by the prison guard. I lifted up my head and took a grim look at the metal gate, the only gate to get into this rat-cage. What I saw was outrageous. I couldn't believe what appeared right in front of my eyes. There was a large group of very young Thai girls. Most of them were under 25 years of age by my best guess. They were just marching into the rat-cage. Some of the girls were walking right into the other cage and the majority of them were walking into our cage.

I was speechless, as was my mother, but the rest of my little brothers and sisters were in their own world. They just carried on with their playhouse. All the girls just kept marching in. I was asking myself, "How many people could fit into these two little rat-cages?"

While the gates were open, these people just kept coming, one by one. They marked their own little space wherever they possibly could. I was so amazed at how many people could fit into these two little rooms. I was counting each head. There were a total of 52 young girls. They were dressed mostly in blue jeans, mini-skirts, T-shirts and tank tops. Some were wearing pajamas as if they had just rolled out of bed.

As soon as these young girls marched into the jail cell all the prisoners in the cell stopped playing their chess game. They didn't seem to be surprised. It seemed as if they had seen a lot of this kind of thing. The interesting thing was to see the sparkle of excitement in the pupils of their eyes. At this particular moment, I didn't quite understand what this was supposed to mean.

Out of curiosity I made an effort to talk to a little skinny girl who had just marked her narrow spot, just big enough for her to sit next to me. She could have been the same age as I was, or maybe a few years older. I was 16 at this time.

This girl told me that her curry-house had been raided, and they all were arrested and were being sent away for rehabilitation at a detention center in another province. I was confused when she told me, because I didn't really know the meaning of the slang "curry-house." She leaned over to me and whispered into my ear, "Whore house—you got it?" I was speechless and in shock, then the alarm in my head went off. Oh my God! They are all prostitutes!

Just a few hours after the 52 prostitutes were crammed into that rat-cage, they turned it into a living hell. At first there were two girls fighting over the sitting space. They were scratching each other's faces with their nails and pulling each other's hair out of their heads. One of the male prisoners was angry, and he slapped both of the girls' faces and broke it up.

About an hour after that, another fight broke out. This time it was between two prisoners fighting over a girl; another prisoner broke them up. Their mouths and faces were bruised and bleeding. Blood was splashing all over the floor and some was on the wall. After that heated moment everyone in both rat-cages calmed down and kept quiet for a few brief moments. Soon, however all hell would break loose again.

I felt very badly for my little brothers and sisters. They had no way of knowing the reason for what had just happened. I could see they felt sympathy for the big people's world. It was written all over their faces, but nothing could stop them from being as innocent as they were. They would just pick themselves up, go back to their playhouse and continue to play with their imaginary friends. They were giggling and joking around among themselves as it nothing had happened.

I thought to myself, I am only 16 years old and I don't have any innocence left in my veins. All afternoon and into the evening I kept thinking and asking myself what the worst case scenario that could possibly happen. Would someone get raped or killed right in front of us? Will there be fighting like this every day? How long will they be staying here before they will be shipped to the detention center?

All different kinds of crazy questions were pouring down hard and deep inside my head. Because of the fight that had broken out, the prison guards had gotten mad, and they decided to punish everyone in both rat-cages. The prison guard was banging his solid wooden stick against the metal bars and announcing, "None of you *Dearasarn* deserve to have any food for dinner tonight. No one, I repeat. No one." *Dearasarn* is the Lao word for animal, and the Thai also used the same word for the same meaning.

As soon as I heard this harsh announcement I immediately thought about my little brothers and sisters. If they cried for food in the middle of the night, what would happen to them? What could I do?

It is very hard to come up with a creative idea when you are in a dead end. I knew I wouldn't find any compassion from a heart that is numb. I was wondering if there would be the possibility that some food would be served for the little children. As for me, I could go for a day or two without eating. I could take this kind of punishment with no problem. I kept thinking and thinking—I was wandering around inside my own head for hours. I still could not come up with anything.

I asked my mother if she had any idea to beg for sympathy from the prison guard. Mom was quiet; I could tell that she was also caught up in her deep thoughts of a master plan. It had been a few hours after dinnertime, and I was wondering when my little brothers and sisters would start to cry for food. I was praying to Buddha in my heart asking if he could create a miracle to let all my little brothers and sisters fall asleep without being hungry for the night, then, hopefully, food would be served again tomorrow as usual.

On this night the miracle did happen. All of the children were very tired from playing and joking around, and they fell asleep while they were sitting and leaning against the walls waiting for food. They slept through the night peacefully and quietly as if they had taken sleeping pills, in spite of the fact that all the prostitutes were chatting and the other prisoners were playing chess all night. I was very pleased that Buddha had answered my prayers.

That entire night I went without food, and I slept in a sitting position, because I couldn't stretch my body out. We were packed into the room like sardines in a can. I remember the morning after, I woke up with the sound of my stomach screaming and *"choking the chicken,"* the Lao expression for being hungry.

The next morning I woke up with massive aches, pains and soreness all over my body. I felt so empty; I kept hearing the sound of gas in my hungry stomach. I tried to ignore it, but I couldn't. It sounded like a battlefield, like a war had gone off in my stomach. I was starting to worry about myself now. Even though I thought I could go a day or two without food, I had forgotten that I had a very bad case of anemia at the time.

Thanks to the Lord Buddha, food was served again that morning as I had prayed for. Everyone in both rat-cages was calm, and I was hoping the situation would stabilize.

As the day went on it wasn't as bad as the day before. I thought to myself things will get better from now on. Yesterday was just a day of adjustment. Everyone was anxious over his or her displacement. I thought this was kind of a normal situation.

So, that day nothing serious happened except a couple of girls were teasing each other and that turned into a small argument. Dinner was served again as usual. The prison guards seemed to be very pleased with the effect of their punishment tactic. My mother and I were especially pleased, because all of my little brothers and sisters at least had some food in their little tummies, and they were playing and joking around with each other as usual.

My mind was calm, and again I hoped and prayed it would stay this way. On that very same night, at about 1 or 2 a.m. I woke up to the unusual sound of human flesh colliding and a girl moaning. I wasn't quite sure if this was moaning in pain or in pleasure. At first I thought that I was just having a nightmare, but I realized that I wasn't, so I tried to wake myself up to be on full alert. I focused on the sound that I was hearing, and within a split second I looked out of the left corner of my eyes. I saw a prisoner, the guy with the busted lip and bruised face, engaging in a sexual act with a prostitute in the rat-cage next to ours.

At first I was in disbelief at what I saw. It was so surreal. While they both were engaging in that sexual act, all the girls in that cage were dazed and trying to disengage from the situation. Some were just pretending that they were fast asleep. Some just kept chatting with each other like there was nothing happening. The rest of the prisoners were watching it as if it were some sort of great entertainment that pleasured them.

I could understand why everybody was reacting the way they were because they didn't want to make the situation any worse than it was. So did I. I thanked Buddha for keeping my little brothers and sisters asleep so they did not see the bad behavior of the big people's world.

The next morning, everything seemed to move slowly and smoothly. Whatever had happened the night before was just a *thing* that passed us by. I tried to forget about it, but every time I looked at the girl who been engaged in the sexual act the night before, I just couldn't get over it. In my head I was praying, "Please, Lord Buddha, do not permit this inappropriate behavior to occur during the day while my little brothers and sisters are awake.

Sure enough, though, on the very same day that I prayed for bad things not to happen, the worst case scenario magically occurred like a nightmare. Soon after we had lunch, while everyone in the rat-cages was trying to take a moment to rest or take a nap; it happened. Another prisoner was harassing another girl. This time it was the senior prisoner. They called him senior prisoner simply because he was there longer and had been a big shot in that rat-cage longer than anybody else. His name was Loukphee Yoa—(it means big godbrother; Yoa means long.) He was the big hot shot; no one dared to even take a look at him because we were all scared of him. He was a very scary looking character. He had a big tattoo of the Monkey God on his chest. Both of his arms were also tattooed. One arm had a picture of a mad cobra and the other had a dragon wrapped around it. On his back was a picture of a naked angel. His hair was as long as a hermit's.

Besides the prison guards he was the one that everyone feared the most except my little brothers and sisters. They were insisting on seeing what was going on in the other rat-cage while Yoa was physically and verbally harassing this skinny little girl. Because this was a very offensive action occurring in broad daylight, my mother, my older sister and I commanded our younger siblings to close their ears with both hands, face the wall and close their eyes.

They were so young, and they were very curious about why all of a sudden they had been commanded to follow such an order. Some of my little brothers were trying to move one of their hands to uncover their ear so they could hear what was going on in the background. They stopped doing that after I smacked them on the head. In this way, I was able to block them from seeing and hearing evil. This kind of behavior went on for seven long days until they all were sent away to different provinces for their drug and prostitution rehabilitation.

Two days later there was another Lao family who were thrown in jail with us. They were also refugees who had just escaped from Lao the night before. My mother was very excited to see them; my mother knew them from back in our hometown, Thakhek. They were all chatting non-stop since they had stepped foot into the rat-cage. Now my mother wasn't feeling so lonely.

My mother felt much better now that she had a friend who was also a wife of a former RLA soldier. Her friend was there with her five children, and she told my mother that her husband had been executed in the re-education camp near the Vietnam border. One thing the lady said to my mother stuck in my head like glue: *"I couldn't wait for a dead man forever."*

When I heard that from her I felt very hurt, because my mother was also there alone with all of her young children. In our case I wish there was a way of knowing for sure what had happened to my father after they took him away. I would rather know what had happened, like the lady with us. She knew for sure that her husband had been executed. For us it was even more torturous to let our hearts and minds wander for years. We kept hoping and guessing whether he was dead or alive. Every day the number of Laotian prisoners increased. The rat-cage was getting tighter and tighter.

The prison guards used the vulnerability and desperation of the Laotian refugees, who were flooding all over their border. They made extra cash by extorting money from the refugees, threatening to send them back to Laos or suppressing their living conditions while in custody.

First, the prison guards reduced the size of the food portions down to almost half of what we were used to having. Now, almost every day my little brothers and sisters were crying for more food. The longer we stayed there the more our daily hunger was accumulating. Most of the time when my little brothers or sisters cried for more food, either my mother, my sister Mok, who was few months pregnant, or I would give our portion away to the young ones to keep them calm. We would go hungry until the next serving time, praying that nothing bad would happen so we would not be punished.

The more times that we gave away our portion to the younger ones, the hungrier and weaker we became. I remember one particular dinner when my mother and I were so hungry we could not afford to give away our own portion to the young ones. My youngest sister was crying for more so my mom decided to beg for more food and the guard was cursing at her. He said,

"You already ate four or five mountains in your country, and you are still hungry and ask for more? You greedy Lao Tarkhao." (Lao-Tarkhao means Laotian white eyes—no pupil. It stands for—dumb or stupid.)

My mother was choking from his insensitive and inhuman words. I didn't know that such words could easily bring tears out of my eyes. Every drop that passed down to my lips I refused to let drop on the rat-cage floor. I swallowed every drop.

Then that night the prison guard came to take my mother out of the rat-cage. They took her to their office in front of the building where their headquarters was located. This was part of their usual procedure. They asked my mother for money, gold or silver, jewelry or whatever valuable belongings she had to speed up the illegal immigrant process so they could release us from jail and send us to a refugee camp. My mom couldn't offer them anything because she had nothing left except 800 Baht that she had saved for medicine for my little brothers and sisters in case they got sick.

My mother refused to make any offer. They were mad at her, but there was not much they could do that night. After they tried very hard to extort something out of her they just threw her back in the rat-cage like a piece of trash. The morning after, I could tell that my mother had been traumatized by what happened. She was a very smart woman with a strong will, and she was stubborn when it came to the principles of right and wrong and protecting her children. I knew she was very frustrated and angry with the prison guards for leaving her with no other options. Her eyes were glazed over with her thoughts as if she were a distant star far away from the horrifying rat-cage.

I knew that the prison guard was trying to break her will, but my mother was too strong for that. I knew that it would not be easy to break her sturdy will and hard, stubborn principles. Through her body language and facial gestures I knew that my mother was very nervous and scared, but her strong will kept her composed. A few nights later, they took her out of the rat-cage again and they asked if she had any relatives on the border that she could borrow money from to pay them off. If not, they said they would take our whole family on a boat, drop us off in the middle of the Mekong River, let us swim back to Laos and be persecuted or executed by the communist Pathet Lao.

These were the kind of things they often did. Just the thought of the cruelty frightened my mother's gentle soul, and they broke down her vital spirit. So, she begged the head of the prison guards for sympathy and made an offer of 800 Baht (about $20), which was all she had left for medical emergencies. The head of the prison guards was glad to take whatever my mother had to offer. So, she gave him the 800 Baht that she had hidden inside her bra.

The next morning, after taking all we had left, the prison guards rushed to get us out of the rat-cage. They put ten of us into the back of their pig farm pick-up truck. The floor was full of dust and some pig waste. It smelled like pig feces, but we were glad to be sitting in it. At least we could smell the fresh air and look up to see the sun. After 22 days in the rat-cage without seeing the blue sky and sunlight, we were temporally blinded from the sunlight. When we were walking out of the building, away from police custody, we were bumping into trees and electric poles on the sidewalk. Our eyes were blurry and temporarily colorblind. I had double vision and was lightheaded from hunger. I felt so physically weak, I felt like I was going to faint while trying to get up into the back of that foul-smelling pick-up truck.

We arrived at a place they called "Napho." We thought this was supposed to be a refugee camp like the prison guards had claimed, but instead it was an illegal immigrant detention center. As soon as we arrived at the headquarters of Napho, we tried to get out of the truck as fast as we possibly could. My legs had fallen asleep and I couldn't move fast enough; as I was trying extra hard to move faster, all of a sudden I heard this irritated voice in the background directed at me,

"*Leoa Leoa Noi, Leoa Leoa Noi ai Khouiy*"
"*Hurry up, hurry up you dumb ass water buffalos.*"

In my head an alarm went off. Oh fuck no, not again!

We had just bailed ourselves out of the wild lion's mouth, and now we had landed in the claws of the tiger. "What else could possibly happen?" I asked myself.

As soon as we got out of that foul pick-up truck, we were called to form a line in a little room where one of the Paramilitary Forces also known as Or Sor (Volunteer Defense Corps) was sitting holding a list of our names in his hand. He told us to raise our right hands straight up toward the sky as he called our names. He slowly took his time calling each of our names. Before he called out each name he seemed to examine it carefully with the intention of seeing if our names were fake.

He read out loud one of my younger brothers' names--Sethy, which again means "Millionaire." He was laughing sarcastically at the name and he said out loud to himself, "Why would you name this little rat, Millionaire?" My mother had no words to respond to him with. After he was laughing for a while he decided to take us to the building where we were supposed to stay. He said, *"Your family will be staying in building #2."*

Then he told us to grab our belongings and follow him. We got to Building #2 and he was looking for Slot #29, which was all the way at the end of the other side of the building. It was hard to determine which lot was #29 because there was no divider. It was just an open space. Each refugee family that was there before us had just used pieces of cloth, mosquito netting or blankets as a divider so they knew which lot belonged to them. Finally, he found Slot #29, and he indicated with a hand signal to let us know that this was our little space. Before he left us there, he made an effort to emphasize the rules and regulations of the place. He said, *"First, you must know this is not a refugee camp, it is an illegal immigrant detention center. You are in Thailand and you must obey the Thai authorities. Our rules and regulations are expected to be holy. If any one of you dares to break our rules, we will break you. If you don't follow our regulations we will force you to and we will punish you.*

You will be inspected and checked by our Or Sor five times a day.

9 a.m., 12 noon, 3 p.m., 6 p.m. and 9 p.m. before everything is shut down and everyone is expected to go to sleep. Food will be delivered once a week, and we expect that whatever portion you receive will last for a week. You must cook it yourself. We have our cooking facility out there." He pointed to the small building next to the main building where all the other refugees were cooking their food as a group.

"For the time being, before next week, we will provide you with some rice and dried fish and some cooking materials. For pots and pans you must borrow from other refugees."

My mother, my older sister and I took all of these notices into our hearts. We were concentrating and trying to stay focused, and we almost forgot to breathe just so we could hear every word he said. After he finished delivering the rules and regulations he left us there. The rest we had to figure out how to do on our own.

This time it wasn't too bad, compared to the first moments when we had originally walked into Thai police custody. At least in the detention center there were plenty of other Lao families to give us a hand. So, as we settled down, we felt so much better. The building was overcrowded, but at least we could breathe fresh air and look up at the sky and see the sunlight. We were simply waiting to be transferred to a refugee camp: "Ubon Refugee Camp" in Ubon Ratchathani province. We didn't know exactly when this would be.

According to the Lao family who lived in the slot next to us, whenever the refugees accumulated to 500, they would send all of us at once. But as long as we numbered less than 500, they would keep us here until whenever. We might be trapped in this hellhole until kingdom come.

Although our new Lao friends made this sound very harsh, I was still quite pleased with the number 500. In my naive estimation I thought to myself that it would not be longer than 20 to 30 days, because both of the buildings looked quite packed, and we were not that far away from 500.

Boy! I was so wrong with my estimation. Instead of 20 to 30 days it turned out to be 3 months and 12 days. This was 102 days of living oblivious to everything. I had no clue as to what was going to happen. In the first week that we got there we were trying to recuperate from our Thai police custody trauma and, at the same time, we were learning to adapt and cooperate with the rules and regulations of the detention center. We tried to make friends with the other Lao families. I had a couple of new friends, who were my age, and I was very pleased. Roughly, we made it through our first week.

At our first food receiving session, I was excited to see what kind of food would be provided to us. In my heart I had assured myself that whatever we would be given would definitely be better than the food when we were in police custody. Here, one person stood in line for each family and waited for the food truck to arrive at the detention center. I was the one who was standing in line to get the food for my family. Everyone on the line was holding a plastic, 4-gallon paint bucket and a clear plastic bag. I had nothing, because we had just gotten there.

Everyone was standing there anxious and excited. I was probably more excited then anyone else. Finally, two pick-up trucks were slowly pulling into the building at the center of the detention building. The building had no walls. It had a tin roof and hard cement floors and pillars. The pick-up trucks came to a full stop. The heads of each building were in charge of dividing the food equally, by averaging out the food per family member for each family.

The head of the building and a volunteer assistant, also a refugee, would empty all the food, vegetables and rice from the trunk of one of the pick up trucks. This person had a list of families and the number of family members. He told his assistant to begin spreading all the food out on the cement floor and to divide it into different piles. There was one of each item in every pile from raw fish and vegetables to cooking supplies. When he finished dividing each pile, he would call the name of the head of each family or whomever the representative of the family was to come and pick up their portion.

Each family's clear plastic bag was used for their raw fish, vegetables and cooking supplies. The assistant would use a soup bowl to scoop out the sticky rice grain from a 100 kg sack, filling each family's 4 gallon plastic paint bucket, either full or half full, depending on the number of family members. My slot number was 29 so I had to wait until they finished serving 28 other families first. Then came my family's turn. Of course, I was the last person on line. The head of building #2 finally called out my mother's name, "Oraday Phrasavath!" I then presented myself as the representative of my family instead of my mother. The head of building #2 asked me where my plastic bag and bucket were for my rice grain, and I told him that I had nothing because we were new arrivals.

He was very nice and helpful—he found an extra plastic bag for me to put my raw fish in, as well as vegetables, cooking supplies and some basic ingredients, such as non-iodized salt, a cheap brand of fish sauce and a small can of corn oil. He couldn't, however, find an extra bucket for the sticky rice grain. This was the sole source of our survival. I was in a panic. I didn't know what to do and I tried to offer him some suggestions such as using my T-shirt as a sack. He gave me a silly look and said,

"No! I don't want you to spill all your rice and then starve your family to death. Whatever we give you today you will have to make last for the whole week."

Each grain of rice was just like a piece of gold over there. I really appreciated his point blank honest suggestions. From his accent I could tell that he was from Savannakhet. He told me to just wait there until he finished wrapping things up then he would find me a bucket. But after a moment of waiting I was humiliated by the look of one of the Or Sor, who was standing a few meters away from me. He was the one who kept his eyes, ears, nose and mouth on everything that went on in our food distribution session.

The good man with the kind words finally found a plastic bucket and filled it for me without counting my family members. I was very touched by his giving attitude. I brought back all the food supplies to building #2 for my family. My mother and my older sister tried to figure out how to preserve our raw, half-spoiled Mackerel from the fresh market.

There was no refrigerator or freezer to keep it from becoming completely spoiled. Just looking at the worn-out Mackerel made me feel sad. There was probably no nutrition left in this Mackerel—not even a soul of it. But, regardless of its condition, my mother and my sister, Mok, who was five months pregnant at the time, still tried very hard to figure out how to preserve it for the whole week, so we could use it for tricking our minds when our desperate hunger would spin out of control.

Even though the 4-gallon bucket was full of sticky rice it wasn't as much in actual volume as if it had been Jasmine rice. This was because sticky rice grain is less saturated with water than Jasmine rice grain. My mother with her expertise in survival skills came up with a great idea of how to preserve the soul of the Mackerel and extend the life of the sticky rice bucket to last longer than or at least one week for our family of ten. My mother said,

"Rice we must boil and make soup out of it. Fish we will dry using sunlight to dry it. Vegetables we will wrap with newspaper then soak in some water, and the wet paper will kept them moist, and will preserve them for at least half of the week or more."

That was the master plan, but regardless of how well we could preserve it, the food already had no nutrition left in it. It didn't matter how much we ate, we still felt hungry and tired. My stomach was never full. I was hungry all the time. Every day, all I had was sticky rice soup with salt and a small piece of dried worn-out Mackerel. Sometimes at night I was so hungry I broke out in a cold sweat, was light-headed and had severe pain from stomach gas.

One time, I was able to convince two of my good friends in the detention center who were from the Pakse province in the southern part of Laos, to break the rules. We had all had very similar lives. Both of them were fatherless like me; both of their fathers were former RLA soldiers who had also been taken away right after the Lao revolution of December 2, 1975. We were crazy enough to dare to break their rules. We snuck out of the detention center to find some fruit, vegetables and whatever we could get in the nearby jungle.

I knew this could be possible because I saw a couple of people sneak out, and they would be gone for a few hours before the routine inspection time. If the Or Sor didn't see or they didn't get caught at the barbed wire fence, then they were off the hook. There were only about ten Or Sor guarding the detention center. Most of their daily routine, besides checking and inspecting us, was just hanging out in their main office, drinking their Mekong (a popular Thai hardcore whiskey) and watching Thai boxing on their black and white TV all day.

Two or three times a week they would come around and take their frustrations out on us. I knew, however, there were plenty of times I could utilize when the Or Sor looked the other way. One time three of us were out scavenging for whatever was edible in the jungle nearby. We found a small shallow creek. We dipped into the mud in this creek to search for clams, snails and crabs. There we found fresh water clams, small snails and some rice paddy crabs. We were so happy to also see all of the edible vegetables alongside the creek, so we climbed up the mango tree and grabbed as many of the young mango leaves as we could, and we wrapped them in our T-shirts.

We took whatever we could find and tried to rush back to the detention center with a hope and a prayer that all the guards were looking the other way. None of us had a watch, so we had no way of knowing how long we had been out in the jungle. We got carried away with excitement at the moments of freedom we were stealing from the guards.

We were taking very calculated risks and had faith that we would bring some nutritious foods and vegetables to share with our family and close friends. As soon as we crawled under the barbed wire fence to the other side, we heard the sound of a hammer banging on the metal rim of the car tire hanging in their main office. The Or Sor were using the rim of a car tire instead of a whistle—simply because the sound of a hammer banging on the metal rim was such an annoying sound. Every time I heard that sound I had to cover my ears—because if I didn't, I was afraid that I might go deaf from the irritation. This was the signal that instructed everyone to be with his or her family, get into formation and be present at his or her assigned slots. My assigned slot was #29 at the other end of the building.

We all were rushing to our slots to make sure we made it to our family formation. We made it on time, but the problem was far from over. When I got to my family formation I didn't have enough time to change my clothes. My pants and T-shirt were still full of mud, dirt and stains. The Or Sor asked me,

"What the hell happened to you, little rat?"

Then he panned his eyes around and saw clams, snails and young mango leaves. He asked my mother,

"Where did you get these from?"

Before my mother tried to lie or make some kind of excuse for me I took full responsibility for my own actions. Although my heart was pounding, my mouth was dry and my jaw was stiff, I had to bite the bullet and be brave. I kept encouraging myself with my own inspirational thoughts in the back of my mind. I am the son of a soldier—I am the son of a soldier—I shall not be bowed by fear.

I told him exactly what I had just done. "Sir, I was sneaking out of the detention center with friends, and we found all of these edible vegetables and things, so we brought them back with us for additional food supplies." He looked at me, but he didn't seem to be bothered by what I had said. He seemed to admire my honesty. Then I looked up at him so he could look me in the eyes and see that I was telling the truth. As soon as my eyes were engaged with his I could see a little crack of a smile on his face. Then he gently tapped his palm against my cheek and gave me a warning,

"You, little rat, will not be as lucky if you get caught by the other Or Sor."

Then he slowly walked away. I was immediately gasping for fresh air and took a long deep breath. I was very damn close to being punished without mercy. While I was trying to gather myself to confront him with my honesty, at the back of my mind I still remembered what had happened to some older guys who had snuck out of the detention center to pick some crabs and clams. When one of them got caught they made him do 50 push ups, kicked his butt with a military boot heel, and made him jog 50 times around building #2 carrying a clamp in his mouth. They threatened that if he dropped the clamp from his mouth they would double the number of rounds. Just remembering what had happened was enough to make my legs tremble, but again I had to keep reminding myself that I am the son of a soldier, I shall not be bowed by fear. I was blessed on that day.

Two months after we paid tribute to this hardship there were two Lao guys that had both come from Thakhek. They were my brother in law's friends. They had come to the detention center a few months before we got there. One day they were very hungry, perhaps more hungry than I was.

They decided to escape from the detention center. In the middle of the day they snuck out to a nearby village to ask for food. Two days later, local Thai police caught them. They were sent to police headquarters in the city of Nakhon Phanom. The police from the city headquarters contacted the Or Sor from the Napho Detention Center. The Or Sor went to pick them up with their pick up truck.

Napho was in the middle of a jungle at the time. There was no paved road from the main road to get into the center, except the old water buffalo path turned into a road which was paved with this gravel rock--in Lao we called: *"Heen Narmnor"*. This means brown thorn stone, the kind of stone that you can't walk barefoot on unless your feet have very thick skin. Instead of driving them into the detention center the Or Sor parked their pick up truck on the main road and commanded the two hungry Lao refugee escapees to crawl on the brown thorn stone gravel--wearing only their underwear—to the main office building which was centered between buildings #1 and #2.

The two escapees crawled on the brown thorn stone gravel with their semi-naked bodies, while three Or Sor, each of them with an M-16 and a leather belt with metal buckle, walked after them while kicking and stepping on them with their hard-heeled military boots. The Or Sor were constantly screaming and cursing at them while they crawled on the brown thorn stones gravel toward the main office building.

Even though the crawl was a distance of about a quarter mile, by the time the two escapees made it to the main office building, they had almost passed out from the heat, pain, bruises and cuts. They were both bleeding all over their pale, skinny and weak bodies. When they got to the main office building the Or Sor tied them up on a pole with ropes, then constantly punched the escapees with their bare hands. They hit them with their belts and the butts of their M-16s.

From a distance of about 150 meters away – with every full blow of bare hands swinging against the escapees' naked bodies - I could hear the collision of flesh against flesh. Every time I heard the thick leather belt hitting against the escapee's bodies and legs I could hear the sound of their rib cages absorbing the blows. Every time the two escapees passed out during their punishment, the guards would pour icy water on their faces to wake them up and carry on the punishment.

I stood with a group of other Lao refugees by the edge of Building #2 watching this whole event of cruelty. The Or Sor wanted us all to see it. This was a way they tried to mentally humiliate us and break our spirits. An old Laotian expression called this act of cruelty "killing chicken in front of monkey," which meant using an act of cruelty on one victim out in the open with a wish to create fear in others and break down their spirits. After both of the escapees were severely punished they put them in detention center confinement for two weeks.

After they were released the one that was my brother in-law's friend had severe brain and nerve damage. He was only 20 years old at the time, and he was already half blind from the punishment. On that day I was stunned by my own overwhelming sadness. On that day I felt very hurt inside. From that day on I knew I had a deep cut with a permanent scar on my soul. I knew that every other Laotian, who was there to witness this cruelty, felt more or less the same way as I did.

But there was no way of saying anything back to the Or Sor, because we were the landless people, we were put down and degraded below the level of their domestic animals. Every day was a trial, struggling to survive under the mercy and breath through the narrow nostrils of the corrupted authority, with hopes and prayers that we would make it through their process alive.

After two and a half months had passed by, my brother-in-law Tou and I began to lose the feeling in our legs. Every day our legs were swollen and getting bigger. The feeling in my legs was almost completely lost. Every time I squeezed my leg I would leave my own handprint in my skin as if it were a ripe mango. By the time we got transferred out of Napho detention center to a refugee camp called "Ubon Refugee Camp" in Ubon Ratchathani province, I could hardly move my leg. I was dragging myself on a homemade bamboo stick crutch to get into the bus. That was the worst case of malnutrition that I had ever experienced.

After all the hassle and hell that we had to endure we finally arrived at the first official refugee camp, Ubon Refugee Camp. The Ubon Refugee Camp was still operated by the Thai authorities, but was under UNHCR (United Nations High Commissioner for Refugee) supervision with additional support from many other international non profit organizations and religious institutions like the IRC (International Rescue Committee), ICMC (International Catholic Migration Commission) and many more.

The Ubon Refugee camp was very crowded in mid 1979. It was estimated that 15 to 16 thousand refugees from almost all parts of Laos were there. When we arrived in the Ubon Refugee Camp there were a couple of Lao men waiting to assist to get us to our assigned housing division. If I am not mistaken, I think the camp was divided into 36 divisions. My family was assigned to the 16th Division, since three of my family members were in need of immediate medical assistance. My older sister was seven-and-a half months pregnant, and my brother in-law and I were both on bamboo crutches.

The Lao volunteer workers assisted in getting us to Division 16 immediately, and they advised my brother in-law and I to get help from the refugee camp hospital right away. One of the volunteer workers told me that if my problem was not properly taken care of I could lose both of my legs. My brother in-law and I were both frightened by this warning.

Right after this we settled down in the unit where we were assigned. After being on the bus for six and a half hours that day my leg was getting worse. All day long I was worried about my legs. Deep in my heart I felt liberated; I was out of Thai prison. I was now in the refugee camp under the supervision and in the eyes and sight of an international rescue organization.

I felt safer, and I felt there was hope and some possibility that our life was only going to get better. The Ubon Refugee Camp was ten times better in comparison to the Napho detention center. But this refugee camp was a refugee camp regardless. All the refugee camps in Thailand were more or less still operated by some corrupt government officials, but at least the Ubon Ratchathani Refugee Camp was not as corrupt and inhumane as

Napho detention center.

At Ubon Refugee Camp food and cooking supplies were distributed twice a week. The fish was not as spoiled, the portions of vegetables and rice were more manageable for a family of ten, and they didn't have the strict rule that we had to be inspected five times per day. There were no camp guards walking around with their M-16s to intimidate us. The camp guards just stayed at the checkpoint at the main gate of the camp. If we called for help or if we had any major problem, for example, if a refugee needed major medical attention outside the refugee camp hospital, then they might come to assist, depending on the situation.

After a month and a half at Ubon Refugee Camp, my older sister gave birth to the most healthy and precious baby boy. We were very happy. Our lives seemed to blossom with joy and hope, although my brother in-law and I were still walking on our homemade bamboo crutches. The feeling in our legs had begun to come back. There was time to think further ahead. Here we were at the refugee camp, but where were we going from here?

Seeking asylum in a third country? Wait here until whenever?

Mom, my sister Mok and I were going to make the ultimate decision together. We decided that we wanted to move on to a third country for the sake of a better future and education for the younger siblings. Every four to six months there was a third country (every country that opens its door for the refugee to have legal resettlement, we called a third country—such as US. Canada, France, England, Germany, Switzerland, etc.) that would come to interview the refugees about whether they wanted to seek asylum in their country or if there was anyone else who would be interested in asylum or resettlement in their country.

First and foremost though, before registering for resettlement in any third country, we had to go through a scanning interview process. The Thai authorities along with international committees gave these processes three color codes. The first screening process, called the White Screening, was when the refugee family would go in to register their names, dates of birth, places of birth and the total number of family.

The second screening called the Green Screening, was when the families were called for an interview with the refugee camp official worker. Usually these official workers were mostly white westerners from America, Australia, France or Canada. Here the refugees would be photographed. There were two different types of photographs, UB and T number. The refugee had to give each type of photograph to a different post. Most important of all, the refugees had to decide which country they wished to seek asylum or resettlement in.

The third and the last screening was called Tor Mor. This was a Thai abbreviation that stood for Immigration Interview. This was when the refugee finally met and was interviewed by the representative of the third country that they had applied to.

Before we went in for our White Screening no one gave us any advice or clear information. We went in completely unprepared. On the day that we went in, we were standing in line for about an hour and a half or two. We were sitting on a bench right in front of the Thai official with a Lao refugee volunteer translator. He looked at the list of my family members that had been written down by the Thai police before we were put in their custody at Nakhon Phanom. He asked us to confirm if each of our names, our places of birth and the total number of family members was correct. After all of this basic information about our family was properly written down on the form he said,

"Oh, we almost forgot, we need each of your family members' dates of birth."

I looked at my mom; she just went blank. I thought to myself, "Oh shit." We had no list or any written information regarding our dates of birth. This kind of information had been taken care of by my father, because my mother couldn't read or write. I had to come up with something creative, and quick, otherwise we were going nowhere. From what I remembered, my younger brother, Sethy (the one born after me), was six years younger than I was.

Back in Laos I was old enough to remember my father had told me my exact birthdate. From using my birth date as a reference, I figured out that my younger brother Sethy's date of birth was six years different then mine. I was then able to come up with a simple numerical system, which remained easy to remember in all types of situations, without a list for the rest of my life. For my three younger brothers and three younger sisters the date I was starting with was 3 and the month started with 2 and the year I started with was 1970, because I was born in 1964 and Sethy was 6 years younger than me.

For the dates I started with = 3, 6, 9, 12, 15, 18; for the month I used 2, 4, 6, 8, 10, 12 and for the year I used 1968, 1970, 1971, 1972, 1973, 1974 and 1975.

After I came up with the numerical system in my head I asked the Thai official if he wouldn't mind if I wrote it down for him, because there were too many numbers for me to dictate. It was close to his lunch break, so he didn't mind. He handed me a blank piece of paper and a pen. I just created a complete list of names and dates of birth for my family, and the Thai official completed his form.

After he finished completing the form he gave us our UB number. UB stood for Ubon. It is a family identification number. Before he let us go home and wait until we got called for our Green Screening, he explained the procedure to make sure every time we looked at the posted information on the bulletin board, all we needed to do was look for our UB number, not our names.

We were one step forward on our journey to the third country, but we hadn't decided which country. We didn't have any idea which country we wanted or qualified for resettlement in. My mom kept insisting that we should look into resettlement in America instead of Australia, France, England, Canada, Switzerland, Germany, Belgium, Argentina, Japan, China and some other nations. Mom insisted on coming to America because Dad used to work for the Americans during the war and she said, *"If we go to America we will have a better chance of being taken care of because we are the wife and children of a soldier who served them."*

So as acting representative of my family, I looked into resettlement in America for the reasons my mom had given. It was about four months after our White Screening that our UB number appeared on the bulletin board, posting the date of our Green Screening. We were very excited. We couldn't wait any longer to get out of the refugee camp in Thailand. We were exhausted with the life of a refugee. We had nothing important to do. My mother and I were especially worried about my younger siblings, because they were at the age where they needed to have some basic education including learning how to read and write.

There was some schooling and ESL (English as a Second Language) classes for kids and adults run by a third country NGO (Non-governmental Organization), but there was no proper school with an academically trained teacher for the children in the refugee camp. It was rather urgent that we get our family out of the camp as soon as possible.

Finally, the day of our Green Screening arrived. Of course, as usual, before we could meet any officials we had to stand in line for hours. After over two hours standing in intense heat and thick humidity, by the time we got the call for our Green Screening interview I was already exhausted, thirsty and hungry. Thank goodness by this time my malnutrition condition was almost fully recovered; I was strong enough to walk and stand on my own two feet without homemade bamboo crutch.

While we were standing in line waiting for our UB number to be called, I was thinking of all the possible crazy questions the interviewer could ask me. For some reason the absence of my father led me to think there could be an issue, but whatever would happen on that day, I was willing to accept it, and I had to make sure I had some room in my heart for disappointment if the Green Screening didn't go well.

There were eleven of us. I was the one who my mother had chosen to be the spokesperson for the family. I was very shaken by my thoughts that the worst case scenario could happen.

I still clearly remember our first time meeting with the westerner. His name was Mr. Charles. I don't remember his last name. He was a slim, tall, white American, and he worked there in Ubon Refugee Camp. He was a quiet person, but seemed to be a very kind and caring person with a soft-spoken voice. Despite this, I still couldn't help but be frightened when I was in his presence. There I was, standing right in front of Mr. Charles and his Lao interpreter. The first question he hit me with, was regarding my father.

(Through interpreter)

Mr. Charles:

"Why is your father not here?"

"He was taken away by the Communists two months after the revolution." I replied.

Mr. Charles:

"What was your father's occupation before 1975?"

"Soldier! Soldier, sir!" I replied.

Mr. Charles:

"What kind of soldier? Do you or your mother know?"

"He was an RLA soldier, sir." I replied.

Mr. Charles:

"What rank, Do you remember?"

"I think he was a captain or commander or something. Honestly, we didn't really know him in terms of his work and duties, sir." I replied.

Mr. Charles:

"All right, that is very good. I just want to make sure that everyone's dates of birth are correct. Could you please give me each of your family members' dates of birth?"

I knew by western cultural standards that remembering dates of birth was very critical, and basic, but for me it was a challenge. I came from a country where date of birth is not an emphasis of the society. I didn't have the privilege of access to proper records, lists, or even personal handwritten notes of our parents. To avoid my numerical system from being noticed by Mr. Charles I carefully dictated the dates to him one by one without him realizing my numerical invention system. I was off the hook, and I was very pleased. So far so good!

Mr. Charles:

"Not bad for remembering your entire family's dates of birth. This is very important in the third countries; I am very impressed," he praised me.

"Thank you, sir," was my response.

Mr. Charles:

"All right, let's talk about the third countries now. Do you have any family members or close relatives in the third countries - America!

Canada! France—No!

"None, sir," I replied.

Mr. Charles:

"Did your family decide what country you want to go to?"

"My mother insisted that we should look into resettlement for our new life in America sir." I replied.

Mr. Charles:

"Why America?"

"I don't know, sir. But my mother said that we would have a better life in America." I replied.

Mr. Charles:

"Well, if this is the case than I will sign up your family for the American immigration interviewer. I think the next American immigration interviewer will be here four or five months from now."

"Thank you very much, Mr. Charles." I replied.

Mr. Charles:

"You all are done for today. You may leave now. Good luck to you all."

Mr. Charles handed us a sheet of paper. On it there was a UB number and a T number. Our UB number was UB05520 and our T number was

T155286. Then the Lao interpreter led us to the photography unit, so we could have our UB and T number photos taken. These were the two different types of photographs required by all refugees for identification. The refugee had to give one of each type to a different post. The T number photograph was a half body shot of the each person holding chalkboard with their T number written on it. It looks like a police mug shot of a criminal. The UB photo was a family photo in which we were all lined up as if we were ready for execution by fire squad.

That day we left the Ubon Refugee main office with happy hearts full of hope. America was on the list of our final destinations we had wished for. Our life went on as usual, refugee camp style. There was more crowding, more chaos. Everyday the number of refugees kept increasing. The more the numbers increased, the smaller the portions of our food supplies became.

Again, the fear of hunger and malnutrition was hitting home, especially for my brother-in-law and me. To prevent this from happening again, my quick thinking mother who had managed to save two ounces of a pure 24K yellow gold chain even after what we had gone through Thai police custody, sold it to start a little business.

In Ubon refugee camp there was a small fresh market where every morning the Thai food and vegetable merchants went to sell to the refugees who could afford to buy. Most of the refugees who could afford to buy extra food were the ones who already had family members or close relatives residing in the third countries who sent them money. There were plenty of buyers.

My mother saw an opportunity, and she grabbed it. From the money that she received by selling her two ounces of 24k gold, she was able to start a little dried food store. She bribed the camp guard so she could go out of the refugee camp to downtown Ubon Ratchathani to buy different kinds of dried fish, noodles, cooking ingredients and whatever else the refugees demanded. We would sell it at double or triple the price. From the little profit that we made, our life improved.

I was the one who ran our little food shop. Every morning I had to wake up at 5 a.m. to prepare the product and give my mom the order of what our shop needed. Then, she would go out and find it. I had great admiration for her merchant skills—for someone who couldn't read or write and only knew how to talk and count numbers. Here we were in a different land,

and she managed to give us a sense of security and a life that was better than most of the refugees in the camp, who been there long before we arrived.

Now my life was not boring at all. I was constantly busy taking care of the shop, helping Mom with whatever she needed and looking after my younger siblings so they would be safe. Instead of the average of 4 to 5 months wait, it turned out to be 8 1/2 months later that we were called for Tor Mor screening (Immigration Screening) with US immigration.

Before we had the Immigration Screening with the US immigration officer, we heard a rumor about him. Nobody really knew his name, but many people, who failed an immigration interview with him, remembered what he looked like. From their description he was a heavy, white American with a big, red face and a short-fuse attitude, who knew how to speak Lao very well. He had a tattoo of a rooster on his arm. Some called him Mr. Kein Lai-Lao for Mr. Tattoo Arm. From his reputation I was very intimidated, and I couldn't fall asleep for days before the interview.

It usually took two to three weeks after the UB number was posted on the bulletin board before the actual date of the interview took place. Within this three-week period I was gathering all my resources and figuring out in my head how to write out all the possible questions and answers in such a way that would make sense for myself. I was asking people all around, especially those who failed his interview, what kind of questions Mr. Kein Lai liked to ask.

I got some clues. In this way my third, last and final judgment day had arrived. I couldn't fall asleep the night before the interview. I was worried sick about how I would make it through. I knew that I had never been in America or even knew anything about America. Just hearing the name - America - was already making me hyper. I don't know why; it seemed as though this was our destiny, and that destiny was calling us to fulfill its need. It was a weird experience I couldn't quite explain. It was a *calling*.

Here we were in the same routine, standing under the radiating heat of the equator sun, wiping our rivers of sweat, breathing in the thick humidity, waiting in line with at least a hundred families ahead of us. We were waiting to meet my ultimate fear and challenge. I felt like a contender waiting to go into the ring with Muhammad Ali. The chance for me to withstand his full-blown punch and make it out alive was 1000-to-1.

I thought escaping across the Mekong with a narrow margin of 500 feet from the mouth of the Pathet Lao soldier's AK-47 assault rifle, B-40 shoulder rocket launcher, and machine guns was frightening. There was no comparing that fear to the fear that processed in my imagination of this US immigration officer, this big dude with a rooster tattoo on his arm. I couldn't figure out at the time why I was so frightened of a person whom I had never met. After three and a half hours, I finally heard the voice of a man calling our UB number from a room a short distance away. I couldn't quite see the person who was calling us because the room was divided by a bamboo wall. As we were walking toward this room my heart was pounding heavier and heavier. I could hear my own heartbeat; it sounded almost like an old stream engine. Clunk! Clunk-Clunk! Oh shit! Here I am.

When we got to his table it seemed like that old stream engine came to an immediate halt, but in slow motion. It seemed like everything went blank and silent. Here he was—he looked almost exactly as the other refugees had described him—except his face was much redder. I was so nervous and scared I totally forgot to take a look at his arm to see if there was a rooster tattoo or not. I did not know for sure if this was Mr. Kein Lai, but in the back of my mind I was subconsciously sure that I was seeing him as Mr. Kein Lai.

My mind was so dulled by fear and confusion. After a moment passed I came to realize that he was a different immigration officer. Even so, the intimidation and intense fear continued to grow. I became even more fearful of this man than of the one I was expecting because all of my mental preparation was now shifted onto a completely different target. Anyway, this man was right there. I felt as if he were right there in my face. He gave us a grim look, and took a long, deep drag of his half-lit cigarette, while he examined the list of our names and dates of birth. As he blew out the smoke, his big head with curly blonde hair was silhouetted against the sunlight that leaked through the bamboo wall.

The room was filled with cigarette smoke. When he raised his face and looked at us, even before he asked any questions, he frightened me. There was no translator, only him alone in the room. Since I never knew for sure who he was, I named him Immigration Officer X. Within a few seconds he asked the first question,

Immigration officer X:

"Your father's name is Mr. Santy. Is that correct?"

I was blank for a split second, and then I was able to compose myself and concentrate:

"Yes! Ah, Yes, sir! Mr. Santy. Santy Phrasavath was indeed my father sir!

I am his first son and these are my siblings. This is my mother and this is my brother in-law." I replied.

He was quiet for a moment; he might have thought that I was a cassette tape player, just press one button and the motor would keep running non-stop. He seemed to be cool with my enthusiasm, although he still looked mean, and frightened me with sharp glittering sparks in his big blue eyes. For a few seconds our eyes engaged, and I felt like I was looking into a magic crystal ball. It was a brief moment of an out-of-body experience. Then he pounded me with his second question,

Immigration officer X:

"How do I know for sure that you are really his son and this is his real family?"

I was choked by his question. This was the question about proving our identity that I was worried about. At that very moment, it was hard to come up with a straightforward answer. I paused for a second, then I started to panic, because my mind had blanked out. A moment after that, the unexpected words just came out of my mouth:

"We carry his family name, Phrasavath, sir." I said.

Immigration officer X:

"What else?"

"Sir, I can give you a couple of names of his military bases where I used to go visit him during wartime."

Immigration officer X:

"Go ahead!"

I was stuttering and shaky:

"Chinaimo.

Narm thorn.

Pou Louang.

Atapeu."

Immigration officer X:

"OK, that is good enough. What about giving me all of your family's dates of birth!"

I took a deep breath as I felt slightly better about his second question. For the dates of birth I was well practiced since the day I had invented my numerical system. I was fully confident in it. I just recited straight from my head exactly what I had listed on the paper.

"2 / 3 / 1969
4 / 6 / 1970
6 / 9 / 1971
8 / 12 / 1972
10 /15 / 1973
12 /18 / 1974"

Immigration officer X said with a little crack of a smile the size of a sewing needle on his lips, "I am very impressed, but I am curious about how come all the years are arranged in such order?"

As soon as I heard that question I wished I could dive through the solid ground, drop dead and get it over with. The alarm went off in my head. Shit! Shit! Shit! I think he just got me. No, no, no, I am not going to let him. No, he won't!

This was the internal discussion that went on in my head. Then I took a lightning flash look at my little brothers and sisters; the one thing that struck me and sparked a thought was that they were all standing in such a way that they looked like the slope of a mountain from the shortest to the tallest. One answer that bumped into my frozen brain was that they were all nine months apart from each other—that's why.

By the time I had been run over by this good thought—I wasn't quite sure how long I had been lost deep in my own head. I immediately and excitedly responded to him:

"Sir! They were all born nine months apart, that's why the years are arranged in such a way."

Immigration officer X made an effort to glimpse at the slope of the mountain, and he nodded with approval. Then he quickly signed the paper and ripped off the bottom sheet which was separated by carbon paper, and gave it to us. It was all written in English; I had no knowledge of what it meant.

"Good-bye!" Immigration officer X said to us. That was all he said. We just awkwardly walked out of the room, more or less confused. Perhaps he assumed that we understood what had just happened.

Right before we stepped out of the door, one of our Lao volunteer translator brothers asked if he could see what was written on our carbon copy. He just took a quick look at it and congratulated us. He said "You passed!" I was like, oh no you don't, you're just kidding us with this mean joke. To me, when immigration officer X had said good-bye, I thought he meant for us to say good-bye to going to America.

After I realized that we had just scored the home run for America—I thought, hell yeah, let's lose our heads for the day. My brother-in-law, Tou and I drank at least a bottle and a half of Mekong whiskey, until we crawled on the floor like catfish in the monsoon. This was one of the fondest moments, from all I could remember, while dreaming of coming to America.

The next day we began to pack our belongings and get ready for the day we would leave Ubon Refugee Camp. America was on my mind. After we got approval to come to America, I thought we would be transferring out of the Ubon within the next few weeks, or at the longest, a month.

After a month passed, our T number wasn't showing up on the bulletin board. I wondered what was happening. After two months passed we still had not seen our T number on any bulletin board. I began to worry, and thought of the worst things possible. This could have been a mean joke by the translator, because on the day of the interview, Immigration Officer X hadn't said anything about whether we had passed or failed. I had doubts.

After three months had passed by, I began to lose hope for coming to America. I began to ask people for advice; besides America, what other country was good to go to? Someone told me that I should look into the possibility of resettlement in Canada. Although it was described as cold and snowy, they said the government was good. I was thinking seriously about this possibility. I went into the UNHCR office and asked when Canadian Immigration would be coming to the camp for resettlement interviews.

One of the official refugee workers told me that Canadian Immigration wouldn't be in the camp for three months. I didn't know what to think. I decided to stay put and be calm about it. I just let life flow as it pleased. The best I could do was just live life and wait around as usual. Our dried food shop was still in operation. My mother decided not to close it until our T number with a definite travel date appeared on the bulletin board.

Not until six months later did I finally see our T number show up on the bulletin board. When I saw it I couldn't believe my eyes. I went back to check it three times just to make sure that was really our T#155286. Indeed it was.

Even though I was hanging on the edge of limbo for six months the excitement of coming to America wasn't lost at all. It was exactly two weeks after our T#155286 appeared on the bulletin board that we were sitting in an air conditioned bus on the way to the Rangsit Transit Center, located at

Chonburi Province right across the road from another refugee camp called Phanat Nikhom, about 20 km away from the capitol, Bangkok.

After approximately five hours of a smooth bus ride, the convoy of refugee buses was pulling into the Rangsit Transit Center where there was a group of camp guards waiting to receive us in front of the main office building, just outside the fence. As soon as the buses came to a complete stop and engines were turned off, we were about to grab our belongings from the overhead compartments, when a camp guard hopped into our bus and banged his stick against the metal frame of the bus seats. Some refugees who were still asleep woke up to their nightmare.

"Wake up and hurry up, all of you water buffalo."

Immediately, I had this bitter taste in my mouth before I had even gotten out of the bus. This place reminded me of the Napho Detention Center. As we were stepping out of the bus—sure enough—there was the same type of hard-faced camp guard almost exactly like the one who sent us to a living hell once before in Napho Detention Center. He was standing there to rush us off of the buses. I felt bad for the little kids and elders who didn't have the capability to mobilize at a quick enough speed to satisfy him. He would scream right in their ears to make them move faster. He acted as if he were a drill sergeant drilling an army of poor and helpless elderly refugees and children.

We were then ordered to form a line and get ready to march with all of our belongings to our assigned living units. While we were marching along, he gave us the instructions on how we should follow the rules and regulations. Most of us couldn't pay much attention. Just walking with the hard-faced guard along the tall, corrugated metal fence with barbed wire coiled around the top was more than enough for me.

The Rangsit Transit Center was the temporary holding camp before moving on to resettlement for our new life in the third country. This camp was for all groups of refugees from Laos, Cambodia and Vietnam, who were finishing their immigration process and completing their ESL (English as Second Language) and CO (Cultural Orientation) programs from other refugee camps within Thailand other than Phanat Nikhom. It was also for large refugee families who couldn't easily find a private family sponsor in a third country. Due to crowded condition in the Thai refugee camps, the large families were sent away to complete their ESL and CO in the PRPC (Philippine Refugee Processing Center). These large family groups were dependent on non-profit organizations, churches and religious institutions or agencies like the IRC (International Rescue Committee) and CWS (Church World Service) to sponsor them.

My family was one of thousands that was assigned to complete our ESL and CO program in PRPC. According to word of mouth information, the maximum holding time in the Rangsit Transit Center was approximately two months. The rules and regulations were usually extremely strict, especially for the Vietnamese and Cambodians. As for the Laotians, it wasn't as bad by comparison, due to our closer relationship in culture, religion and language.

The Rangsit Transit Center had a typical corrugated metal fence with barbed wire coiled around the top. The buildings were without room dividers, had hard cement floors without mattresses, no beds or baths and no cooking space. There were eleven people in my family—the place that they had assigned for my family had about 1.5 square meters of hard cement floor space for each one of us. It was so crowded, that I think at the time we were there, there must have been at least six thousand refugees packed into this condensed space.

Food was served twice a day; lunch and dinner. Most of the time whatever we had for lunch was what we were going to have for dinner. Most of the food we got was tofu soup, served pig farm style. A 4x4 pick up truck dragging 400- gallon military water tanks full of tofu soup would pull up. The service man would stand on the side of the soup tank with a big, extended aluminum dipper at hand. He would scream very loudly so everyone could hear him.

At serving time, all the refugees—Lao, Cambodian and Vietnamese—would run after the soup tank with our empty cans, pots, pans, plastic or aluminum buckets or whatever we could use to bring food for our family. Every time I ran after that pick-up truck and stood in line with other refugees waiting for my chance to fill up my bucket, I felt like I was on a pig farm, living in a cage, waiting to be fed.

As for water, there were several large aluminum tanks which they refilled a few times a day. I would go to get it with a plastic bucket that they had provided, and bring it back to our assigned living space. We would drink, clean our dishes, wash our hands and faces and do everything else with it.

For bathing, there were only about five or six open bathing water tanks for the entire Rangsit Transit Center, which was packed with close to six thousand refugees. There was no privacy in our bathing system. Most of the time I was too shy to take a bath. Within the period of two months and three weeks that we were there, I bathed in the open bathing tank less than six times. Most other times, I would bathe myself differently than the usual way. I called it the "dry-bathing" style. All I needed was a piece of cloth soaked with water, and I would clean every part of my body with it. With dry-bathing I felt so much cleaner because I took the time to really clean myself. Every time I had bathed at the open bathing tank, I had to rush, because other people were waiting in line. I was extremely uncomfortable with this arrangement.

The smell was indescribable. There were toilets, but they were all squat toilets. There was no toilet flusher; everyone had to dip the water from the same open bathing tanks to flush down their own waste. Most of the times there was no toilet paper. People had to bring their own toilet paper. Sometimes when my family ran out of it or couldn't afford to pay for it, I had to use my best God-given tool— five fingers and a plastic dipper.

Two months and three weeks of living with these conditions was already enough to tear any dreams out of any man's skull. But we hung on and kept our dream of America alive. Beyond the conditions and obstacles that we had to endure daily to just get over the peak of the hump, I couldn't help but think about the Vietnamese and Cambodians who were falling into even worse situations then we were.

I understood and spoke Thai very well, sometimes I felt so hurt deep down in my soul, when I heard the camp guards cursing at the Vietnamese and the Cambodian refugees, who did not understand Thai. The camp guards would curse at them over minor misconduct due to the language barrier as if they were valueless being. Some of the words they used were so inhumane.

The camp guards provoked me to think, and I couldn't help but ask, why do we all have to be treated worse than their domesticated animals? We were just the victims of war, seeking civil liberty, begging for mercy and crying out to be treated humanely. We were not Communists or terrorists; we were just helpless refugees.

Although the Rangsit Center was fully funded by the UNHCR (United Nations High Commissioner for Refugee), we were still under the Thai authority. The living conditions were still very poor and unsanitary due to corruption, and the authority enforcers were very cruel and unforgiving.

Because the living conditions were physically and mentally harsh, as well as stressful and unsanitary, many refugees who were stuck there for a short time or who were just passing through, contracted some intestinal diseases that produced severe diarrhea, vomiting, dehydration and gastric pain. Eating low quality food, and drinking water from resources that were not chlorinated and were contaminated with some bacteria caused this. My seven month-old nephew, my two younger sisters and I suffered from some of these symptoms while we were at the Rangsit Transit Center. Luckily, we weren't the worst cases.

The maximum waiting time at Rangsit was normally two months, but we didn't get out until two months and three weeks later. The three weeks seemed like 30 extra years of solitary confinement in maximum-security.

We headed to another holding camp, called Lumpinee, which is right in the heart of the capital, Bangkok. This was one of the holding facilities before we boarded the plane at Don Mueang International Airport. The maximum wait was two days to two weeks. The condition of the facilities was indescribable. Thank God that we were only there for two nights. These were the last two nights of my bitter dream, thus ending a chapter, which many refugees called: The Twilight at the Land of Cry.

Note to reader:

I want to clarify that I do not intend to generalize or try to convince people that all Thai people are bad. All the horrible experiences that we—the Lao, Vietnamese and Cambodians - went through as refugees in Thai refugee camps was an act of a very small group of corrupt officials. This should not concern the rest of the good, kind-hearted, loving, and most generous Thai, who had nothing to do with this corrupt authority. My intention is not to criticize or try to jeopardize the reputation of the Thai; I just want to share the true story of what happened behind the closed gate and barbed wire fence of the refugee camps in Thailand while I was there. In this way my children and grandchildren will understand the hardships that I had to endure before I got an opportunity to live my life in such a privileged nation—the United States of America, the land that gave me freedom and civil liberty. It is my hope that the generation I am planting in this country will never take their pride and the price of freedom for granted, or degrade its value in any way during their lifetime or in the generations to come. The journey to the "land of the free," for me took much more than years of enduring horrible hardship, dehumanization, hatred, ethnic prejudice, fear and loss. It took a soul of faith and a heart full of trust in the existence of humanity on the planet.

Again, what happened behind the closed gate and barbed wire fence should only concern the abused refugees who were permanently scarred by their acts of inhumanity, the corrupted refugee camp officials, the bad camp guards. These small groups of people are not representative of what Thailand is all about. I have many close relatives, dearest Thai friends who I love and have a great respect for all over Thailand.

I was anxiously and impatiently waiting for the boarding to be completed at Don Mueang International while our fellow refugees from Laos, Cambodia and Vietnam were searching for their seats and putting their personal belongings in overhead compartments. I had a thousand thoughts wandering around in my head; my tears of happiness were unexpectedly overflowing.

As the engine of the plane was starting and the giant eagles were pushing out of the gate my heart was pounding with excitement. It was the moment that I had dreamt about for the longest time. The giant eagle began to slowly crawl, then run, before it gained maximum speed and was ready to fly. I looked out of the little window, as the four gigantic jet engines were about to lift some 360 tons of weight off the ground. My heart was pounding faster, and I was feeling lighter as the giant eagle was about to lift off the ground. A moment later we were airborne.

As the landing gear was folding into the big belly of this giant eagle, we were elevated above the monsoon clouds, high up in the sky, a long distance above the face of Mother Toranee (the godmother of the earth). As my sight was stretched over a great distance in miles, I recalled for the first time in a while the fond memory of my grandfather telling me that our world was round like an orange. I was holding that thought close to my heart. It was the first time in my life that I believed it. My feet were now completely off that ground. The question I had for myself at that very moment was, when will be the cycle of my return, or will it ever be?

After two and one half hours crossing the ocean's sky, we landed at an island on the eastern edge of the South China Sea. It was Manila—the capital city of the Philippines. There was a convoy of buses and a troop of refugee officials waiting for us to arrive at the airport. As soon as the main door of the Boeing 747 opened, one official refugee worker walked into the plane and gave us instructions on how to get onto the buses.

Most of us didn't understand a word of instruction, because it was in English. We just followed the crowd and hand gestures to get on the buses that were parked in front of the airport. Each bus had a sign, "PRPC." (Philippine Refugee Processing Center). Soon, we were packed into the buses, the

Laotians, Cambodians and Vietnamese. After we were seated, the convoy began to move. We were heading to PRPC. After about a 20-minute ride from the airport the whole convoy suddenly pulled into a rest area and the refugees were instructed to leave their belongings and get off the bus. My family was in luck, because on our bus we had a Lao man in his 50s who was a former USAID worker, and he understood English. He volunteered to translate all the instructions, so we could understand the officials and the bus driver.

We were let loose to hang out in the rest area for a few hours before the convoy resumed. There was food, water, juice, cookies and candy for the kids. After two months and three weeks in the Rangsit Transit Center and two nights in Lumpinee, my family and I were very hungry for some variety of nutritious food. We stuffed ourselves to the max. So did other refugees. We ate everything that they gave us, juices, water, fruit, bread and cookies. While we were waiting, the Lao man who understood English went to ask the bus driver a question. Then, he came around and told all the Lao that the reason why the convoy had stopped and let us hang around at that rest area was because the driver preferred to travel at night for safety precautions due to road conditions.

I couldn't quite comprehend why the night was safer than the day. The phrase "road conditions" triggered an unforgettable childhood memory. Once, when I was about ten years old I was traveling to Vientiane with my family at the peak of monsoon season. Vientiane is the capitol of Laos. We were traveling on the one and only main Axis Road Number 13 that ran through the entire country from north to south. This was the only road left from 60 years of the French colonial period when the French were building for their own military purpose.

The road was not tar paved; it was like a horse and carriage path. I was riding on an old commercial bus, traveling all day from sunrise to sunset. Wherever we arrived at sunset, was where the bus would stop. To travel a distance of 350 km from Thakhek to Vientiane took us two days and one night, traveling through the intense heat, thick humidity, heavy rains and monsoon storms, deep potholes of mud, ferry crossing rivers and crawling on crumbled left-over bridges from colonial time.

This was my unforgettable trip to the Lao capitol. In my head the worry alarms went off. I was praying that the road to PRPC wouldn't be the same. At about 7:30 PM we heard the bus driver's whistle signaling us to get back to our bus. We boarded the bus excitedly. With stomachs full of food, some good rest and fresh air, we were ready.

The convoy resumed with the refugees clapping hands and applauding the driver. The driver laughed, and we were on our way to the PRPC. After about two hours into our destination. I began to understand why the driver chose to travel at night. The Philippines is an island country and most of their roads and highways are built over mountaintops, with summits, rocky hills, and snakelike twists around the edge of cliffs. The roads curved along the mountain slope, up and down along the elevations of mountains; it was a rollercoaster.

Almost everyone in the bus, kids, the elderly and pregnant women were bus sick. I thought three of my younger siblings would die from the worst bus sickness; it was surreal. The seats were soaked with saliva and spit, the floors and walkways were flooded with vomit. All of those boxes and boxes of food and drink were now coming back up, and it was spreading out all over the bus.

For two hours toward our final destination of PRPC, I smelled nothing in that bus but vomit and Tiger Balm. I heard nothing else but kids and women crying and elderly people praying and chanting charms for safety. We more or less felt as if we were having a near death experience from the dizziness, even up to the point where I began to hallucinate. The trip took about four and one half hours, and over half of that felt as if

we were riding on a rollercoaster. We finally arrived at the PRPC. My pants and shirt were soaked with my brothers' and sisters' vomit and spit. As soon as we got out of the bus almost everyone lay down flat on the ground. Everyone was pale, weak and soft like steamed vegetables. We had survived this miserable bus riding experience, but it was one hell of a rollercoaster ride.

PRPC was a very peaceful place. It was set on a mountain slope about a mile away from a town called Morong in Bataan province. We were a distance of about ten to fifteen miles from the US Navy base at Bataan. In PRPC's natural environment I found peace and serenity, but seeing the US Navy jet fighters take off and fly by almost every day seem kind of odd. It reminded me so much of my childhood wartime experiences. Once in a while I had a weird flashback of war. This was the first time I realized that my childhood war experiences had had an effect on my psyche. Sometimes when I heard the sound of US Navy jets flying by the camp I broke out in a cold sweat without knowing why.

Life here was considered great compared to Thailand. In PRPC all the refugees (Lao, Cambodians and Vietnamese) were free to go about and do whatever they pleased. There were no significant strict rules; we didn't get the hard-faced expressions of hate from the police and military guards, and I didn't feel intimidated by them. They were around all the time; every time we saw them, they would raise their hands to say hello or wave good-bye to us. They were very nice.

One of the few easy rules that we had to follow was that the refugees had to attend all of their ESL and CO classes and do public service work. Some of the public service work was volunteering to help with whatever the PRPC needed, like cutting grass, cleaning their offices, and cleaning the shared refugee bathrooms once a week. Every night all the refugees had to be in their rooms or at least in their assigned building. Compared to the refugee camps in Thailand's rules, I could follow these nonrestrictive rules, while doing a headstand. I was so pleased with all the PRPC's rules and regulations.

I began attending my ESL classes; I was put in grade one since I had no prior English background. I started from A, B, C, one, two, three. Most of my classmates were Vietnamese and Cambodian; there were only three other Laotians in my class. I had a great time in my ESL class. My ESL teacher was Mr. Mateo. He was very patient and kind. He was very passionate about his teaching. I will never forget my first day in his class; before we started Mr. Mateo gave the class his big dimpled smile and delivered his welcome,

"Welcome to P R P C."

We all loved Mr. Mateo. After three and a half months of ESL, my English was still zero. I just couldn't get the hang of it. It was so hard. It sounded very fast, and every time I tried to translate or understand the structure between Lao and English everything was dyslexic or backward from each other. For me to think in English I had to be dyslexic in Lao. That was like Leonardo Da Vinci writing his secret code backwards, which then could only be read in the reflection of a mirror.

At the time, my mind was so disoriented that I had a very tough time even functioning in a normal straight line–forget about commanding it to function in dyslexic mode. So, for me, it was three and a half months of wasted time and mind wandering in la-la land. After the ESL program was over, I had two weeks off before the cultural orientation class started.

Cultural orientation was a special class for all the refugees. The purpose of the class was to teach us how to cope with our new environment in America. It would teach us: How to turn on a gas stove, flush a toilet, turn on the shower, turn on the heat or air conditioning, use a telephone and intercom in an apartment building, call 911 for emergency help from the police and for medical assistance. It also taught us basic American mannerisms such as: Americans love to talk, so practice your English when you get there, then you can talk to them. You can say hello, but don't get too close to them, because American don't like people they don't know being physically close to them. In America men and women are considered equal. Touching someone's head is OK as long as you don't step on their feet. Never ask people their age and how much money they make. Also, never make any comments if they are fat. (For the Lao, commenting on someone's weight is complimenting them on their wealth and good financial status.)

When I was in my CO classes I had a couple of Lao friends who had a close relative who had been already resettled in America for a while. Sometimes after our CO class they would invite me to their room to hang out, drink beer and smoke cigarettes with them. They would read to me the letters from their relatives encouraging them to endure the hardships of refugee life and hope for a more beautiful life in America. In the letters they would make comments like:

"If you made it to PRPC that means you are one footstep away from paradise, hang on tight in the limbo etc..."

They would show me photographs of their relatives in America. The photos showed a group of young Laotians playing in the snow wearing heavy coats, scarves, ski hats, and boots with a snowman in the background. These images gave me dreams of America, and made me believe what America would be like. My dream of America was beyond extraordinary.

6

Coming to America

With the beautiful vision of America in my heart, and great hopes and expectations in mind, coming to America was a dream.

I got great news from the bulletin board at the headquarters of PRPC on May 11, 1982. Again, our T#155286 appeared on the list. As soon as I found this out I made the exciting announcement to my family that we would be leaving PRPC for America within the next two weeks. I remember seeing my mother's tears streaming from the corners of her eyes.

The next morning after the T number had shown up, we had to go into the main PRPC office for our final destination information meeting. We would be getting the name of the sponsorship, the exact date of travel, and medical check ups, which we would all have to have, along with X-rays. Early in the morning we would be standing in line to meet with the official refugee worker to get our package; after we got our complete information package we were sent to another line for our X-rays. Three days after we finished our X-rays we had to go back to meet with a medical official to make sure that we were all healthy and had no contagious diseases such as TB.

If the X-ray of our lungs was clear then the official would approve our travel date. If any one of our family members was having some medical issues then the official would hold the whole family until the medical issue was clear. I had 11 people in my family, and I hoped and prayed that none of them would have any contractible disease or other weird disease. Thank God, all of our X-rays and blood tests were clear. We were all healthy and free to go. Within that week and a half of waiting, every night before I went to bed, I prayed for the safe journey of my family to the new country.

The day of our leaving was May 22, 1982, early in the morning. It was the morning that summed up all of my emotions, the morning of my greatest happiness, sadness, worry and fear. All of our friends and next room neighbors were gathering in front of PRPC headquarters to say good-bye before the convoy of buses came to take us back to Manila. We would be on that same hellish roller coaster highway. I couldn't help but think about the highway.

The more I thought about it, the more I got worried, because this time we would be traveling back to Manila during the daytime. But, from the love and well wishes for my journey from friends and next room neighbors, I was able to encourage myself to compose my heart with peace and calmness throughout the entire trip back to Manila.

By the time we got to Manila International Airport there were only a few people in the rear of the bus who were sick. Everyone in my family was fine. This might have been because we were physically getting a little stronger. The past six months in PRPC were six months of good health, being well fed and being happier by refugee standards.

As we arrived at the airport before we boarded the plane, the Official Refugee Worker was standing at the gate, handing out a big, thick, white plastic bag with large red letters written on it. It read " ICMC" and on the plastic bag was a shield. I had no idea what was in it. Each refugee family that was boarding this plane had an "ICMC" bag in hand along with a small amount of personal belongings. I remember that between my family of eleven people we only had three bags of old, outdated clothes that had been donated by some NGOs and some Christian church organizations. None of us even had shoes; we were wearing flip-flops when we stepped into the airplane.

Once again, the giant eagle took to the skies crossing the Pacific Ocean toward the North American continent. From daylight through moonlight the giant eagle was floating in the air. Through endless sky from one edge of an ocean to another it flew. By the time we landed in Alaska, we were cold and exhausted alongside the giant eagle that also needed to rest for a short while and to be refueled. All the refugees were informed to stay put wherever they sat until our flight resumed.

We were all mumbling and chitchatting among ourselves to kill time. With hearts trembling we knew that our final destination was near. The feeling of excitement, fear and uncertainty was overwhelming. After two hours of wondering and mind wandering, the belly and gates of the giant eagle were reopened. The flight attendants resumed their intercom, new passengers were boarding and looking for their seats; they were mostly business people. Some were wearing suits and ties, and nice dresses with sparkling jewels. We were shrinking back into our seats trying to hide that we didn't have proper shoes and clothes.

We were not embarrassed by our status, though, because we knew who we were; we were refugees. I assumed from the looks of wonder from the new passengers who had just boarded that Air France flight, that they couldn't help but wonder where all of these poor Eskimos were traveling to.

A few hours after the giant eagle took to the frozen sky and flew over parts of the North Pacific Ocean, we finally approached the border of California. We then landed at Oakland International Airport at about 11:30 a.m. Right after the plane landed, the passengers who were not refugees were rushed out with their carry on luggage, briefcases and overcoats.

As for all of us refugees, we landed and entered America in refugee style; ICMC bag in hand, flip-flops, UNHCR t-shirts, outdated jeans, yellow teeth, pale eyes, many were very skinny and mulnutrious. Everywhere we moved, we moved in a group—in line like a flock of ducks or herd of sheep.

We were just sitting still, waiting for further instruction. There was a Vietnamese and a Cambodian male official refugee worker and another lady, who was our Lao speaking lifesaver. Their mission was to help us get out of the plane and go through U.S. customs. Then, we went to a small holding place in the airport before we would be shifted out on a convoy of buses to Hamilton Field, which is formally known as Hamilton Army Airfield, before our transition to New York City. This was the Southeast Asian transit center on the U.S. mainland.

At the airport our Lao lady official refugee worker got us through customs and led us to the holding place along with the rest of the Cambodians and Vietnamese. There they gave us warm jackets to wear. I remember mine was blue with three stripes, white, red and yellow. I could see the smiles of satisfaction written on all of our faces. These were the first brand new jackets we had since leaving our home country. The warmth of the jackets comforted us on the bus on our way to Hamilton Field. I thought about the kindness and generosity of all the American people. What a wonderful way to welcome us to their land. Brand new jackets, "fuck yeah! America—me love you longtime."

The convoy of buses emptied us off at Hamilton Field. We were led by our Lao social worker who gave us instructions in our mother tongue. We were comfortable and even more excited after we were led to our rooms; then they took us to get more clothing in a small warehouse across from the building.

Now, we had new shoes (sneakers) and some extra decent clothing.

We went to a cafeteria with so many kinds of food. There were vegetables, beefsteak, roast pork, steamed and fried rice. The list seemed endless. There were drinks of all kinds. Coke, Pepsi, Mountain Dew, 7-Up, Sunkist, Schweppes Ginger Ale, etc.

At Hamilton Field there was one pivotal moment that I remember. This was my very first time feeling that in life there were many choices, and that I could actually choose between Coca-Cola and Pepsi. Using my pointer finger is freely allowed for communicating my needs, but after being a refugee and living under oppressive authority and in fear of rules and regulations for too long, I actually forgot that I could use my pointer finger to ask for the piece of beefsteak that I desired.

On the day we first arrived, we did nothing except eat and experiment with different kinds of soda until we were hyper. Our entire blood streams were frenzied with caffeine. All night long I could not fall asleep from caffeine agitation, excitement and wondering what would be the outcome tomorrow. I for sure believed that by tomorrow we would all be landing in New York City, and would be welcomed with warmth and open arms by our sponsor.

Life from here should be a good new beginning. We would be settled and no longer displaced. Of course, the curiosity and fear of uncertainty were buried deep in my heart and soul as usual, but I was always optimistic with a positive and patient attitude toward life and reality.

I was able to comfort myself with all that had happened on that one great day we already had in America. Ever since we were in the refugee camp in Thailand, the day we set our goal to seek an opportunity for resettlement in another country, America became my inspiration, hope, dream and possibility. All of this good hope and optimistic expectation got me through the first night in America. Early the next morning one of the Lao official refugee workers knocked on our door. He had come to tell us that the van would come to pick us up to take us to the San Francisco airport, and we needed to be ready within an hour.

Of course, we were ready within 20 minutes. By that time we were more or less considered "semi-professional" refugees. Whenever we got orders to move, we were ready. On our way to the airport the Lao official refugee worker gave me some tips for traveling through the airport, plane boarding, using the toilet and asking for food and help whenever it was necessary.

I took neat notes in my head. By the time we arrived at the airport in San Francisco I had learned a few new things about America. This was 19 years prior to September 11, 2001. All airport and security personnel were laid back and easygoing. Everyone could accompany his or her friends and relatives all the way to the gate. The Lao brother was very kind as he got us our boarding pass at the counter, walked us through security all the way to the waiting area next to the gate and left us there. Before he left he took a brief moment after looking at our boarding pass. He told me, "When you see people start boarding, all you have to do is just follow the line, then give your boarding pass to the airline official at the gate. When you are inside the plane, look for your seat number. All of your seats should be all the way in the back."

When boarding time came I just followed his instructions and boarded the airplane. Everything went smoothly and the plane was half empty. I didn't know exactly where to sit. When we walked onto the plane the flight attendant wasn't paying attention, so we just went to the back and grabbed a seat. After about four hours into the flight, my mind began to wander and many questions were entering my head. For the rest of the flight I kept asking myself, why does it take so long to just cross one country. This couldn't be right.

The plane landed sometime around 3 p.m. As soon as the plane landed there was only one thing on my mind or on my family's mind. This was our wonderful, white man sponsor, who would be right there at the door of the plane waiting to meet us and perhaps give us a big warm hug welcoming us to America, and take us to his home. When we got the letter of approval in the refugee camp no one really explained to us who exactly was going to be our sponsor. All they told us through the interpreter was—CWS (Church World Service) was our sponsor. What did I know about CWS? I didn't even know what it stood for at the time. All I knew was we were accepted to be resettled in America, and before we were going to America we had to go to PRPC for our ESL, CO and WO (work orientation) courses.

The reason they sent us to PRPC was because our family was so large that there was no private sponsor who could sponsor all of us. Also, the Phanat Nikhom Refugee Camp in Thailand—the place where most refugees from Laos were supposed to have their ESL, CO and WO—was completely jam-packed. We were blessed that we were sent to PRPC.

After the plane landed, all the passengers left the plane. We were the last group of people left on the plane. I was informed that my whole family was to stay put and wait for further instruction, but none of the flight attendants realized that we were the refugees, so they assumed that we knew what to do. After some minutes passed I decided to lead my family out of the plane hoping to see the sponsor outside in the waiting area. So we proceeded.

We walked out of the plane, but no one was there waiting for us. We didn't know where to go; we were just standing right in the middle of the walkway. Many people passed us by. I could see that they were very annoyed and sort of disgusted by our public manners, because we didn't know where to go. We were just stuck in the middle of the crowded human traffic. After one hour passed by, the intensity of the crowd was heated toward us. Some of the people were purposely bumping into us to knock us out of their way. Someone rolled their suitcase over my little sister's toe. We were very confused, anxious and scared. My heart was starting to rage against myself. I began to blame myself that I could have led my family onto the wrong plane when we were boarding. After almost two hours, finally, an Asian man showed up. He asked us if we were the Laotians.

"Are you Laotian?" he asked.

I said, *"Yes. Laotian!"* Because that was only one of the few words I knew in English—**LAOTIAN**.

He gave me a hand gesture to follow him. Then he put us in a van and we headed to Brooklyn, New York. When we got to Flatbush Avenue, my family and I started to panic. We thought that we had definitely gotten on the wrong plane and landed on the wrong continent. We were sure that we were somewhere in Africa. This was because back in our home country, I had learned that black men lived in Africa and white men lived in Europe and America.

I never realized what America was all about; how America was such a big melting pot with people of all races. It was totally unexpected. Suddenly the van stopped, and the man pointed out this old, crumbled down building. I remember the address was 420 East 21st Street. Then the Asian man signaled us to get out of the van and follow him. He took us into a hallway. The hallway was so dark; there was hardly any light. Most of the light bulbs were either dead or broken.

There were people hanging around in the hallway. They were smoking, drinking, listening and singing along with this weird kind of music from their boom boxes. The way they dressed and carried themselves was out of this world. They all were very dark, but I still could see the sparkling light in their eyes and teeth. They were looking at us with their eyes glazed over, and it seemed like they were all a distant star away.

I asked myself how could we possibly live here? What is this place?

The apartment was very small, and there were only two rooms. A Cambodian family of six, who had just come a few weeks before us, already occupied one room. There was also a Vietnamese guy, and now my family of eleven. So, there were Laotians, Cambodians, and Vietnamese, the three Southeast Asian ethnicities who were not always friendly to one another in the past. Now, here we were, in the middle of New York City next door to a crack house.

The Asian man who worked for the agency left us in this hellhole with $40 in food stamps, a bag of Wonder Bread, some hotdogs and a bag of Jasmine rice. From what we had, we managed to live and survive through our first two weeks. This was an immense achievement. Our Cambodian next-room neighbor was the greatest help in getting us through that two-week period. Every time he cooked his food, I watched to see how he lit the gas stove with matches, turned on the toaster oven and electric water pot. Every time I needed help with anything, he was always there to help even though we had no way of understanding each other's language. We used sign language to communicate, hand gestures, body language and smiles. He was so helpful to us.

Every one of us who was dumped in that apartment, was a resettler with the same sponsor. We were trapped there together; we had no choice but to help each other in whatever way we could. On our first few nights a group of angry, drug-addicted people were knocking at our door and trying to break into our apartment in the middle of the night. There was no telephone in the apartment. Even if we had one, it might not have meant anything, because we didn't know how to speak English and we had no one to call.

None of us knew who our sponsor was, who was working for the agency, or who was in charge of taking care of us. We were all scared to death. All we could do was move chairs, pieces of wood and metal, and whatever else we could find in the apartment to reinforce the main door. This was needed even though the main door already had at least four locks on it. During the night there was constant pounding on our door. This happened almost every night. We all were very frightened of nightfall, as if we were living in the land of the vampire.

To secure our families' safety all of the male adults would eat and sleep during the day, and stay up all night to make sure our door was guarded with our lives. After a week and a half, the same Asian man who had picked us up from the airport, took my family and a few other smaller families of Vietnamese and Cambodians to apply for food stamps, welfare, Medicaid and social security cards.

He took us to midtown Manhattan in his van. There we met a very wonderful Laotian lady. She told us that she worked as a social worker for the IRC (International Rescue Committee), but she had come to help out because there was no Lao translator working for the CWS, the organization that had sponsored us to come to the U.S. She gave us much insightful information regarding where the other Laotians who had come with the same agency were located. She also told us that she knew all of them, and she was willing to introduce us to them. I was so pleased to know that there was another small group of Laotian in the middle of New York City.

Through her connection we were able to make new friends, and luckily, one of the families who had come eight months before us, lived just two blocks away. That family became our immediate adopted family. They were the ones who helped us learn the basic way of life in NYC. They taught us how to ride the bus and subway, to get to an Asian grocery store in Chinatown. They showed us around the neighborhood; they showed us how to use our food stamps, and where to cash our welfare checks.

Now that we knew someone who was Lao, they would come to visit us at our hellhole apartment. Every time they came, they would gather all of their brothers and sisters to come with them, because they were very afraid of walking through the hallways from hell. We felt so much better by that time; now our life wasn't as lonely.

I was brave enough now to walk around the neighborhood. Every time

I walked around, checking out new territory, I was consistently harassed. At the time, however, regardless of what they said, it didn't matter because I didn't understand English. Through their body language I could tell that they were making fun of my crooked teeth and slanted eyes. Whatever they did, I just didn't pay any attention to them so they wouldn't have the satisfaction of knowing that they were annoying me. Even if I did, I kept it in my heart and hoped someday they would come to know the true reason of why I am here in the United States.

As every other immigrant before me, I set my feet in this great nation—America. I had hopes, expectations and—most important of all—the American Dream. Upon arrival in my so-called paradise and dream place, America, my dreams were immediately turned into nightmares. Despite this, my American Dream didn't just drop dead right on the spot, instead it became the core of my inspiration and ultimate goal for me to achieve. I was very blessed when I stepped foot in this country; for some reason I almost automatically knew that all my dreams and my ultimate goal could only be achieved by creating my own opportunities. I would have to create my own path and trails and pave my own road to glory. I knew it wouldn't be easy because there was a thick and chaotic jungle full of hatred and prejudice. When I first arrived in America, the public was so unaware of what really happened to Southeast Asian countries that were part of the Vietnam War—especially Laos.

Who is a Laotian?

Where is Laos?

Why are the Laotians suddenly flooding this country?

Being told to go home and being called "Chink" became my greatest inspiration. I discovered my duty and obligation. As a citizen of this country I realized that I had a responsibility. It was to be an activist, and create awareness regarding the subject matter that meant the most to my life including the condition of my environment. My goal became educating and communicating with other people and communities—opening up and making myself available to be accepted by others, as well as being ready to accept them.

It was a basic principle that I believed was the key to moving forward in unselfish ways in American society where individualism existed in the majority of the population. One thing I had to always keep in mind in this vast ocean was that I would have to widen my mind, to think big and dream big. Besides having the ability to think big and dream big, I also have to stay alive. I had to always remember an old Lao proverb:

"Falling in with the group of eagles you must be an eagle.

Falling in with the group of crows you must be a crow."

Through the words of this proverb I derived the intellectual strength and wisdom of this survival principle:

Flexibility and extreme adaptation are the true methods for surviving.

I eat whatever food I can find or whatever is provided for me.

I sleep wherever I can stretch out, flat on my back, straight on the floor.

I work at whatever job pays a little or more.

7

Life in America

It was one late morning a few months after my arrival. I was cruising around Flatbush Avenue—checking to see what was in that strange neighborhood. After being trapped in that hellhole for a while, I was bored to tears. I was so inquisitive and eager to see what was beyond the walls of that loathsome apartment. As I was about to turn the corner, I saw this little grocery store just across the street at the corner of Cortelyou Road and Flatbush Avenue, just one block away from my hellhole apartment building. That store caught my attention, because there was a little Chinese character written on the corner of the store's sign. Out of curiosity I crossed the street to get a closer look. As I was standing in front of the place, I decided to peep through the clear glass door and take a good look. There I saw an Asian man standing at the counter. I walked in to check it out, because there were hardly any grocery stores run by Asians in that area.

While I was looking around inside his store, I heard the man speak with his wife in Thai. I couldn't believe what I had just heard, so I walked up to him and introduced myself. We ended up having a very brief, nice conversation. He told me that he was Chinese Thai from Thailand. He asked me if I was Thai; I told him that I was a refugee from Laos. Because my Thai was very fluent, he wondered where I had learned how to speak it. I told him that I knew how to speak Thai even before I escaped to Thailand. I learned how to read and speak Thai through Thai comic books, Thai radio and Thai TV.

He asked me if I knew another Laotian family, which happened to be the one that I had just adopted to be as my own. "Yes!" I told him—I knew them very well. He told me that three kids from that family were working part-time in his grocery store. As soon as he finished telling me that I saw a little crack in the window of opportunity, and I wasn't hesitant to break my way in. I asked if I could also work in his grocery store—and he said, "Yes."

I was so pleased that I would have a job. I would do anything rather than sit hopelessly in that hellhole. That damned apartment was getting into my head; it distorted my thinking and imprisoned my imagination outside the actuality of my American Dream and the true realm of America's paradise. Everyday I felt like I was a prisoner of fear. I was glad that I was making that brave discovery. Walking just one long block through that strange neighborhood at that time felt to me like walking onto a battlefield.

The morning after I met Mr. Chin I was on my way to his grocery store and ready to work. While I was walking, I could feel the vital spirit of hope, and the sparkle of the American Dream sprinkling some comfort into my inner thoughts.

It was the first time I could remember since I stepped foot in America that I was able to assure myself that I could crack a smile in the face of my terrible despair.

Now, I was a full-time worker at "Mr. Chin's Grocery and Candy" store. I was so pleased with how I had just been blessed. Speaking no words of English, having no skills, no working experience—I had landed the job. I was more hopeful now than I had ever been. I was immediately beginning to see my tomorrow. Every day I was encouraging my family to hang tight and hope for a better tomorrow. Soon, I would be saving some money from work in addition to our welfare checks. Then we would be able to get out of that hellhole apartment.

After three months of sharing the apartment, the Cambodian family got some help from the Cambodian community and they got out. The Vietnamese guy managed to relocate with his extended relatives to another state, so he also got out. We were the only family still trapped in that hellhole apartment. It didn't matter how long we had been living there. There was never a moment that I felt comfortable, and there was never a time that I walked through that hallway from hell without thinking that I could be mugged and killed.

Miraculously, no one got hurt in the six months we lived there. Finally, we managed to move out. Our new apartment was two blocks away and next door to our newly adopted family. It was 800 Ocean Avenue, Apartment #1B. Even though it was only two blocks away from the old apartment, it was so much different. It seemed like two different countries. Now, all of our new neighbors were so much nicer. I was able to find peace and harmony every time my little brother and sister looked out of the window. There was nobody throwing rocks and empty bottles at them like there used to be at the old apartment. When we moved from that hellhole apartment, we moved out with a few small garbage bags full of clothes and we just walked the two blocks. There was nothing in our new apartment. It was just an empty apartment, but that didn't stop us from being happy. We were thrilled to get out of that hellhole apartment alive.

In order to build our new nest and make it more comfortable, we had to be very creative. In the evenings we would go around the neighborhood and pick up all the mattresses in the Dumpster, open garbage cans to look for discarded clothes, and collect kitchenware and housewares from Dumpsters and trash.

We were scavenging almost every day until we got whatever was necessary. We found mattresses for every room and for everyone to sleep on. There was no more sleeping on the hardwood floors with a thin piece of cloth. We found window fans to keep us cool, a desk for me to write on, a dining table with chairs of different sizes, styles and colors. I used to call our dining set "the mosaic of an American carpenter." We even found a convertible sofa bed and convertible couch—the kind that you could pop out the footrests and armrests. It was so awesome; every time I sat on it I felt like a king. My little brother and sister called me "the king of New York scavengers."

After we picked up so much garbage and scavenged so many Dumpsters, our neighbors must have taken notice of us because after awhile, before they would throw out any of their cooking utensils or clothes, they would just put them in a garbage bag and drop them off in the hallway right in front of our apartment.

We were so happy with all the treasures we found from other people's trash; we couldn't believe what people threw away in this country.

Even our first 19-inch black and white TV came from a Dumpster. With the assistance of a coat hanger rod and a piece of aluminum foil, that TV was able to entertain my whole family for years.

That black and white TV from the Dumpster was a window that gave us insight into the edge of American society. It certainly introduced us to American idols and heroes. Through its screen we found our first American hero, idol and role model. There, we found an escape route into a momentary painless realm, where we were able to forget about our grief, conflict, displacement and chaos.

I have so many fond memories of moments with my family—from enjoying our naughty old man, Benny Hill, to our heartfelt loyalty to the WWF (World Wrestling Federation). There was so much hype about the WWF during the 1980s. Almost every Saturday night my mother would prepare food, and all of our family members, our Laotian friends and neighbors would gather for the WWF extravaganza. Mom was definitely the cheerleader of the pack. All of us were die hard in rooting for our beloved good guys—Bob Backlund, Andre the Giant, Hulk Hogan, Jimmy "Superfly" Snuka. Every time our beloved good guy got beat up mercilessly and unjustly by our most hated Iron Sheik, Mr. Fuji. Mr. Nakasaki, King Kong Bundy and, with the support and decision of the semiconscious referee, it stirred us to madness. Sometimes we went for a day feeling bad about an unjust decision.

Everything that went on in the ring and in the circumference of that 19-inch black and white screen—was what it was. At the time it was so black and white to us—the injustice in the WWF's ring perpetuated the perfect American stereotype as we were experiencing it. We were in the discovery process of figuring out what is truth versus what is stereotype; we were getting to know what American society, mentality and the American entertainment business were all about. From what we saw on screen we were convinced that the American mentality was surely to worship injustice -- where good guys never win -- but instead, bad guys are glorified with a championship. The WWF fans on TV were furious, and we were devastated in front of our screen. How could so many viewers possibly be deceived by such injustice? What's wrong with the justice system in this country? We screamed and cried out loud, feeling so devastated over the defeat of our hero.

How can we forget the WWF Saturday night main event—when Rowdy Roddy Piper was bullying our most beloved Jimmy "Superfly" Snuka. We were all insulted when Rowdy Roddy told Superfly to go back to Fiji, and, to remind him where he came from, Piper dropped a pineapple, banana and coconut on him. Then, Piper did a sneak attack and smashed Superfly's head with a coconut, rubbed his face with banana and hit him with a belt while he was crawling on the floor. In our living room all the Laotian fans were screaming and yelling at Rowdy Roddy and wishing him to be condemned to hell for his acts of inhumanity and for having no soul for sportsmanship. Then, the following Saturday night main event would be a Superfly revenge episode. As usual, all the Laotians at the Ocean Avenue apartment would get together for the extravaganza, cook our favorite dishes for the feast, and hope and pray that our Lord Buddha would hear our prayer to bless our beloved Superfly upon his revenge. We expected and hoped that Superfly would rip Piper into a thousand pieces and condemn him with justice so we could celebrate with greatest satisfaction. Of course, when the moment we were waiting for finally arrived, once again all the Laotian fans were humiliated and totally devastated with the result of the revenge—when Rowdy Roddy Piper was beating up our beloved Superfly mercilessly with a metal chair until he was out cold. While the team of paramedics dragged Superfly out on the stretcher we felt so betrayed.

Over and over again what went on on screen really affirmed our conviction of what America was about, and convinced us that that was the true mentality of American society. At the time, our perspective on America was limited to the bandwidth of the TV signal. What we saw was what we believed. But our first love-hate relationship with the WWF was surely an ingredient that helped us to relieve some of our pain.

At the time, we received food stamps and welfare checks, and our health was taken care of by Medicaid. My $2.75 per hour job at Mr. Chin's Grocery and Candy was just to keep us from being hungry. Still, with the size of my family, from time to time we needed some additional food. My next-door-neighbor, whose family I had adopted as my own, was a widower. He had lost his wife in the refugee camp in Nong Khai, Thailand, and that left him with nine children.

I called him "Uncle," and I loved him as much as if he were my own uncle. His name was Khanty Vatthanavong. He was my first, best friend in America and my fishing partner. He knew where to fish for big fish, fish so big that just one could fill the stomachs of a whole family of eight to 12 people. On my days off from Mr. Chin's store, my neighbor and I went every place where there was a pond, bay or ocean.

We went to Prospect Park's pond, Sheepshead Bay, and the Coney Island ocean. As long as it was located within a manageable distance from our neighborhood, we went there. Sometimes we would ride a few miles on our bicycles from our 800 Ocean Avenue apartment building all the way down to Sheepshead Bay to pick up blue mussels and clams, and to fish for snapper at the Coney Island pier. We would stack all the fish we caught in the freezer or fridge. Sometimes we brought them back still alive in our bucket, and kept them in our kitchen sink or even our bathtub. That way, whenever we cooked them, they were fresh.

Speaking of capturing livestock from the pond, one of my fondest moments is of fishing in the heart of New York City. One day, my adopted Lao uncle and I decided to walk from 800 Ocean Avenue to fish at the pond in Prospect Park in Brooklyn. After we fished for an hour or two, together we caught a gigantic fish. It was almost the size of my leg. We decided to bring it back to our apartment alive. For some odd reason a policeman happened to be walking by at the exact moment we dragged the fish out of the water. The policeman approached us in an aggressive manner. He tried to stop us, but we didn't understand the reason why.

We decided to run away with the fish jumping in our jackets. At the time, we didn't understand why the police would always try to stop us. Back in Laos, anyone could fish in any river or pond anywhere they wanted to. We assumed that wherever the water was clear, the fish must be clean. We didn't take serious notice of American industrial land where almost every pond, creek, stream and even the ocean shoreline was polluted. After that harrowing episode we were stuck between a rock and a hard place. In order to survive we had to use desperate measure, but beyond just surviving, we had to do it in a safe and secure way.

Our stomachs were full; our bodies were covered with decent and warm clothes. Life progressed forward, carrying with it our optimistic hopes and the call of our American dreams. We endured all the obstacles of adaptation among strangers in the hazardous environment of our strange new land. Maintaining the tight screws to keep our heads on top of our shoulders was the ultimate challenge. New York City was a very unforgiving place, especially if you were at the bottom of the bottom. New York City was an extreme place that tested the strength of our willpower and determination.

After ten months of living in Brooklyn, one of my Lao next door, adopted family members told me that one of her ESL teachers was about to create a special program for Southeast Asian refugees who came to the states in their late teens—young enough to be in high school, but too old to be in elementary school. My sister, Mok, and I were able to enroll in the ESL program at Martin Luther King Jr. High School at 66th Street and Amsterdam Avenue. This was all the way to Manhattan Island, which was about a one hour and fifteen minute subway train ride from the borough of Brooklyn at the Cortelyou Road subway station. I was 19 years old at the time, and my older sister was 21. Every morning we would have to wake up at 5:30 and be at the Cortelyou Road subway station by 6 a.m. sharp, so we could make it to school on time.

At Martin Luther King Jr. High School, if I am not mistaken, I think my sister Mok and I were the first two out of 15 Asian students that had, more or less, ever stepped foot in that school. We were there for an experimental ESL program. From what I understood, the mission of the program was to see how long it would take us before we could attend regular classes at an average American high school level.

During the time that we were in the ESL program we were allowed to take one or two classes at regular high school levels with American students. Most of the classes that I took outside the ESL program were art, math and science. These subjects were in more of a universal language to us. My sister and I both did very well in art, math and science classes, but we didn't do well in our English classes.

Despite our struggle with English as our second or third language, we carried on with our mission with pride and determination. Whenever we began to do well, there was always some jealousy by the American students. There were daily harassments, either physical or verbal, since the first day that we stepped foot into that school there was never a day that passed without some kind of trouble. There was always something.

All of the Asian students were called "Chink." Regardless of which Asian country we came from, we were all labeled as Chinese. Sometimes I got robbed in the bathroom while I was standing taking a piss. Other students would threaten me with their Swiss army knives, and take all my money, my watch, a pack of cigarettes, and subway tokens. My sister couldn't wear any of her jewelry to school because the girls in the lunchroom would snatch the chain off her neck.

Back at home I had to deal with the family life of a teenage refugee. I had to take care of my family. My mother, who couldn't speak a word of English, was alone with eight children. Out of these eight, six of them were very young. Raising eight children, without knowing a word of English in this strange country, was beyond my mother's capabilities.

Now I was a full-time student at Martin Luther King Jr. High School, and a full time employee at Mr. Chin's store. I had no time to sit at home after school and do my homework. Everyday, during the hour and fifteen minute subway train ride back to Brooklyn, I would finish all of my homework. When I got back to my apartment, I just dropped my book bag, said hello to my mother, told my younger brothers and sisters to finish their homework, and ate whatever my mother had cooked for lunch. Then I had to be at Mr. Chin's by 4 p.m. at the latest, and I would work my full eight-hour shift.

My job varied depending on the day. I would do everything: cleaning, assisting at the cash register, filling shelves and stocking the refrigerator. Whenever I finished doing all of these, I acted as security, watching customers to make sure there was no shoplifting. That was the hard part of the job because that was the kind of thing that happens most of the time.

I called my boss, Mr. Chin, although his actual name was something else. The store was named Mr. Chin, and was legally under the real Mr. Chin, but my Thai boss was the one who ran the business. I loved how Mr. Chin had a tactic of keeping everything in the right order, and claimed respect from all the local regular customers. I could tell from the behavior of the customers—especially the ones who knew who the real Mr. Chin was—how much they respected him.

It seemed strange to me that there were baseball bats hidden in every corner of the store and two licensed, loaded handguns in the drawer under the cash register. The store was legally armed with weapons and ready for anything. Although I had grown up in the middle of the war zone in Laos, compared to New York City in the 1980s, Laos was a war zone, but New York City was a battlefield. Fire trucks and police sirens went off every five minutes. The sound of gunshots was constant and, every so often, fighting broke out on the street, sidewalk, school grounds and subway. Everywhere I turned there was a sign of potential danger. Every day on the news there was almost nothing but murders and robberies, shootings, drugs and the pathetic city's other violent crimes.

New York became a surreal world to me. Every day that I saw what happened, I couldn't comprehend how all of this could possibly happen in the nation that was labeled as one of the richest and most powerful on the planet. In my head, none of this could possibly happen, for example, a person killing another person just for his overcoat. All of the things that happened on the streets of Brooklyn reminded me of the old Lao prophesy that had been recited and preached to me from the lips of my grandparents since I was a little child and had begun to learn the words of men.

"The time will come. The time where in every big and
small country around the globe.
People will become scavengers.
Desperate for power to survive.
Greed will exceed morals of humanity.
City Streets will become war zones and battlefields.
Killing, torturing and dehumanization
Will appear in very naked eyes in broad daylight on the streets of civilization.
The wisdom of human life will be vague.
Everywhere in the future, you will see these deep cracks in the soul of
our humanity."

Every night I got back to the apartment from work at 2:30 a.m., sometimes 3 a.m. Mr. Chin's store closed at 1:30 a.m., but after the store closed I still had to clean the floor, refill the groceries, milk, other dairy products, beer and soft drinks before I could call it a night. These tasks usually took me about an hour or an hour and a half to complete. Every morning I had to be up by 5:30 and out of the apartment by 5:40 or, at the latest, 5:45. It was an eight-minute walk to the subway station, one to two minutes to go through the subway cashier booth with my student pass and get down to the subway platform with just four or five minutes to spare before the train arrived at 6 a.m. sharp. That was my routine.

After a year of living in America my English was much improved. Things were looking up for my family and me; all my brothers and sisters were in school. Although they were experiencing the same kinds of problems I had, they were hanging on. We remained on public assistance because my mom still couldn't work and all my brothers and sisters were very young. It was not our preference, but we had no other choice. I owe you, America.

By this time, through my observation and self-teaching, I became knowledgeable about social service systems, immigration processes, school systems and how to go about town. The other Laotian families came to me for help, because the agency that had resettled us here still had no community outreach. No one followed up on what happened to us. We were left alone to find our own way to survive in a place where we couldn't even speak the language.

Since the day we arrived in New York City we had to learn how to adjust, adapt and deal with an overwhelming number of aspects of city life that were previously unknown to us. The list of challenges seemed endless: social conduct, politics, city bureaucracy, cultural differences, lifestyle, racial discrimination, crime and street violence, chaos, poverty and a society seemingly made of fear.

All of these alarming factors, as well as the hazardous conditions that were simply part of the nature of New York City, became reminders of our familiar past. Almost every element and component that made up the New York City environment began to trigger memories of the pain and the indescribable tragic experiences that we had endured. It began to penetrate -- weakening and deteriorating our psychological and mental defense boundaries. We left one war and now we were entering another one.

In addition to all of these difficulties, now we had to face an even more serious dilemma due to the affects of our war experiences, including our wounds, our scars, the trauma we witnessed, and the atrocities we lived through, as well as revolution, fear of persecution, chaos, dislocation, separation, sadness, disappearance of our loved one, homesickness, despair, the multi-stage resettlement process (from refugee camp to America ghetto), and the struggle to survive with the support system of Medicaid and Public Assistance -- living check to check and hand to mouth. If we were lucky, we would get a job in a factory or washing dishes for minimum wage, trying to pay the rent on a rundown house or apartment either in a low-income housing project or a ghetto. This was a severe shift of cultural traditions, and a radical change in our way of life -- from self-subsistence in the rural areas and jungle of Laos to a cash-dependent lifestyle, where we needed to sell our services in the form of job skills for the modern industrial and technological complex. This had to be done without vocational school or experience. Many of us had just been farmers, civilians, blue-collar workers, housewives and children of war. We came here with almost no education. Some of us were from the city and many were from the countryside. It was very hard for everyone to adapt to mega city life and deal with welfare, food stamps and hospitals.

These problems were only a small portion of our daily dilemma. They were more or less just physical and mental challenges that we had to endure with the strength of our will and determination.

Also, as refugees, we were treated as if we were imaginary people with mysterious ancestors from an unknown land that hardly anyone had ever heard of or knew any history of how it related to the cause of our migrating to America.

In addition to all of the above, we still had to deal with our own psychological warfare and spirituality, which tangled and convoluted deep within so many layers of our awareness, sub-consciousness and consciousness of our past, present and future.

This war was very different from the last one, because we had to fight it on two fronts: spiritual and psychological. We were insightful, but this enemy was totally invisible to us. It lived within our hearts, our minds and our spiritual environment. We couldn't really see it, but felt every essence of its presence. It was just like our own intestines had turned into maggots that were eating us alive from within.

Of course, all of this occurred at the very moment when we were caught in the middle of reconstituting our life and fighting for the existence of our traditions, culture, and national and personal identities; while, at the same time, feeling the pressure to adapt, assimilate and become American. We were now on the verge of a point break.

The psychological and spiritual warfare that we were fighting, was so buried within our innermost being and tangled in layers of our awareness, that it could only be analyzed and interpreted through the elements of faith, culture, tradition and mentality, but unfortunately, we didn't seem to have a strong enough immunity to fight it. Furthermore, because it was so internal, it became invisible to even ourselves, and to those who were there with some expertise and experience in helping us deal with the situation.

Even though we were the only people who could possibly understand what was happening to us, we couldn't necessarily see our own demons that perpetrated their black magic against us. Those demons, who tracked us all the way here to the end of our death-defying journey in order to haunt us, were nothing more than the essence of our ancestors. The awareness and recognition of our ancestral spirit, as well as the customs of the faith that we inherited and processed internally and externally, created tremendous anxiety, uncertainty and internal fluctuation in our daily physical and spiritual life.

The effect of this was believed to have claimed some lives in our Laotian community in America. This is known by the western medical profession as "Sudden Death Syndrome," or among the Lowland Lao as *Phi Zuae*, "the ghost or the spirit of our ancestors." The spirits of our blood related past-relatives (beginning of our roots and clan, our great-great grandparents all the way down to our parents' generation, the ones who vowed to protect us) were responsible for our spiritual prosperity and happiness.

This puzzling and frightening phenomenon strikes when we, the descendents of the ancestors, begin to ignore their voices and no longer follow the traditional rituals or make merit as we did back in the home country. The unhappy spirits of our ancestors furiously launch an attack against their descendents to remind us that we must carry on with their heritage, faith, and rituals. We are also to continue our spiritual communication with them and listen to their needs. That is why in the Laotian culture we have *Heed Seepsong*, 12 rules of traditional rituals that we conduct, one in every month of the year.

Since our Theravada Buddhism is intertwined with ancient Lao Animism, many of us interpreted and transformed the 12-ritual tradition into our own superstition. That is why in many Laotian living room or master bedroom, whether in the US, Canada or elsewhere, you will always see a little altar on the wall accompanied by a picture of a deceased grandparent, parent or some holy Theravada Buddhist monk. This altar is a place to honor the spirit of our ancestor, and to communicate with them through prayer.

We still practice the 12-ritual tradition, but it is very hard for us to follow exactly on the proper date and time. Based on our lifestyle and our busy schedule we can only do our best. Many of us can attend only the most essential traditional rituals, because we don't have a Buddhist temple in every town and village as we did in Laos. At every important temple event we make an effort to bring various offerings of food and supplies in order to earn merit by offering them to the spirit of our ancestor, hoping for their well wishes and blessings. At the end of the blessing session we follow with what we call *Yard Narm*, "Dropping Water Ritual." This part of the ritual awakens the spirit so they will be aware that an offering is being sent to them. At the end of *Yard Narm* we pour water from a bottle or cup into another cup, then pour it onto the ground, while asking *Toranee*, the mother god of the earth, to be our messenger and carry our offering to wherever our ancestors' spirits reside. In return for making an offering and making merit, we believe we will be rewarded with a life of peace, harmony, prosperity, and happiness, but -- most important of all -- we will have prevented their sneak attack against us. However, not all ancestors are angry; some really don't care if we make merit or not, they never bother us. Others, though, become angry and complain about every little thing— such as a guest or visitor who is not related, staying overnight without the family calling first to their spirit for permission.

The extent of the unfortunate effects caused by the ancestral spirits depends upon how deeply the family or individual allows their spiritual state of being to get involved with the ritual beliefs. That's why in every Laotian community throughout North America, Europe and Australia there was an urgent need to have a Lao temple where everyone can worship, make merit, pay respect to their ancestors and carry on their customary beliefs and traditional rituals. But, at the early stage of resettlement in the new country, this was nearly impossible until we established and stabilized our lives as a family and a community. The lack of a temple meant the lack of social support, which meant increased psychological and spiritual stress.

To insulate ourselves from the frightening phenomenon of ancestral haunting, and cope with physical hardships, mental distress and spiritual pain, we had to allow ourselves to be vulnerable, susceptible and accepting of the influences of our new environment. To sustain ourselves we had to seek the right balance between what we could afford to gain from our new way of life in our new country, and what we could afford to lose or neglect from the heritage of our ancestors—which included our faith, way of life, culture, tradition and identity. The deeper we dug into our innermost-self to find what we could afford to neglect or lose, the more pressure we felt from our heavenly ancestors. The demand on our endurance to sustain every element of our past was tremendous, but so was the force to continue our assimilation into all of the elements of our present as well as our future.

Our ancestors are indeed alive and well, existing in a parallel dimension deep within our own innermost-lives. We see their vision through our dreams and hear their voices through the echoes of their words of wisdom -- words which are the principles of our giving, sharing and passion for humanity. Their co-existence with us is truly our primary concern for our own peace and harmony with the cycles of the universe.

Our primary concern was for our physical and spiritual state of being due to the dreadful conditions we were facing, including culture shock and acculturative stress. This caused many of us to suffer from severe depression and anxiety.

Many of us developed gastric symptoms such as peptic ulcer disease from being in the stressful environment of New York City. My mother and many friends of her age suffered from severe psychosomatic disorder. Almost every other day she complained that she was sick with some kind of disease, but after multiple tests and examinations by respected specialists, the tests always came out negative, thus freeing her from any obscure disease that she thought she had. There were so many people in our community -- the elderly widow or widower, or the orphaned youth (here alone or with a distant aunt, uncle or old family friend), who didn't acknowledge that they were having some kind of psychiatric symptoms. All they knew was that they were susceptible to self-abuse, such as continuous consumption of alcohol, gambling, chain-smoking, or episodes of extreme explosive violence.

I remember three of the worst cases of post-traumatic stress symptoms. One was my Lao friend's father who became schizophrenic; he was talking and debating with himself and our ancestors all day. Another older Laotian man was so traumatized that he literally became mute after losing all his money the day the Pathet Lao changed our currency during the Lao Revolution. One Cambodian woman in the Bronx became blind after seeing so much torture and atrocity in the killing fields of Cambodia.

Domestic violence also took place in our community, generated in many cases by changes in socioeconomic status. We were coming from a patriarchal world to a society where men, women and children have equal rights, equal power and freedom to be whoever they want and live the way they want. In many cases the wife became more resourceful and had more capability to generate income. Also, the children were better able to assimilate, and their acculturation was much different than their parents'. This caused cultural and intergenerational conflict in the inner circle of the family, creating disorder of the traditional family structure. Often, this caused a chain reaction which erupted into a severe case of domestic violence. Many of these men were accustomed to being important figures in their community, in the military, in business or in their clan; but when they came to America, they became common factory workers, janitors, or in many cases were just dependent on public assistance. Thus, their status became subordinate to their wife and children who often were more capable of speaking and understanding the English language.

In our Laotian and Southeast Asian community I encountered many cases of domestic violence with deadly consequences -- cases often involving jealousy, severe child and wife beating, separation, divorce or suicide. Most of these acts of explosive violence, in my personal opinion, had to do with displacement of personal guilt on to a loved one. These violent, and sometimes deadly acts, broke down the family bond, widening the distance of physical and mental separation. Adding to the breakdown of the family, was the generation gap: a result of fear, miscommunication, lack of shared interests and lack of the same retrospect. While the children often adapted very well, had a great ability to see their future and move forward in their new country, the parent -- in many cases, the father -- was still caught between neither here nor there. His thoughts and emotions may have been focused on his family and brotherhood at war back home, in limbo someplace else, or somewhere between two worlds -- the past-homeland and present-America.

The community was in desperate need of many kinds of help, so I began to seriously volunteer. I helped by being their translator, brother and community leader. I opened the door to the living room of my apartment as the place where friends and neighbors would gather for open discussions regarding daily matters and crises. This included filling out social service and immigration forms, children's school work, etc.

One day, while we were drowning in the waves of all the crises, I got a call from my blood-related uncle who lives in St. Petersburg, Florida. He told me that he would introduce me to the New York branch of same Christian church that he had attended in St. Petersburg Florida. They had been his sponsors, and he said they were great caretakers. If I joined their church, I would be well taken care of as well.

Of course I was born and raised as a Buddhist, so this was not an easy decision for me; I slept on it for two weeks. I made this critical decision while keeping in mind the desperation and needs of my family and the rest of the Lao community who were in even worse shape than we were. It was two weeks of agonizing and questioning myself regarding my faith and beliefs.

Am I betraying my own faith and religion?

Am I deceiving anyone if I commit my physical being to Christ while my heart and soul are Buddhist?

After two weeks of sleepless nights, I called my uncle to tell him that I would join his church just for the hope of a better life, not for the wealth of faith. So, I joined the church, and brought everyone in my family and almost every Lao family in the area into the church as well. This was to get help because that was the only place that welcomed us with open arms and gave us free food, clothes, and free English lessons. The minister even came to our house to give us the English lessons.

I was a full-time student with a full-time job, and was now involved with the church. My life began to get even busier. I was now a sophomore in high school; I had a lot more homework and demands, while at the same time there were many more problems happening in the Lao community. Laotian kids were having crises in school; there were social services problems, such as food stamps and welfare checks not showing up; families were getting evicted from apartments, and police stations needed an interpreter. The list of problems accumulated as the days went by—from teen gangs to teen pregnancies, from police brutality to a grand jury court case, from domestic disputes to nervous breakdowns, from unusual physical and emotional illnesses to psychosomatic complaints—crisis after crisis, day and night. All that happened during this small increment of time would normally have taken at least three lifetimes for most people to see.

There are several cases that I remember fondly.

One in particular was a typical case involving a medical condition. One day I had to take a Lao grandmother to the hospital for a medical disorder. She was 70 years old at the time, and she had had vaginal bleeding for at least two weeks. The grandmother was too embarrassed to tell anyone until her condition got much worse. Finally, one of her daughters intervened, and called me for help, so I took the grandma on the subway to St. Luke's Roosevelt Hospital in Manhattan. When we got to St. Luke's Roosevelt I took her into the emergency room. After we filled out the registration form at the front desk the nurse told us to wait.

As usual, in almost every emergency room in any hospital in NYC, people were standing and waiting in line. After about 40 minutes the front desk called Grandmother in for a quick blood pressure check, weight check, and to answer a few questions.

What was the reason she was coming to the emergency room?

How long had she been sick?

Did she have any allergies to any medication?

After the nurse finished writing down this basic information, she told us to go back and wait again, so we waited. After two hours we still didn't get the call to go in. The grandmother was getting very agitated and frustrated, and her lower abdominal pain was getting severe. I walked up to the front desk and notified the nurse. I wanted to make sure the nurse knew that the grandma's condition was getting critical. Her bleeding was getting heavier; she had dropped some blood on the floor. I was very worried, because she had been losing a lot blood during the past two weeks before I took her in. So, about 15 minutes later, the front desk nurse finally called the grandma in, and we were led to a big open room with many rolling beds. Each bed had a rolling curtain surrounding it so they could easily convert it into a private little room.

Here was the grandmother in a converted private space with a rolling curtain and a rolling bed. The nurses and doctors were roaming and running around, going about their life saving business as usual. I could see the grandmother was getting more nervous and more uncomfortable with the whole environment. Before the nurse left us inside that little cubical, she handed us a hospital gown and said,

"Please tell your grandmother that she must take off all of her regular clothes, and put on this hospital gown before the doctor can give her a checkup. Please! She has to do this right away; our doctor is very busy, and we don't want to waste his time. She has to be ready when the doctor is here; he should be here soon."

Here I was in a little cubical with a nerve-wracked grandma, who was feeling extremely weak. Her embarrassment was indescribable—even before the doctor came to check her, she was already pale from fear and discomfort. Talk about embarrassment: here I was, trying to figure out how the hell I was supposed to tell the grandma to take off all her clothes and put on the hospital gown. I tried to give her a hint in the most polite way possible because I didn't want her to be more embarrassed than she already was.

"Grandma, the nurse was telling me to tell you that you must change all of your clothes and put on this hospital gown. Don't worry, when you are ready to change I will go and wait outside the cubicle," I said to her.

I could see the Grandma was already overwhelmed by the commotion going on in a nearby cubicle. About a minute or two after I told her, I be-

126

gan to see that she was turning her face against the cubicle curtain and had begun to take off her top. As soon as I saw this, I immediately stepped out of the cubicle so she could have a moment of privacy. I waited outside for about five minutes, then I called out to Grandma to see if I could come back into the cubicle. I wanted to make sure I didn't walk in on a naked grandmother.

About 20 minutes after we had been left in the cubicle, another nurse rushed in and asked if the grandma had changed her clothes. She took a brief moment to take a look at Grandma to make sure all of her clothes were off except the hospital gown.

"You must take it all off, make sure your bottom is off too."

I cut in—"Miss, she doesn't speak English. I am here to translate for her."

Nurse: "Okay, then, make sure there is nothing beneath her gown."

"Okay, I will tell her that," I replied.

Here I was—again trying to figure out how to be more direct, and at the same time culturally correct, so she wouldn't feel physically and spiritually violated. I totally understood where she was coming from. She was 70 years old; in all her life this was probably the first time that someone other than her husband would be seeing her naked. While I was figuring things out in my head, the same nurse rushed in and asked me directly this time,

"Did your grandmother finish taking off everything under her gown yet?"

"Please give her a few more minutes" I replied to her.

I was staring blankly at the grandmother from across the cubicle. I couldn't think of the proper words. If I found one, I was still puzzling about how to deliver it to her. Grandma was getting really shaken; her face was changing from pale to white; her mind seemed to be even more distorted. I could see her lip vibrating, and she shrank back to the corner of the cubicle where she stood still like a scared little child. I was feeling terribly guilty that I had taken her to such a place. While I was in the middle of getting caught up in my awkward feelings, there came a doctor and a team of nurses storming into the cubicle.

Before the doctor started to examine the grandma I told the doctor that I would face against the wall to prevent Grandma from being too embarrassed while being examining.

For over 20 minutes I was stared at the blank wall trying to help doctor and team of nurses interpreting and tried to figure out many ways to get Grandma to put on the hospital gown with her top and bottom off.

After 20 minutes of trying, by that time I think we were all getting very frustrated with the poor grandma. The doctors ran out of time, and I ran out of ways to say things so that she wouldn't feel culturally violated.

So I decided to ask the doctor if I could do my last attempt to explain to Grandma, with hope that she will not carried on refuses to take off her cloth.

"Grandma, it is okay to let someone like a doctor or medical professional look at your body, checking and touching different parts of your body when you are sick. You have to let loose and make an exception sometimes, especially when it is necessary, like right now. All you have to do is just peel off your pants under the hospital gown, then get up on the rolling bed. Lay down on your back, then the doctor will take a quick look to see what is wrong with you. After that he might give you some medicine, then we can go home and you will feel much better. Don't worry; the last time I took my own mother to see the doctor they did the same thing to her. It is really okay, Grandma. Don't worry; I am here to look after you. Just try to do what you have been told. Okay, Grandma?"

Grandma still responded with silence.

I just couldn't hold back any more. Softly, directly to Grandma I said, "Grandma, can you just please take off your pants."

Everyone in the cubicle was silent. After a brief moment I still could hear no action-taking place, and I said to myself I would try again one last time. Maybe the grandma was too scared and too nervous to hear me. Blasting my voice with the essence of some frustration I said, "GRANDMA, DROP YOUR PANTS—NOW!"

The next thing I heard were the voices of relief from the doctor and team of nurses, "Here you GO!"

This story of "Grandma drop your pants!" is told to inform the reader that in the early stage of our Southeast Asian refugee resettlement in the United States, American doctors and the medical profession were unaware of our cultural traditions. As simple and basic as it should have been to get a grandmother to drop her pants for her own serious medical condition, it took a huge effort from an interpreter to a team of nurses and doctors with years of skill and experience.

Many refugees were unfamiliar with the concepts: psychology, psychiatric and psychosomatic, because the way we Laotians look inside ourselves is very different than the westerner's perspective of their life and world. For the western health professional to be able to understand our needs, as the interpreter, I had to find a way to explain to both doctor and patient through very specific examples or re-framed in culturally appropriate terms. The hardest part was finding proper terminology in order to respect our cultural tradition. Oftentimes I ran into a brick wall because many western doctors were unaware or didn't try to acknowledge the bilingual and bicultural differences. In many cases the doctors lacked treatment methods for the refugee, especially for the patient who had physical and mental health issues at the same time. As a matter of fact, most physical health issues were caused by psychological and emotional stress. In these cases Western psychiatric methods would not necessarily work or even be relevant to a refugee, due to the fact that we perceive our mind and body in a completely different way. Every time I took my Laotian friends and family to the doctor, I made an extra effort to make sure he understood the bicultural issues that they were dealing with. I made it very clear that I wasn't just an interpreter, but was there to help him have a better understanding of his patient's cultural background, tradition, ethnicity, way of life and behavior. I also strived to ensure that the doctor recognized his own personal culture and that of his Western medical practice, so he would take all of these components into account before making a clinical decision. It usually took a lot of time to do my homework to prepare for these appointments. Ultimately, this was good for me, because it forced me to learn and acknowledge more about my faith, values, Laotian behavior and cultural sensitivities.

From all the experience that I had dealing with the issues and crises that went on in the Lao community, I was the one who had some ability to help. Also, I was willing to volunteer my time to help others. I ended up spending more and more time and cutting classes two to three days a week. In one particular worst case situation I was absent from my class for three weeks.

This case involved a minor conflict between a Laotian husband and wife in the Bronx, but ended up in a NYPD shoot out. One evening, the husband and wife were arguing with each other over a small family matter. The husband was frustrated, and he ordered his wife and two children out of the apartment so he could have a moment to resolve things inside the apartment alone.

A few hours later the wife and kids returned to the apartment and knocked on the door. He refused to open it. The wife called 911 for help, so two New York City policemen showed up and ordered the wife and children to wait in the hallway downstairs. The next thing she knew, her husband was being shot six times by two policemen who were over 6-feet tall.

They claimed that the frustrated husband was running after them with a knife. Instead, the husband was eating ice cream to cool himself down from the minor agitation—while the police were breaking into the apartment. The husband was in shock, holding the silver spoon in his hand. The police had mistaken the spoon for a knife, so both policemen had maliciously pumped six bullets into his helpless, frail body. He was only 5-foot-1-inch, 125 pounds, and spoke no English.

After the man was shot, the wife went to the police precinct, and with the help of her nine-year-old son, filed a complaint against the police department. She ended up being talked into filing a complaint against her own husband. So, when I got a call from the wife, I jumped on the subway and got myself across the borough of Manhattan to the Bronx as soon as I could.

Here I was, as a friend and translator, at the office of the assistant district attorney, trying to have the case of the wife's complaint against her husband dropped. At the hospital, where the man had miraculously survived the bullet wounds, almost his entire body was wrapped with bandages. He was barely capable of moving, but they handcuffed him and had a 24-hour police guard at the door. He was being treated like a guilty criminal. My heart was broken to see my fellow countryman having to endure this pain and suffering, because of a misjudgment based on racial and ethnic profiling, and miscommunication because of a language barrier.

He had six bullet wounds from our own public protectors—the policemen, whom we respected, admired and trusted the most in our society. How could this be an accidental shooting by the NYPD? How could this be considered resisting arrest? How much force or strength did two six-foot tall men really need to take down a 5-foot-1-inch, 125-pound man? One bullet in the arm or leg I could possibly understand, if there was a life-threatening situation, but six bullets? To me, that was shoot to kill. This was beyond my common understanding. To me, it was a case of intentional shooting, not accidental shooting. It was one of the racial profiling cases of the 1980s that no one heard about. Since we were just imaginary people from Laos--who would give a damn? The police department? Hell no! I ended up spending three weeks volunteering my time to translate for the family at their lawyer's office, at the assistant district attorney's office, and for the attorney at the grand jury hearing to drop the case of the wife pressing charges against her husband.

When I returned to class, I was called in to meet with the principal of the school; he wanted to know what my situation was. Why had I been absent so much? I explained everything that had gone on in my life, my family's life and in my Lao community. After I told him about my involvement with the Lao community, he understood and encouraged me to cut down on my volunteer time. He said I should try to focus on graduating from high school, so that I could go to college and better myself, then I could help improve my community. Despite my very bad attendance, I was still able to keep my grades very high for most of my important classes.

A few months after the NYPD shooting case -- which ended without a proper resolution -- I was safe from being kicked out of high school. I desperately needed to take a trip somewhere away from New York City to breathe fresh air. I decided to visit a close friend in Charlotte, N.C., with my best Lao buddy, Souvanh, who liked to be called "Ronny."

Right after I confirmed the date for traveling, the phone began ringing off the hook with calls from Charlotte, N.C. One call was from the friend I planned to visit, and many calls were from his girlfriend who was asking me to bring Southeast Asian cooking ingredients for her special recipes. On the list were many different kinds of rice powders and flours.

At the time, both Ronny and I had dreams to be punk rockers and rock stars. We were drug free, clean and lawful residents, but our outfits were out of this world. Even in our neighborhood, all the brothers kept reminding us that Halloween is in October. But who cared? I was in America -- the free world -- where there was freedom of expression and freedom of speech. Who cared what other people had to say?

During my early time in America, I did everything I could to camouflage myself, to blend in – by changing my body language, learning the local American expressions and slang, adapting to the style of clothes.

Sometimes, when we were so frustrated with our inner voice, the voice that needed to be heard and needed to be released to blow out the flame that was blazing inside our hearts. We would use Sharpies and markers to write it out on our white T-shirts: FTW (Fuck The World), BTK (Born To

Kill), BTR (Born To Rock), ALB (Asian Lover Boy) and so on. We thought we would be accepted and fit into the world of sex, drugs, rock and roll, heavy metal, punk, new wave and hip hop -- whatever was out there. Being imaginary people, we had to do whatever we must to get our voices heard and get our point across.

Sometimes, when I tried too hard, I ended up with a Duran Duran hairdo and the personality of Bobby Brown, wearing MC Hammer pants, Michael Jackson glove, and Gene Simmons boots, cruising up and down Flatbush Avenue. Even I began to ask myself, who had I become? What am I about to be?

It didn't matter what or how I tried, the harder I threw myself against the arm of American society, the harder I bounced back against my own self. And there I found myself asking bigger questions regarding my ancestors' roots, my own identity and political history. What had happened to us? Who had started all of these things? I was not trying to fabricate evidence for judging anybody, but to gain a better understanding and a higher value of my own integrity. I tried and I tried. I came to realize that America is not the big melting pot that I believed it to be, but rather a gigantic wok of races, ethnicities and individuals – stir-fry. Being of an imaginary people in a strange land, a man without country or dignity, it didn't take long for America to frustrate me. Out of this frustration, desperation and confusion, however, I began to search and seek out the answers to all of my innermost questions.

For us at that time, to be *cool* was to be popular—looking tough, rough, dangerous and hard-hitting were symbols of strength and power; they meant we mandated respect. Despite all the facts, this was what I thought the mentality of American society was all about. I believed the American attitude was: Who cares? Why care? Nobody cares. So, why should I care or why should I give a damn? As naïve as I was, how would I know any better?

This was the kind of city mentality that was rising up at the time. In the eyes of the law and authority, we were nothing but poor, dumb refugees, the scumbags of the ghetto, the leeches that fed from the bottom of society, second-class citizens. Wherever we went, people always perceived us as troublemakers or criminals. The police especially, loved to harass and intimidate us just for the hell of it.

The night of our traveling had arrived. Upon our trip to Charlotte, N.C., we both were ecstatically happy just to get out of the crazy city for a change. We slept all day during the day, so we could travel at night to avoid the traffic hassles.

We left Brooklyn at about 10 p.m., hoping to arrive in Charlotte by the next morning. It was an 11-hour drive. Here we were with an old Pontiac 1980 Sport TransAm with black tinted windows. We were humming and singing along with our favorite rock band, AC/DC's "Highway to Hell." Who else would it be?

Rock groups and heavy metal stars were our inspirations and idols, more or less our dreams and our influence in life. That night was typical. That rainy, spring night, we were on the New Jersey Turnpike near the border of Pennsylvania cruising with our cruise control set at the speed limit: 65 miles per hour. We were rejoicing with one of our favorite songs from another favorite band, Motley Crue's "Shout at the Devil." We were just starting to have the greatest time of our life—enjoying the freedom and liberation from city stress. We were both shouting and shaking our long porcupine hair. Our hair weighed almost as much as a whole can of Aqua Net hair spray.

Many times in the past when we were all traveling together as a group in the same car, we would have to ban smoking inside the car to prevent our Aqua Net porcupine hairdos from catching on fire. Back at that time, in order to be *cool*, we would have to do whatever it took to make sure our hair always stood up like porcupine quills. To achieve that, every time we did our hairdos we would have to lie down on the floor with our hair lying flat, straight out on the floor. Our *homeboys* would then spray the hair for us, and we would just stay fixed in that position on the floor until our hair dried completely. When we got up, we would have a perfectly sculpted, porcupine hairdo and be ready for action.

Besides our hairdos, super tight jeans were another thing that we had to deal with. As part of the style, the long porcupine hair was incomplete without the super tight jeans—so tight after we put them on that we couldn't drop our pants without the help of our homeboy pulling them off for us. Many times I ended up wearing the same jeans for three or four days, simply because I couldn't take them off. It's kind of funny when I look back to the 1980s; we took the hard rock, heavy metal and pop culture to an extreme. Being first generation immigrants, we liked to extend the margins and break the boundaries just to prove that we could. That was the period where I was running from what I tried to remember and what has already been forgotten. As my journey drifts further and deeper into the core of America, I became a traveler moving in and out of dreams and nightmares.

As we were having a great time cruising within the speed limit and keeping cool, all of a sudden I saw a New Jersey State Trooper tailgating us. I told Ronny, "Hey, homeboy, why don't you just move to the right lane so he can pass us; he seems to be in a hurry. I think the Dunkin' Donut store is at the next exit and will be closing down in five minutes."

"Okay man!" Ronny replied.

As soon as Ronny was switching into the right lane, the trooper was also moving into our lane and flashing us with his high beams – commanding us to pull over. Ronny gave me a blank look, I looked at him, then I laughed just to annoy him.

The next things I remember, we both were ordered to get out of the car with our hands on our head at gunpoint. We were commanded to stand still while they were searching Ronny's beloved 1980 Pontiac TransAm. He had put his every penny into it, just to make it look good and function at all times. That TransAm was his pride and a winning ticket to his girl's heart, his baby, is now being checking inside out. I could see the feeling of violation and invasion of his very privacy in his eyes.

I was the one who had packed his TransAm trunk with all the food supplies and cooking ingredients before we left. I spent a few days shopping around New York City's Chinatown to get all that my good friend from Charlotte wanted. In my head I was beginning to wonder, and started to ask myself a question, what does he want? He must be so damn high on Dunkin' Donuts or he's up to something weird.

After what I had just been through with the crisis of the Lao family and the NYPD, I couldn't believe the situation I was in, standing outside in the chilly night in the middle of a drizzling, spring rain. I thought to myself, "Oh shit! Very soon the Aqua Net will melt and drip down into my eyes, and I will have a burning sensation. Then, if I try to wipe my eyes and face, he might shoot me. Oh shit! What I am going to do now?"

I was praying to God and the Lord for Aqua Net not to fail me so easily. As I was deep in my own thoughts, all of a sudden, I heard shouting from the top of the lungs of the police—the one that was checking the trunk of Ronny's car.

"Down on your knees! Now! Down on your knees!"

The other officer, who was standing about 10 feet in front of us, kept quiet with his finger on the trigger.

As we were both kneeling down, another shout came from the same policeman to both of us.

"Hands off your heads and roll up your sleeves—then stretch both of your arms forward and stay fixed—nobody move."

After those very harsh words of command, I said to myself, why are these assholes making such a big fucking deal out of a routine stop?

Then he ordered his partner to come around to check our arms. His partner did as he was told. He came about three feet away from Ronny and me. He flashed the light from his flashlight on both of my arms and Ronny's arms; he was panning them up and down searching for something, but I had no clue what they were looking for. He didn't seem to find whatever it was, then he just called out to his partner,

"Negative!"

Then I was confused. I didn't know why I was having a physical checkup by the police in the middle of the night on the shoulder of the New Jersey Turnpike.

Then both of them came up to our face.

The police (the one that check Ronny's TransAm trunk):

"Where are you folks heading tonight?"

We both coincidentally replied together at the same time, "Charlotte, North Carolina, sir!"

The police:

"Very funny. So, tell me exactly where did you get all the goodies in your trunk?"

I didn't hesitate to call out to the police. "Chinatown, sir!" I replied on behalf of Ronny.

The police: "Ah huh! That's why it's all labeled in Chinese?"

"Yes, sir," I replied.

I was cracking a bit of a smile as I was answering his questions because I found his comment and question to be ridiculous. I could see his face and tone of voice begin to change immediately. He seemed to be more explosive and meaner.

The police (seriously, with his big, straight, red face turned towards me): "I am not going to play with you. All I want to know is where you got all of this stuff? And who supplied it to you?"

"Sir, I don't know what you are talking about. I am honestly telling you. I got all of the stuff in the trunk in Chinatown. We are not selling it; we are just bringing it to our friends, because they asked for it. They told me that there are only a few Southeast Asian grocery stores that carry these kinds of items. So we are bringing it for them. Sir, I don't believe this is illegal." I replied.

The police: "Not illegal! You can be put away for a very long time for all the stuff you have in that trunk."

(I cut him off.) "Sir! Would you please let me know what is going on here?

What do we have in our trunk that is illegal?"

He grabbed my arm and dragged me to the TransAm's trunk, where he pointed directly at all of the cooking powders that my best friend's wife had requested for her special recipes. By now, I had a clue as to what they had been trying to get at.

"Sir! I really mean it—these are for cooking," I tried to explain.

He was just ignoring me.

"Sir! If you don't believe me you could sniff it.

Within a brief moment after that, he was accepting my advice. I thought to myself, "Oh, no! This is getting to be really stupid! Don't tell me that he is going to open the glutinous rice powder and sniff it; he is going to sneeze like hell. Hell yeah!"

I almost couldn't stop myself from laughing, but I knew I couldn't fuck around with New Jersey State Troopers. I had heard all kinds of rumors of how rough they were—so I held myself back.

He was kind of mad at me for being so gullible to take my advice. Than both police went back into their car for at least ten minutes more, while we were left standing in the drizzling rain. By this time I was getting cold and wet. The Aqua Net was melting and getting into my face and eyes. I was so upset and angry, but there was not much we could do. We were in *New Jersey*; what *could* we do? Regardless of the injustice, the rookie police had no heart; they still gave us a ticket for $80 claiming that we were going 73 m.p.h. in a 65 m.p.h. speed zone.

They stopped us, because back in the '80s, based on our race, tattoos, rock and roll porcupine hairdos with the weight of a whole can of Aqua Net, black leather pants, long neck boots, belt buckle in the shape of a human skull and spike, Pontiac Sport TransAm with black tinted windows, bags and bags of white powder in the trunk, and traveling on the highway in the middle of the night, the police thought we were drug dealers. This description or profile perfectly fits the typical dealer who gets high on their own supplies. The only problem was that there were no needle holes in our arms, as all the policemen expected and hoped to see—so they could really give us hell.

We drove on that night, and ultimately had the time of our lives in Charlotte, N.C. We drank like fish and ate like monsters. We danced like it was Lao New Year. We chatted like a couple in love. All day and all night we did nothing but celebrate our friendship and catch up on each other's lives. Again, it was one of those trips, out of the house at the wrong hour, and all possible things going wrong—from one bad thing to another worse thing—from laughing to crying and back to laughing again.

On the way back we were both somewhat tired from partying and having such a good time. I was the navigator, reading the map and telling Ronny where to go. He was just driving; he loved to drive. Halfway back to New York I couldn't keep my eyes open any longer, and I was fell asleep. Ronny just kept driving and listening to our favorite AC/DC music, while I slept. He kept driving and driving. He let me sleep, as he was confident that he knew the way back to New York City. He managed to get us back to New York, but *upstate* New York. We were heading North—way, way North. When I woke up, I asked Ronny,

"Yo homey! Where are we man?"

Ronny: "We are in New York. I don't think we are that far from New York City."

Without paying any attention, I took him at his word. I always trusted his instincts, and I was still feeling sleepy. Ronny suggested that I go back to sleep; so, I did. I must have slept for another 10 or 15 minutes. I woke up in the middle of a traffic jam; I felt relieved that we had made it back to New York City. As I was looking for someplace to get a soda to help me stay awake, I looked out of the side window. That was when I realized, we had just missed the last exit to turn around before we got to the checkpoint at the Canadian border. That trip was hilariously fun, as well as a nightmare. (I called this event: K-9 and Fine Police Squadron)

Now, it was time to get back to life in the Big Apple.

As for my life involving the Christian church, we were all about to be baptized, and become real members of the church. We went to church three times a week: Sunday morning services, Sunday afternoon services and Wednesday night services with choir rehearsal. I did a very good job of organizing and gathering all of my Laotian community along with some of my Vietnamese and Cambodian neighbors. The minister saw great potential in me, so they ordained me to be their first Laotian sub-deacon.

Eight months after my sub-deacon ordination, I skipped the deacon level, and was ordained to be a minister to serve the Laotian community in their church. As the first Laotian minister, and the youngest minister to ever be ordained by this denomination in North America, I was quite popular. Every time they had a large service and communion in North America, the church members would fill Carnegie Hall and the Hilton Hotel auditorium in New York City. Sometimes they would broadcast to at least 52 countries around the globe, and the head of Apostles would ask me to serve alongside him at his high altar in front of more than several thousand audience members.

For a 21-year old who barely knew how to speak English, it was a huge honor to be a recognized and highly-respected figure. The serious consequences that I had to face though, were that I knew nothing about the Christian Bible or even the basic principles of Christianity. Every time the ministers were at the altar preaching about John, Mark, Peter or whomever else he mentioned, I knew nothing about these names. Who is John? Who is Mark? Who is Peter? Who is Sister and Mother Mary? Forget about other brothers such as Andrew or James; I had no clue. Every time I was asked to speak at our local church when the minister was preaching about John or Peter, I would just find a reference to some disciple of Buddha so that I and all of my Laotian brothers and sisters could have some sense of Christianity's principles that had some similarities to Buddhism. What did I know—I was the one who had been kicked out of Catholic school from second grade for insulting nuns and priests regarding their sexuality.

Many times when I walked up to the altar, before I spoke I looked down at the benches and saw that all of the Laotian brothers and sisters were asleep from being bored to death. I would blast them to wake them up with my usual—Come on Peenorng Lao (Lao brothers and sisters), wake up. I can hear all of your snoring all the way up here at the altar and for all you kids please stop drooling. Some evenings when the service went on for too long my own little brothers or sisters would fall into such a deep sleep that they would wet their pants. From all the way in front at the altar, I could hear the sound of their urine dropping on the church's hardwood floor in the middle of services.

With all the activities that I was involved in, I was under tremendous pressure to fully function. It had been almost two years of living and struggling in Brooklyn. By this time my family had been able to save enough money to move to a new neighborhood. My family, along with a couple of other families who lived along Ocean Avenue and East 23rd Street, moved to Parade Place, which was located across the street from Prospect Park. There were many more Southeast Asian refugees (Cambodians and Vietnamese) in that area, along with many other Asian descendents -- Chinese and some Koreans. Before we moved there, the neighborhood seemed to be much better than our old neighborhood. In the end, though, it didn't matter where we went; it seemed like problems were traveling along with us.

After living in America for two years and a few months, one my very close cousins, Soulivanh, arrived in the United States from the Ubon Refugee Camp in Thailand. A Christian family in Conestoga in upstate New York sponsored him, and he was not happy with the way he was being treated. So, one day I asked one of the ministers from the church that I was attending in Brooklyn to drive me to Conestoga to take him away in the middle of the night. We brought him back to New York City to live with my family.

That reminded me of the time I was trapped into living in that hellhole apartment. I wish I had had some cousin or someone to come and rescue me. Now, we had a new family member added to the eleven already living in a small three-bedroom apartment. There were so many of us packed into this tiny three-bedroom apartment, that we turned our little dining room into another bedroom, which I shared with all three of my younger brothers, as well as my cousin, Soulivanh. Every day we turned our tiny living room floor into our dining table where twelve of us could sit in a circle on the hardwood floor and eat. During the summer we would turn our fire escape into a sleeping space at night as a way of cooling off from the heat of the day.

Four months after cousin Soulivanh came to live with us, his old friend, who used to be a volunteer nurse in Ubon Refugee Camp in Thailand, called him and said there was an American lady friend of a friend who had an interest in learning how to speak Lao. My cousin asked me if I might be interested in teaching this woman. He suggested that I be the one to teach her since my English was already much better than his.

So, one day this woman called and left a message. A day later I called her back, and she told me that she wanted to learn how to speak Lao. I was thinking to myself, why in the world would she be interested in learning how to speak Lao? Every time people asked me where I came from and I told them that I came from the country called "Laos," almost no one had even heard of it. Even the former president, John F. Kennedy, didn't pronounce it right—many time out of my frustration I have to emphasize how to pronounce it Lao—L-A-O-S not LAY US or not GET LAY (Sometimes I made up a story for an inquisitive stranger that I came from a place called Laos, a small country next to Canada; people believed me because they thought I was one of the ethnic minority Eskimo tribes.) Here was this stranger—she wanted to learn how to speak my language. Out of curiosity I went to meet with her, and I soon became her Lao teacher.

This woman, as the world has come to know her today, is one of the greatest female cinematographers or DPs (Director of Photography) in the movie-making world—Ellen M. Kuras. As I was beginning to teach her how to speak Lao, I was also teaching her about the Lao culture and traditions. One thing led to another, and I ended up helping her write her first documentary film script about a young Lao girl who lived in Rochester, in upstate New York.

During the production of this documentary project I volunteered to help out as the production assistant, to do whatever I could. The production went on for about two months, then the main subject decided not to go on or be part of the project. So the production stopped. When the production stopped, I carried on with my teaching as usual, twice a week. Again, one thing led to another. From being a teacher to being a good friend, I ended up spending a lot of time sharing my Lao view of the world and universe. This included life, death, and beyond -- the realm of faith, the spirit, the soul and religion -- all the way from the old Lao Animism to Theravada Buddhism.

In the course of all these conversations and discussions I came to realize that I had absorbed so much from my parents and grandparents when I was a child growing up in the middle of the war zone. Of course, my good friend was using her Sony TCD 5M to record most of our conversations so we could extract a story regarding ancient Laotian knowledge, philosophical ideas, Laotian myth and legend. How I ended up becoming a partner, one of the creators and the subject of The Betrayal (Nerakhoon) never really came from a specific commitment or any legal agreement; it just happened as it was supposed to be. It seem like it was meant to be our destiny. One day my friend Ellen just said to me, "After all this time that we've known each other, you never really told me your personal story."

If only I could have known it would take 20 plus years to tell the rest of my story, I definitely wouldn't have dared to tell it to her. But I did. The next thing I knew, the camera was on me. Whatever happened after that, it was meant to be and meant to happen. It was not a coincidence. Before I met Ellen, I was already seeking a way to express my feelings about my life and struggles in America. I already felt I was responsible for educating the public about my situation and the story of my coming here. It was not our intention to come to America to steal jobs or exploit the social services and public assistance. We came to America because of the war. Every time people asked, *"Why did you come to America?"* deep in my heart I wished I could tell them that this was the wrong question. The proper question is, *"What did the United States government do over there in your country?"*

This kind of misunderstanding and lack of actual facts or public information regarding US involvement in Laos was present throughout my entire time in high school. It was very hard to ignore, but at the time there was not much I could do about it except keep it in my heart, holding it deep in my soul. Sometimes, when I felt strong and brave enough, I expressed it through words in my poetry, or sometimes in my paintings, drawings and illustrations.

Life went on. I was now a junior at Martin Luther King Jr. High School, a full-time minister, a part-time employee at Mr. Chin's store, and I was involved in a film project. By this time, America was shredding me to pieces -- physically and mentally. Due to the overwhelming effects of economic pressure and worry for the safety of my family and myself due to city crime, I was living in fear: fear to go to school, fear to walk on the streets in my own neighborhood, and fear to play in the park across from the apartment building where I was living. Even inside my own apartment, my life was surrounded by all different kinds of fear—even fear of being my true self and recognizing my own true identity. Due to the cause and effect of pure environmental pressure and discrimination, I felt the urgency to assimilate into American society, a society that, for me being a refugee, was made principally of fear as well as physical and financial insecurity.

Assimilation and integration into a non-homogeneous society is much harder than into a homogeneous one. Who should I become: black or white? I am only one man, born in one place, and given one national identity, which is Lao; but since I was forced to be displaced, I became a man caught between two worlds, living with two different value systems. I was a fish of two waters: fresh and salt. I was a man with questions of identity. I couldn't just throw away all the essences that made me who I was—I had to find a middle ground, a place where I could compromise between my *two* worlds.

I tried very hard to assimilate and to be part of something where I could get some sort of recognition or some human decency and respect. It was hard enough for me to just try to survive day by day in school without being beaten up and shaken down for money in the boy's room. I was just like many other Lao, Cambodian and Vietnamese—we were poor and powerless; we came from broken and separated families due to war.

There were no leaders or male role models in our families, because many of us lost our fathers during the war. We had just gotten away from living in a most oppressive, depressive and abusive refugee camp lifestyle. Many of us had very low self-esteem; we were young, and didn't know much about our history or what really happened to us. Many of us knew we were refugees from a war-torn country, and that there wasn't much for us to be proud of. Back in my home country, during the Lao revolution, people called me "son of a traitor." Over here, for no obvious good reason, they called me a "son of a gun." Thank God I didn't own one, because if I had, I might have used it.

I was at my breaking point; I felt like I couldn't take it anymore. I was so sick and tired of being harassed and ridiculed due to my physical and cultural differences. I commanded myself, however, to persevere; I refused to victimize myself and let the environment and circumstances push me down a crack. I was very lucky that I managed to make it through. Many unfortunate ones, who couldn't carry on with the fight, missed out—they dropped out of school.

We tried to be submissive and lay low just to avoid trouble. Being Laotian, my parents and grandparents taught me not to be confrontational or use hostility, conflict or violence. Rather than avoiding or finding a loophole, they taught me to try and overcome with peace, understanding and forgiveness. I tried almost every possible way to avoid violent confrontation, choosing peace rather than conflict. I forced myself to try to understand the mentality of the predators (the ones that preyed on me) and, of course, to forgive, because forgiveness for the stupid and ignorant is always a must. Many of us decided to form our own group, so we could bond into a brotherhood united for strength in order to empower ourselves to fight for our existence and to protect our human dignity. We needed recognition and respect from the society and community who were constantly putting us down. The more submissive we were in order to avoid conflict, the more we were treated like cowards. I was getting tired of being called a coward and being treated like one for not engaging in any form of confrontation or fighting back physically or verbally.

Some of my friends in the neighborhood and in school, as well as many younger neighborhood kids, had nothing to do once they dropped out of school. There was not much to hope for, so they decided to hang out in Chinatown, where they felt a sense of belonging because of their race, similar culture and traditions. They ended up joining Chinese gangs including Ghost Shadow, White Tiger, Green Dragon, or Born to Kill, seeking protection and guarantees of safety along with the promise of money, power, sex, and status recognition from the *Dai Lo*, "big brothers." Because of desperation and vulnerability, they had to choose one way or the other. Many chose to go with the *Dai Lo*, because these "big brothers" became their instant surrogate fathers or male role models. They showed the boys the affection they needed, giving them a feeling of acceptance, security and belonging, giving them something worth living and fighting for.

As promised, at first they were taken care of by the *Dai Lo*. They had been offered a house or shelter, where they lived and were accompanied by many other guys of more or less the same age who seemed to care for them and respect them as family. The tools for empowering themselves were provided, and they were trained to use those tools. No one forced them to go to school, and they no longer had to deal with any school hassles or harassment. After being oppressed for so long at school and at home, dealing with their parents' strict rules from the old country's culture and tradition, the sense of freedom and liberation for many of them was far more important at the present time than anything else.

It was sad. Many of these desperate kids, who were part of these big brother protection programs, ended up being exploited and used like soldiers of fortune to fight vicious turf battles against rival Asian gangs in Chinatown. They were also used as instruments for criminal gang activity: extorting shopkeepers and restaurants, carrying out armed robberies, being guard dogs for illegal gambling houses and brothels, trafficking drugs and, worst of all, being used as internal residential informers.

After they made a pact and were sworn in as the royal brother's keeper of their big brother or *Dai Lo*, they were sent back to live in the old community where their own family resided. There, they spied on their friends, family friends and everyone else in the neighborhood.

Back in the 1980s they had a special operation network or ring, where a local informer would give specific information to their gang. The gang leader would then bring in the gang's nomadic unit. Their special operation was to travel from city to city in different Asian communities around the United States committing residential robbery. This way, it would be less obvious to the local authorities. This was one of the elusive tactics used by gangs to mobilize their criminal activity beneath the radar.

This special operation was successful for the gangs because the Asian community was reluctant to report or press charges, thus avoiding gang retaliation against their businesses and their families. In so many cases, incidents that occurred in our community went on without any notification to the authorities.

Eventually, this criminal subculture became the routine, and it began to deteriorate our community and family structure. It was unbearable to see the worst cases—when kids were being forced to extort from their own families and friends, and when the parents had to give them up to the authorities in order to save their lives. They feared that their child would be killed while doing something of a criminal nature. The parents hoped that after some form of detention, discipline or serving a short time in prison, they would be tamed down or straightened out.

As a minister in a Christian church, I tried every possible way to bring peace, security, and protection to my community. I ended up conducting my own family crisis intervention and gang prevention programs out of my own living room. I was deeply involved in the core of these crises in my community. I tried hard to correct as many problems as I possibly could until my family and the Lao community were able to establish strength and capability, and to be self-sufficient enough to get back on track. We wanted to get to the point where we could live our lives as Buddhists. Although we were all baptized and attending the Christian church, we still maintained our faith as Buddhists all the way through.

In 1986 I was finally graduating from high school, so it was time to pursue my higher education at a university. There was only one way for me to be able to function with such high demands on my time and to be able to focus on my studies -- I had to leave the church. This was another critical decision, which led to the disappointment of many people. When I left the church, all of my Laotian brothers and sisters left with me.

After we left the church each family began to find a new territory to migrate to.

Many Laotians, who had smaller families and could afford to move out, had left Brooklyn. Some families moved to Stockton and Visalia, California, some moved to Philadelphia Pennsylvania, some went to North Carolina and few moved to Atlantic City, New Jersey. Very few families, who had such large numbers and couldn't afford to move immediately like my family, got stuck here for many more years.

Despite all of the hardships, struggles and desperation where extreme measures were needed, I considered myself lucky for not having chosen the extreme path and falling through the crack like many others who were growing up in the same environment. As much as I wanted to choose the fast track to get to my American Dream, I couldn't betray my mother or my Lao community. So, I put up with the daily hassles, like going through a metal detector every day just to get into my classroom. I wasn't part of any gang, but instead had joined the local brotherhood group who bonded for the purpose of peace and protection without any bad intentions. We were like neighborhood security volunteers. If there was a robbery, fight, argument, conflict or any kind of problem, we would call the police for help.

While I was going through these difficulties of growing up, I was being harassed and ridiculed in school and public places. In my case, it was worse, because of my two crooked front teeth with an overbite. I looked exactly like the comic relief character that we used to see in almost every classic Chinese Kung Fu movie. This was the dude with the slanted eyes and two big front teeth. I was the real-life version of that comical character who made people laugh in the movie. My teeth became the instrument that drew attention from people and inspired them to ridicule and harass me. It was a nightmare growing up in a society where everything had a referential standard and everything was categorized based upon the comparison. I totally experienced all of the growing pains of dealing with an identity crisis, personal sense of self, anger and confusion.

Everytime I was bombarded by strangers regarding my physical and political identity—the harder, the deeper and the bigger the questions were that I got from them -- the more I began to ask deeper and bigger questions regarding my history and what really had happened in my country during the war. I wanted to know more about my father's involvement during the war. It was a sad time for me, being a refugee from a classified war, living in the United States as a more or less imaginary person. Because of this sadness and frustration, I wanted to know more and more about Lao history as well as my family's history. I decided to go on my own discovery mission. I began to have an urge, or I would say it was a calling, a calling that I had to accept and hoped to take action on soon.

By this time it was June 1986. I had finally graduated from high school. After I graduated from Martin Luther King Jr. High School in the class of 1986, I was accepted by several very good universities. Out of all the universities that accepted me, I chose Pratt Institute to pursue my engineering career, because Pratt Institute is a private institution, well known for architecture, art and engineering. At Pratt Institute I started as a chemical engineering major with the hope and dream that someday I would help develop drugs and medicine to cure diseases. I also hoped to perhaps return to my home country some day to help develop a community of atomic scientists, so we could develop our own manufacturing of polymers, dyes, plastics, food and fertilizer. This dream didn't last very long; a year later I changed my major to electrical engineering.

As I was studying engineering in the university, my involvement and work on the documentary film was still crawling forward. I began to take on more roles and more responsibilities as the years went by. Since the day that I became part of the process, there was never a day that I didn't think about the project. It literally became our child. Being one of the parents of this most precious child, I knew that I had a great responsibility to raise this child to be right -- to feel right, think right, walk right and see right -- in the eyes of future audiences and American society. This child was the representative of Laotian history, Laotian life and Laotian obstacles. Even though this child became a burden and obligation for all of us filmmakers, at the same time it helped us to grow alongside it and challenged us to the full extent of our ultimate will and desire.

America and the American lifestyle had such a surreal and illusionary influence on my life. I was more or less dazed through the decade of the '80s. In New York City in the early '80s, gangs, drugs and the dream of being a heavy metal rock star were the name of the game for many refugee teens and youth. Many of the parents and middle-aged men and women were working in factories 12 hours a day for $4.75/hour minimum wage, while trying to raise seven to 10 children in America. This was very much the common denominator for most parents.

It didn't matter who they were in the old home country. Over there, they could have been a captain or a colonel, all the way up to a general commanding soldiers in the army, but here most of them didn't even have enough authority to control or knowledge about the new country to be able to advise their own children. They hardly had any time to be home with their wives and children because many of them worked for such low pay that they had to work two jobs and overtime. Many Lao couples I knew were working different shifts. They lived in the same house and shared the same bed but got a chance to actually be with each other only once a week because they committed themselves to a new lifestyle—fancy cars, expensive jewelry, name brand clothes, big houses, even establishing big bank accounts and a high credit line. They thought this would secure their family and gain a respectable image in a society where the financial and materialistic status could earn them a place in the community. They themselves felt satisfaction with this since this was their personal interpretation of the American dream. They had to pay a big price for that kind of demanding lifestyle here in America.

In my opinion this was what many Lao parents thought they had to do to establish the strong foundation for their children and the next generation to come. Although this is very profound and most honorable, the consequences they had to face were tremendous. Many of their children were growing up with a lack of communication, affection and guidance. Many of them went wild without parental supervision and grew apart from the warmth and comfort of the old Lao family value, culture and tradition.

In many Laotian families throughout America, like my family for example, the children became the parents because the kids spoke English and the parents did not. Parents depended on their children to be their eyes and ears, the extended hand and support system of survival, because many of the parents didn't know how to read, write or understand a word of English. For parents who fell into this category, it was most difficult for them to discipline their kids in the old way or in the new way of life.

As far as my daily life in Brooklyn was concerned, we were trying really hard to find a way to secure our financial needs and safety. By this time my family had figured out completely what our goals were. We had made a new friend in our new neighborhood who was the middleman in a piecework business. Since we had many people in our family, my mother got some piecework for us from that friend. Every evening after all the kids finished their homework, and after our family dinner, we would sit in a circle in our tiny living room. We created an assembly line working on the piecework from 7 p.m. to midnight. We assembled necklaces, bracelets, bead-chains, hair clips, bow ties, etc. We would make 3 to 10 cents per piece. Sometimes we would make 15 cents per piece for the ones that were harder and more time consuming to assemble.

We did this kind of work and kept this schedule for years. My mother saved every penny and dime that we made in the hope that someday we could afford to buy a house of our own. To live in the suburbs and be an American suburbanite was one of our biggest dreams. My mother and I were looking for any possibility to move our family -- anywhere except Brooklyn or the Bronx.

As tough as my mother was, it only took a few years in America to begin to break her down. Her hopes and dreams about America began to fade. Everything changed in this country. Her high hopes, expectations and dreams for all of her children to become lawyers, doctors and businessmen or women were faltering because my younger sisters and brothers were getting discouraged due to the frustrations of racism and violence inside the school.

There was a gang shootout in one sister's high school, and my other brothers and sisters were paralyzed by the same frustration regarding whichever school they were attending. They all suffered with the same problems: school violence, verbal and physical harassment. Some of my younger brothers began to hang out in Chinatown with friends. In this uncontrollable environment, there was nothing much that my mom could possibly do to hold onto our way of life as she used to back in Laos.

As for me, I was a young man caught between two worlds: the old Lao way of life on one hand, and the American Dream and nightmare world on the other. I could only fight so hard to protect and maintain the old values in the hearts and souls of my younger brothers and sisters. I knew I could only win some battles, but I would not be able to win the war. The school playground became a battlefield.

In the minds of young people (15- to 16-year-olds), death, dying and destroying others seemed to be the only way road to honor and respect. How could we possibly enforce our home country's ideology of peace and harmony in the mind of a young Laotian who was having a mental and physical identity crisis, and was submerging deep into an environment surrounded by nothing but substance abuse, violence and fear?

"How? How can we live our lives like this?" I often asked.

We had been stuck in the bottom of the pit as prisoners and slave workers for seven years before we could trust our eyes and ears and truly know how to make the small step of crawling out from the depths below the bottom of the bottom of that pit. Although we tried hard to crawl, the big turning point that forced us to run was two horrendous incidents that occurred in our Woodruff and Parade Place neighborhood.

At this time I was still a junior at Pratt Institute and I was staying at a friend's apartment so I could have some peace and quiet to concentrate on my school work. Engineering school required a lot of research, self-discipline and most of my time working on engineering projects on my own. I was in the middle of my midterm exams, and I had just finished my Atomic Physics midterm exams. My head was still hurting from night after sleepless night of preparing for that exam and working on midterm projects for many other classes. I went back to the apartment, and before I took a nap, I decided to listen to the messages on my answering machine and try to return phone calls. This was my usual routine.

On my answering machine I got a terrifying message from Mrs. X (I call her that to conceal her identity for safety purposes). She was a close friend of my family. In fact, we were more than friends—she and her husband were more like family to me. I treated her two sons as if they were my own nephews.

While she left the message on my answering machine, she must have been terrified out of her soul. I could hardly tell whether it was her, because her voice was so shaky and trembling. She was on the verge of breaking down, even before she got to the point about exactly what was happening. I assumed that someone was dying. This was what she said on the answering machine:

"Thavisouk! Thavisouk! I am so frightened. I am so frightened. The gang forced their way into my apartment early this morning. They managed to break into the apartment while I was about to go out of the house to buy food. They were just there outside my door waiting for me to open it. When they got into the apartment, they tied my family and me up, and demanded all of our money.

I gave them $1000 cash—they also took my VCR and all the other things that we had. They took whatever they could take with them. They still demanded another $4000, and we have to come up with the money within 24 hours. If I can't come up with that amount, they promised that they will come back to kill all of my family. I don't know what to do—please come to help me."

Of course, right after hearing that urgent message I immediately called Ellen to get the camera ready within the hour so we could go to Brooklyn to do a rescue mission and to capture the moment on film or on video or whatever format we could get. (The format was less important to us.) Within less than two hours we were in Brooklyn and had rescued the family from the local gang.

Before I got there, I asked the family if they could just leave the apartment and go to the local community agency where I used to work as a volunteer. I didn't want to be seen in the neighborhood as being responsible for the rescue mission, because I didn't want any of these gang members to know that I was helping my friends behind the scenes. I had to be very careful with everything I did because my family was still living one building away from where the incident took place. So, after we rescued the family, while they were in the car and we were driving them away from Brooklyn, I asked, "So, tell me briefly what happened?"

Mrs. X, in a state of emotional panic and still shaking with shock and fear for her life, said, "Oh God! If I hadn't escaped from the apartment in time, I could have been dead by now. Yes, they would definitely have killed me. Oh yes they would.

"Oh God! I am so frightened—they pushed their way into the apartment while I was opening my door to go out to buy food for my family. They were there waiting to push their way in. They were wearing masks with little holes for the eyes and nose; all of them were armed with guns and knives.

"When they came in, they used the telephone cord to tie both of my little sons and me—my husband was not home; he had already gone to work.

They tied my sons together. My sons were told to sit and watch while they were going to rape me. They really wanted to rape me. They forced me to take off my clothes.

" 'What are you going to do to me? Are you going to kill me?'" I asked.

" 'I just want to take a look at you. Take off your bra!' he said.

"I refused to do what he told me—so he used the knife to cut off my bra. One of the older gang members told the younger one to rape me, but the younger kid, he was too young—he was scared.

"He said, 'I'm not going to do it.'

"Since the younger kid said he was not going to do it, and the older one also decided not to do it, the older kid said:

" 'All right then!'

"Then they touched me a little bit. Then they stopped, and they just left the scene.

I think they were kind of scared after realizing what they had done, so when they left, they dropped one of their masks in the hallway and the police took it with them as evidence. Even though the gang members were covering their faces with masks that had holes for their eyes and nose, I think I still can recognize them.

"I truly believe they are the kids we see every day in the neighborhood. I am so afraid that if I have to go against them, they will definitely come back to kill us. If I leave to go to a state nearby, I know they will still follow me. If I just leave this area and go as far as I can, then they probably won't follow me. If I don't report them, then nothing will happen to me, right?"

She was so agitated and mentally disoriented that she was very much talking to herself. We were video recording them while they were going through this whole crisis. The acts of the gang were so dehumanizing, that in the end she decided to press charges against them. By then it was too late. After realizing that the NYPD didn't have a protection program for the people who pressed charges, I felt that the family was really in great danger. I convinced her to move out of the New York City area as soon as possible before the gang caught up with her. Mrs. X told me that she had a distant relative who lived in another state, so we helped her and her entire family escape safely from New York City.

This was one of the first incidents that tipped the balance in our neighborhood. From this incident I came to realize that there was an internal informer for the ringleader of the rob-and-run gang. Two weeks after that incident, a worse incident occurred. This horrific strike was beyond our endurance. This time it was against one of our Vietnamese friends who lived downstairs in the building next to us.

A couple of gang kids broke into their house and robbed them. The gang took $60,000 in cash, which was hidden under their mattresses—all of the pennies, dimes and quarters that they had made from years of piecework slave labor. As the gang was about to leave the apartment with the cash in hand, the frantic wife tried to break out of the telephone cord and duct tape, and began to scream for help. The gang shot the husband to death right in front of his wife and eight very young children, while they were all tied together with telephone cord and duct tape on their mouths. This incident terrified the whole neighborhood.

A lot of the residential armed robberies, burglaries and homicides that occurred in my Southeast Asian new immigrant neighborhood were the work of those Internal Residential Informer gang members, who decided to act on their own. To conceal their identity from people who were familiar with their faces, who knew their families or knew them personally, they wore homemade masks. Also, if they ever came across any situation where they felt threatened that their identity would be revealed, they shot to kill.

These brutal incidents that occurred in our community were very hard for outsiders or the authorities to comprehend. Being an insider though, I knew that these kids hadn't decided to come to the United States with dreams of becoming criminals; circumstances forced them to the edge and then pushed them over, with the help of Big Brother *Dai Lo*.

Besides the Asian gang-related incidents that terrified all the residents in our neighborhood, we were also having other kinds of disturbing incidents that transformed our residential area into a prison of fear. This was the racial tension that broke out in the neighborhood where we lived and in another nearby neighborhood. Sometime around May of 1990, we encountered the bombardment of this other kind of threat. A racial incident took place in the Korean fruit and vegetable store down the block from where we lived. The Korean store owner was accused of beating up a Haitian woman inside the store. There was a demonstration and protest every day in the neighborhood. Every day when we went to buy fruit and vegetables, the protestors standing on the picket line would scream at us with racial slurs. We didn't have many other choices; this was one of the stores that had fed the whole community for years.

My sister Khaysy was verbally harassed by a group of guys in the demonstration. My younger brother Phoummy was spit in the face by the protestors. Police in full riot gear, angry protestors and demonstrators roamed every day on Church Avenue. Following that incident, there was the Crown Heights riot, which -- up to this very day -- was considered the most serious anti-Semitic incident in American history. Ethnic and racial tension was erupting in different parts of the city. We were so afraid; we never knew when we might be walking on the wrong side of the street or wrong block in the wrong neighborhood and get killed. That was the breaking point for us.

Using everything that my family possessed—manpower, collaboration, love, desire, patience, determination, intelligence, respect and trust among ourselves—triumph and success finally prevailed.

In the winter of 1991 we were able to move out and become Lao-American suburbanites, just as we had dreamt to be while living in Brooklyn. When we first moved out, we got an apartment in Patchogue, Long Island, in New York. A year and a half after moving into the apartment, we found a house that we could afford. We finally had a place of our own. We were ecstatically happy with our new house, which felt like home to all of us. The feelings of comfort, peace and happiness led to a sense of grounding, to a place where we once again could call home after so many years of living as nomads, ever since our journey began in 1977.

One of my fondest moments in our new home was our first Christmas day. It was a very heavy snow day; we had been drinking, dancing and feasting all morning and all afternoon. By evening we were drunk and about ready to burst. We went outside holding onto each other, chain dancing and marching around the house on four feet of snow like soldiers that had just won a battle.

But, we hadn't won the battle; there was no such thing for us in this country. Though we thought the world would stand still and remain perfect like that Christmas day, everything was constantly revolving—and it would continue as long as our planet is fixed in its orbit. Our peace was soon interrupted by the suburban lifestyle. Not much was different. Just like our life in Brooklyn, my little brothers and sisters were verbally harassed by the kids at school, because there were very few Asian students in the class. Many times they got into serious arguments and fights.

Again, the reality of America was awakening us. In this country it almost didn't matter where we went. We had moved from neighborhood to neighborhood and town to town, but violence, gangs, racism and crime were everywhere. It was sad when we came to realize this fact and reality of America. After seven years of hard work and saving every penny we made, here we were, believing that the suburban lifestyle would bring us peace and safety.

Life in the suburbs was even harder to figure out. The problem was, it was harder to know who was your friend or who was your enemy, who wanted you to be in their neighborhood, and who didn't want you there. In the suburbs everything looked and felt innocent. But that could be deceiving.

As for my family, conditions were about to accelerate out of control and into a tailspin. It was more of the same problems that we had experienced back in Brooklyn.

In the meanwhile, it was early in the summer of 1993, two years after my family started living in Patchogue, Long Island. I was still living in Manhattan and commuting to Pratt Institute, but I spent time in Patchogue on my summer break so I could help look after the family. One day, out of the blue, I got a phone call while I was there. I was thinking maybe it was my neighbor, my long lost sister, uncle or some other relative from a long distance. It was totally unexpected that it would be someone we had been waiting for—for all of this time -- until he asked, "Who is this?"

"I am Thavisouk," I replied.

He said, "Do you remember who this is?"

"Who are you? "Please tell me who you are."

And he said, "I am your father. Remember the father who gave you life?"

Because I didn't know it was real, I said, "I thought he died 17 years ago. You must be a ghost from somewhere or your spirit has returned again, either in my dream or in reality."

After that, he asked me about my brothers and sisters: Sethy, Phoummy, Khaysy, Savanhnaly, Bounnhang and Bounnhune. He also asked about my two sisters who had been left behind.

He said, "Where are those two?" Then he added, "I am going to come to visit you."

My whole family was so excited. My mom was kind of sad, yet at the same time very excited and very happy that she would get her husband back again. I was thrilled; it would be the first time in my memory, since being a 10-year-old, that I would have a father. I was now 27 years old, and I really felt that I was going to have a father again.

Before we hung up the phone, he said, "I am coming to America within a month."

After that phone call, the whole family was ecstatic, especially my mother. After all these years of waiting faithfully for him—dead or alive—she always prayed for his safe return. Our happiness was beyond words and beyond description. The emotions and feelings were overwhelming. Everyone was waiting impatiently. We were preparing so we could present our best to our father.

About a month and a half later, he arrived at JFK International Airport. My younger brother and my brother-in-law picked him up and brought him to our Long Island home, where we met him for the first time almost 20 years after his disappearance. It had been way too long for me to not see and know my father. During all those years he had been missing out on everything that happened. I completely believed that he was gone forever. He was just like a ghost that had been resurrected or reincarnated from death.

When he walked into the house I was there with a video camera trying to capture this significant moment in our new chapter of family history. When he walked up the stairs and entered the house, I couldn't just stop the video camera and run to hug him like I used to do when I was a kid. I wasn't quite clear why, but perhaps it had to do with a sub-conscious, animalistic instinct that was kicking in. All of a sudden I felt territorial, as if he were another male bull that had just stepped onto my plateau. Maybe it had to do with my responsibility as a father to this family for 17 years without his presence. I had made my own rules, regulations and goals for the family to achieve while he was missing. Anyway, at the very first moment when we met, regardless of how much I was longing to see him and wanting him to be part of our life again, it felt kind of uncomfortable. So, the video camera was my shield and also my spokesperson during the first day that he arrived. The second day, I was fine with him.

All day and all night we did nothing but cook, eat, drink and get visits from all our Lao friends in the Long Island area. It was a celebration and a delightful moment. After all the years of wondering, doubt, frustration, and longing without hope or any clues, he was finally back in our lives. I asked him a question regarding his disappearance, but before I could ask any other questions, he requested a moment to extend his apology to the whole family for his disappearance from our lives.

"*First and foremost, I would like to take this opportunity to extend my deepest and sincere apologies to the family—I am feeling very happy to see all of you grown up. Being a father, I am very sad that I wasn't here for you, to take care of you as a father should do—I am so sorry that I had to let all of you grow up on your own by the wind and sunlight.*"

A brief moment after that, I gently launched my first question at him. This was the question I had asked myself all of these years.

"So Dad—what exactly happened to you right after they came to take you away on that afternoon?"

"*Right after I walked out with the group of those PL soldiers and sat in the back of that Jeep on my way to the POW camp, I was sure that I would be punished or executed, because I knew how cruel the Communist rule was. I didn't know that heaven would spare my life. I was sure that I would be dead,*" he replied.

Then I went on to ask him point blank about how his life had been spared.

"Why didn't they kill you, Dad?"

"*It wasn't my time yet. Early in the morning, three days after I got to the re-education camp at Boong Boa in the eastern part of Khammouane Province near the Vietnamese border, three little PL soldiers ,each about 15 or 16 years old, came to the cell where my wrists were tied with rope and had been commanded to sleep on one piece of flat hard wood. Both of my ankles were in chains.*

"*When they walked into my holding cell, they un-leashed the chains on both of my ankles and used the rope to tie both of my arms backward. Then they took me out to the river's edge where they had already lined up seven other prisoners. There was another group of PL soldiers there too. As soon as I got there, the soldier screamed out his order to me.*

'*Down on your knees next to the other prisoners now!*'

"*As I was trying to kneel down on my knees, I wasn't kneeling fast enough, so one of the little soldiers pushed both of my shoulders down and kicked the back of my knees so I would collapse onto my knees faster. As soon as I was completely down, they tied this black cloth on my face to blind me from seeing what they were about to do. I knew I was about to die, so I had no fear of the most certain thing in life. Death is number one on the list; I was expecting it—to be a soldier and willing to die for my country -- I knew a true sacrifice time had arrived.*

"*I knew in death I couldn't take anything with me. All I needed to take as a*

156

warrior were the last breaths of peace and dignity. In that very moment, all I was thinking about was my beautiful wife and my ten beautiful children, who were about to become orphans and left to struggle alone in a world that was covered with blood stains and scars from war and conflict. As I was meditating and praying for my peaceful death—I could hear the sounds of a hard wooden stick smashing the heads of the other prisoners. Every blow sounded just like the smashing of a watermelon against a solid cement floor. Within a few short moments after each smashing sound, I could hear the suddenly dead body plunge into the river like a rock. One by one I counted the executions in progress. When the seventh prisoner was about to be executed, I decided to speak out:

"Please, we are all Lao, and we are willing to die for this motherland at any cost, that includes you and me. We are willing to sacrifice our lives and blood for this land. I am your prisoner, but I am a warrior; if you are going to execute me, please do not cover my face so I won't die as a prisoner of war, but will die as a warrior for this beloved motherland."

"As I pleaded with them for my death wish, prisoner number seven's head was being smashed.

"All of a sudden I heard this shaky little voice from one of the soldiers:

"'I am tired already today—seven in a day is equivalent to one per day for the whole week; may I take care of him some other time?' the little soldier asked his superior."

"After about a minute of delay, as I was waiting for my last moment, I could hear the soldiers mumbling to one another as they made their decision.

"Soon, one of the soldiers came toward me, and pulling me up by my shirt collar, brought me back to the holding cell, hands tied and both legs chained. Then, finally, they took off the black cloth that was covering my face. When I thought about it, I realized that I could have been the first person to be executed depending on where the executioner chose his starting point, the head of the line or the tail of the line."

After hearing that brief description a cold chill ran down my spine. Talk about a near death experience.

He went on:

"A few days after that close call, I was taken into their headquarters for further interrogation. They asked me for my true name, the one I used when I was a school teacher. I told them my birth name was Ti, not Santy, as I used in the military."

"I personally think by revealing my birth name saved my life because in the period of political chaos and confusion when the civil war broke out, most of my friends, relatives and formal students were choosing sides—either with Vientiane government or joining Lao Issara.

157

Many of my formal students join the Lao Issara; some of them still remembered my past good deeds and didn't dare to betray the man who was once their beloved teacher.

"*Within a period of one year and a half of my living hell in re-education camp, I laid low and conducted myself according to their rule to establish some degree of trust. By laying low and obeying accordingly, expected someday soon they would lay low on me as response to my good behavior. When I earned that trust then I would use that as my window of opportunity to escape from hell.*"

"*I did just that as part of my escape plan. So I did. When I escaped from the re-education camp (prisoner of war camp) I escaped with six other friends. We had to walk all the way from the border of Vietnam to the Mekong River. It took me 21 days and nights, walking through mountains and jungles, eating wild vegetation as food supplemenst. By the time I got to the Thailand border there were only two left- me and my other friend; the other five didn't make it. Some decided to surrender, some went into the villages and were begging for food. I swam across the Mekong River to Thailand in 1976 and stay put there for various other reasons.*"

"*The whole civil war was a messed up war, especially for ordinary people, farmers and civilian workers. We had almost nothing to do with the war. It was just a war between the royal family and the world superpowers. We, as a people, were caught between two hard rocks.*"

"*Although by principle I was sacrificing my life and blood to fight and die for my country, the internal conflict that I had was we Lao were killing Lao. We more or less just waged war against each other just because our government was having a serious internecine struggle and was so fragmented. Many of us soldiers didn't necessarily have an understanding of what we were fighting and willing to die for. I felt like I was nothing but a fighting puppet, the human war-tool, and the fuel that fed the purpose of civil conflict between different political factions.*"

"*After I was tied down on that piece of wood with both of my feet in chains, I forced myself to think about what I had done during the war to deserve such punishment. To me it was such a contradiction on both sides: the left wing and the right wing governments. We both wanted to free our people from being oppressed by the rules and authority of the foreign invaders and oppressive systems, but we ended up bringing in outsiders to kill and bomb the hell out of our own country and each other. The left wing brought in the Russians, Chinese and Vietnamese, while we on the other side collaborated with the United States and their western allies.*

"*Everyone who stepped foot into this war was not there for the purpose of the greater good of our people and our land. They were there for their own personal self-interest and to use Lao territory for their political agenda. On top of that, they created more conflict and separation within our Lao military."*

He made it very clear to me the United States' secret air in Laos involved all Lao ethnicity

"The US media bias toward the war in Laos portrayed the war as if only one ethnic minority group was involved, the reality is the war involved all ethnicities of Lao.

"The Lao world composed of three main ethnic groups—Low-land Lao (Lao Loum), Mid-land Lao (Lao Theung) and High-land Lao (Lao Soung). These three main groups were made of 68 different ethnicities and 42 speaking dialects. Low-land Lao is the majority of the country.

"For hundreds of years our motherland had nurtured all the various ethnicities with peace and harmony. We coexisted as cousins, as brothers and sisters, and as family until a foreign political power come into our land with their political agenda and interest, interfering and disrupting our peace and unity."

He went on and tried to explain the US involvement in Lao during the Vietnam War period.

"According to the Geneva accord in 1962, Laos was a neutral country. With the assistance of the Communist Pathet Lao, the North Vietnamese went into Laos and used Laos territory as their military supply bypass route to fight their war against the Republic of South Vietnam and American troops. This bypass military supply route was known as Ho Chi Minh Trail—it ran through most of the middle and southern parts, and the rest of the country. The Ho Chi Minh Trail was widespread like a spider web with thousands of footpaths, unpaved roads and submerged bridges, etc. The North Vietnamese were constantly denying their violations of the Geneva Accord of 1962 and the United States decided to intervene. Laos was a neutral country, and the United States couldn't have ground troops there, so they intervened secretly by air. That was the beginning of the US air war and Laos was drawn into the Vietnam War."

"The US went secretly into Laos as a good-will supporter. However there are many questionable issues as to the real U.S. intention. The U.S. excuse was—'Oh! We don't have our military troops here in Laos; we were just a good- will volunteer to help out the good people who believe in freedom and democracy like we do. We were here to help them and to advise them.' But, of course, day and night they were the lords who controlled our sky. Their eagles were wandering the sky and keeping their eyes and ears on everything that moved along the Ho Chi Minh Trail and jungles."

"The US entered Laos no different than any previous power that came into our land. They paved their own way that served their interest by creating and setting up

different agencies making it seem that they supported our interest, when in reality they were serving their own geo-political interest. When in Laos the US set up USAID and SGU, which they funded including the Royal Lao Military. They were the boss of the boss—they did whatever they pleased. All of these separate units or special separate operations created a lot of weakness and confusion within the Royal Lao Army. For more proficiency for their special operations, the US also brought in Air America and the Raven Air Forward Controllers.

"*My service to the US secret air war was that I was one of the commanders who served in a special unit in the southern part of Laos, which essentially was the heart and soul of the US secret air war inside Laos. Our unit was the special unit that sometimes was dropped off behind the enemy line to secretly spy on the enemy along the Ho Chi Minh Trail. We also served as the trail's hunters that rousted out the NVA (North Vietnamese Army) and PL (Pathet Lao). We were the ones who were out there engaging and interdicting the enemy activities or movements, and providing the bombing targets for the forward air controllers. I knew what was going on.*"

From my father's point of view it helped me to make some sense of what had happened to my country during the war. Then he went on with more detail on his most painful, heart-wrenching story about his life in the re-education camp. I asked him to make it brief, so this is his concise personal statement:

"*During the war I called upon the Americans to bomb the Communist strongholds with the hope of saving our land from being invaded by the North Vietnamese and in the good will of saving American lives and blood in South Vietnam as much as we possibly could.*

After the US withdrew their troops from South Vietnam, the Vietnam War ended. Laos was left to defend itself against the Communist Pathet Lao and North Vietnam. It soon collapsed after financial aids and military support was withdrawn. On December 2, 1975 Laos was taken over by communist Pathet Lao and I was abandoned to survive in the palm of the enemy's hand.

"*I was imprisoned and badly punished by being forced to use a small bamboo basket that was just a little bit bigger than the palm of my hand to fill the B-52 bombing craters. The total amount of bombs dropped exceeded the total amount of bombs dropped in World War I and II together. I would say it would take more than 100 years for all of us prisoners to fill up all of those bomb craters. For 14 to 16 hours every day at gunpoint I was a slave worker; we were fed twice a day with non-nutritious food. The rice was full of small rocks and termite shit.*

"*After all of these years my contribution to this country has not been properly hon-*

ored. I am old and there is not much left for me to wish for except dignity as one who served, either directly or indirectly. But what kind of proof do I have to help me to preserve the dignity of my wish? The US will never really recognize our sacrifice and service. Even if they wanted to recognize it, most of us have no credentials, documentation or government-issue paperwork to tie us to US service.

In the chaotic aftermath of the U. S. withdrawal of the troops from South Vietnam and the communist Pathet Lao takeover, it was impossible for me to maintain those documents. Regardless of whatever I have been through and I have done, one thing that I will always be proud of is whatever I did was in the name of peace, freedom and democracy."

"Again all of what I told you is strictly my personal point of view and my brief summation of what I think I know about my own history in 30 years of civil conflicts and eight years of U.S. involvement. There are so many other details I couldn't possibly give you. This is not supposed to substantiate to other people my point of view; other people might have their own opinions, different points of view or different understanding, and many might disagree with me. I just answered your question out of the best of my knowledge as a father to his son. I hope that my answer will help you to make your own conclusion and understand. "

Now, when I look back on that period of history, it still brings me sadness. The covert war in Laos is still considered a classified war. Up to this very day Laos still holds the world record as the most bombed country in the world.

Because all of these Lao men and their families served the United States of America, Laotians of many ethnicities and tribes are here in the USA. That is why I am personally taking the time to do what I am doing. Through art, poetry and cinema I try to create awareness regarding this issue with hope that my work, someday, somehow, will be some contribution in helping those who rendered their service to this great nation, the USA, to be properly honor.

During the first few days after my father returned, I learned so much about my history from the true, honest point of view of a man who had been a participant in that history. His return was all well and good, and so much fun that we were laughing almost all day and night. During one of our dinners I asked my parents to sit down and eat together, so all of us children could watch what they were doing and how they were doing it.

We could see our own reflection through them, so we knew for sure in our hearts that these were the two who brought us into this world. I video recorded all of these events. Besides having fun, just watching mom and dad together was a phenomenal experience for all of us. After all those years that he had disappeared from our lives - most of my younger brothers and sisters didn't even remember what he looked like- yet here he was in person, seated and eating in our living room. My father was a great, loving and very kind man. At the dinner table on the second day of his return he said to us:

"Well! I have to say, as a father I couldn't do my very best to try to take care of you because of my life situation. Disregarding my abandonment by the US government, one hope that I had, while I was out of your life, was that the US government would at least recognize and help the family of a man who served them during the war. I am very disappointed that they didn't."

As he said that, he seemed so sad and hopeless, but we reassured him that we were all okay. We had managed to take care of ourselves. He had nothing to worry about. For us, the past was past, but for him it was nothing but heartbreak and disappointment regarding the entire war era.

One morning, a week after his return, all of us were eating breakfast together, when he painfully delivered the news that was beyond hard to describe. He said,

"I have to go back to St. Petersburg, Florida to be with my new wife and my two children. I have a new family."

That statement alone broke my mother's heart and every one of our hearts.

My mother exploded just like Napalm.

"I am your wife for 29 years.

I was married to you when I was 16 years old.

I was still a child when I married you.

You were my first lover.

You were my beloved husband.

You were my everything in life.

I gave you my life and my virginity.

You promised to take care of me till the end of my life.

After we had ten children together, now you've got the nerve to change your heart and get married to another woman!

How dare you?

How dare you not think about the past that we had together?"

Her broken heart went on. We were all very hurt, traumatized and paralyzed by the pain. I had waited for him for 17 years. I couldn't believe that he was going to leave again. I thought to myself, this is not my wife, and these are not my children. Now I have to carry the baggage of his responsibilities. I became the caretaker when I was 16 years old. When we got to the United States, I became the father figure to all of his children alongside my mother. I helped my mother raise six young children in the harshest situations and most hostile conditions in this strange country, a society that lives by the "dog eat dog" principle. I was very hurt to hear that he urgently, once again, had to leave.

After he left for his new family, there were a lot of bad reactions and trauma that went on in my family. My mother suffered from mental and physical pain. A few months after he left my mother had to have open heart surgery because one of the valves in her heart was leaking. My mother's physical condition reminded me of what my grandfather used to joke about when I was a kid. Quite often he would say to me,

"Watch out for that dimpled smile on that princess's face. That can break your heart and kill you. That's as dangerous as opium addiction."

I used to laugh at my grandfather, and think to myself a broken heart is the word to use for getting a girl's attention. After I saw what happened to my mother, I knew true love does indeed hurt, and it can break a human heart.

I was paralyzed by the whole ordeal. As for the rest of my younger brothers and sisters, they were traumatized by the confusion and disbelief over what had just happened to them. Their reaction was extreme. Two of my brothers and two of my sisters ran away from home as if they had wings and tails. That was the way they relieved their own pain, sorrow and disappointment. It was a devastating moment in my family, especially for me. I had been hoping that I could go on and live my own life and be free from all the household responsibilities. On the contrary, that hope and dream was shattered for me. I had to carry on without any other options.

I was still caught up with three major commitments. I had to carry on with my responsibility toward the family household, finish engineering school, and, of course, the long-term film project needed to move forward. Since there was so much pain and many obstacles in my family, I decided to spend a little more time apart from them so I could focus on my writing and work with Ellen on research for more material, photos and film archives to use for the film. There were also so many other things that I needed to learn and teach myself as soon as possible so I could do more and give more to the project. It was such a very complicated film to do for many reasons and in many aspects.

Filmmaking for me was my destiny. As the first Lao-American generation of my family who had come to this country with bare hands and empty pockets, to be an artist was at first like a dream. Being the first generation is all about being a survivor and establishing the roots and foundations for the next generation. America is the heart and soul of the capitalist ideology. To make it here, all I had to think about was how to make a living. Money, job, and a safe place to live were everything. All I could think about with every subject that I studied in school was what kind of major could I graduate with that would get me a good job offer and guarantee my future financial security? This was the only thing that would help us raise our social and economic status in this country. That's all I could think and dream about; should I be an accountant, an engineer or go into business? These sounded more or less manageable to me. But, as far as thinking about making a living as an artist, it was too inconceivable for me at the time.

I thought that as far as I could be associated with art, it could only be considered a hobby, something that I would do for my own self-interest. This, despite the fact that when I was in high school I had been an award-winning student artist. I had won first prize in a Martin Luther King Jr. national holiday art contest sponsored by the Student Art League of New York. I received a Medal of Honor from The Metropolitan Museum of Art in New York City. I had also received first prize from the American Can Company art contest and various other art contests.

At the time, several collectors were already collecting some of my artwork. Besides painting, illustrating and drawing, as well as having a serious love affair with Lao history, world history and community advocacy, I also had a great passion for poetry. I wrote many poems, and some appeared in publications such as *PASSAGE Magazine*. They were the first ones who published one of my three-page poems: *The Dancing Pond*. It was a poem about my childhood memories of my favorite pond in my old neighborhood in the city of Thakhek, Laos.

Again, I still considered my art to be only a pleasurable hobby, and my poetry was just self-therapy, a healing aid that helped me cope with my war trauma and life adjustment. I took it very seriously, but never really thought that I would make a career out of it. I was even accepted to a pre-college program at Cooper Union, one of the best art schools in the country. Again and again, however, my American first-generation instinct was kicking around in the back of my sub-conscious. It possessed me. Every day it told me that I had to keep focused on a future career that would guarantee financial security. I definitely couldn't deny the fact that our living conditions were considered below the poverty line, so I had to do what I had to do with one main focus in mind—pursue a career that would pay.

That was how I ended up in engineering school at Pratt Institute. I'll never forget the first day that I met with the career counselor at Pratt Institute, Mr. John Silk. I was sitting right in front of him in his office, and he said:

"Son! You better make up your mind what you want to study—we have four types of engineering majors for you to choose from: civil, mechanical, electrical and cemical. Which one of these do you think might be suitable for you?"

I couldn't answer him immediately. He was a little frustrated with me, and then he asked,

"Do you smoke?"

"Yes, sir, I do," I replied.

He handed me a Marlboro Light cigarette and he said,

"Here, go have a smoke; clear your mind, then come back and tell me what you want to study."

As I was taking a deep drag of that cigarette, I had one thought in my mind: the knowledge and the principles of chemistry were keys to the principles of the universe. From what I knew, chemical engineering was often called the "universal engineer." Rushing back to Mr. Silver's office without finishing that cigarette I excitedly told him, "Sir, I am going to be a chemical engineering major—I think that is the most appropriate for me and my future."

He gave me a grin and a handshake as he said,

"That wasn't too hard. I think that cigarette worked, huh!"

So, my first major was chemical engineering. Then, a year later, I changed to electrical engineering due to the boom of the electronic age, satellites, fiber optics, the dawn of the microchip, data and Internet communications, and VLSI (Very Large Scale Integrated Circuits)- the very edge of 21st century technological progress. A diploma in electrical engineering seemed to be a better guarantee for my future. I proceeded down that path with great hopes and expectations.

For some odd reason, however, my life kept intertwining and crossing paths with visual arts (filmmaking). This had started much earlier in a very passive way. It was one of those step-by-step, one thing led to another situations that continued over a long period of time and developed into something else. In my case, the things that happened in my life, the paths I had crossed and all of my hobbies and passions were meant to be part of the making of *The Betrayal (Nerakhoon)*.

I was in high school when I met the American woman who wanted to learn how to speak Lao. That was when my journey toward a filmmaking career began. The making of *The Betrayal (Nerakhoon)* was a very long, complicated process.

I was involved with all aspects of the making of the film, because I was a subject as well as the filmmaker. I was behind the pen and paper, the camera, the Steinbeck machine; then later the Final Cut Pro, Avid Media Composure and Avid Express. From being one of the creators to writing, narrating, editing and being on the directing team, I was involved with all aspects of the making of the movie. Mentally, it was very difficult for me. Every time I sat in front of the editing machine I had to treat the man on the screen (me) as just another character. I had to exercise honor, and be very subjective toward that character and how he would improve the progression of the story that we needed to tell. Again, that was very hard to do mentally, because sub-consciously I was still dealing with my own self-consciousness and was my worst critic.

This film had so much to do with my own life and my entire family's story, as well as the Lao history during the Vietnam War era. It was about how Laos played such a crucial role in the Vietnam War. It was also how the Lao civil war and Vietnam War had such a crucial effect in my life and my family. Of cause at that time any political issue regarding the US involvement in Laos or Laotian issues was considered politically sensitive or controversial. Due to this politically sensitive matter, the secret war in Laos is still considered a classified war even after several decades have passed.

We filmmakers had to find the right resources and accurate materials to accompany our storytelling; this was almost impossible in the early days after the war. We found a number of very interesting, archival footages at the US National Archive, but most of the material was not particularly related to the subject matter of the film or the story that we wanted to tell. That also caused a delay.

Another very crucial element was that the climax of the drama itself needed time to progress and to be captured. To observe how the war affected our lives, the progression of that effect didn't come full circle in a short period of time or when we wanted it to. That's why we were on standby for years, waiting for things to happen. We, as the filmmakers, just hoped and prayed to the man upstairs that he would let us be at the right place, at the right moment, and with the right attitude. We were witnessing history and life as it was occurring right in front of our eyes. We hoped that we would be blessed enough to capture it on film or video or whatever format was available at that moment. Afavorite saying in documentary filmmaking is, " In documentary filmmaking, God is the director. Only in dramatic filmmaking the director is God."

Documentary filmmaking is a true test of self-endurance and self-sharing. It is about sharing our own self-indulgence, passion, faith, deep personal points of view about our own internal world, the voices that we've heard in our heads, what we feel in our hearts and the images that we perceive in our mind's eye. We shared the hope and expectation that we could communicate these thoughts with our fellow humans.

As far as waiting for things to happen in my family, there was non-stop action. It was always one thing after another. Half of my family fell apart right after my father left, and my mother was heartbroken over her loss. Now we had to deal with her emotional and physical illness. Besides her open-heart surgery from her heart breaking over dad's leaving for another wife, she also suffered from diabetic and gastric conditions. Her physical and emotional pain indeed took a toll on our family.

For me, it was hard being a full-time engineering student, working part time and carrying the heavy load of family crises. My remaining brothers and sisters were still acting up, out of rebellion against the old country's cultural and traditional rules, which we tried to impose on them. The functionality of my family was still disrupted due to the resistance of my younger brothers and sisters.

Almost every day my mom had to deal with a teenager in the middle of their coming of age. Most of them carried the heavy baggage of an identity crisis, confusion, anger and the trauma of war. Crises were coming at full scale, practically all at once. It was almost beyond my abilities to manage.

One day I decided to call my father for help. I still remember word for word how I pleaded with him. Immediately after I dialed the number the phone was ringing and a lady picked it up. I asked her if I could speak to my father, and she told me to hold on for a minute.

Dad answered the phone, "Who is it?"

"Me! Thavisouk. How are you doing?" I asked.

Dad: "I am fine; what is happening?"

"I just want to let you know that I had a crisis with the kids. They ran away from home after you left. They were all very upset, and they rebelled. They were out of control. I can't handle this on my own. They're not listening to me, because I am not their father."

Dad: "Which one?"

"All of them. I need you to come to New York. So when can you come? I will send you a plane ticket."

Dad: "I'm working right now. I don't think I can come."

"Dad, I really need your help. You are the father who created all of these children.

They are your responsibility, not mine. Your wife and children need you.

"You should not feel ashamed for not winning the war. But regardless of winning or losing—your wife and children never thought it was your fault. You will always be our hero. Whatever happened is in the past. It is past – just so you know. We just want our father back. You must know that we really need you, Dad."

Dad: "I am working. I don't think I can come."

"Dad, can you just come even for just a week during the Christmas holiday? I will send you an airplane ticket!"

Dad: "Is there anything else that you want to say?"

I was choking with emotion after hearing his question, so I paused for a moment, and as I was pausing he went on to suggest to me:

Dad: "Well then, if you have nothing else to say, then I am going to have to say goodbye to you now. Good-bye."

Then he just hung up on me.

I was in complete shock. From that rejection, I once again felt hurt and very disappointed in him. Even though I fully understood his new family situation, at least he should have given me a little hope, but he didn't. He was just ignoring my crisis. I was so frustrated, and I needed to tell Mom that Dad would probably never return to our lives again in this lifetime. I knew deep in my mother's heart, despite the severe pain and torture she was going through, that she still loved him unconditionally. I felt it was my responsibility to let her know that Dad had refused my request to help the family. I tried to deal with our pain in a mature way. One morning I was sitting with her at the kitchen table, and I told her,

"Mom!

I talked to Dad on the phone.

He said he's not coming.

He has a wife and two children.

We should let him go.

We should go on with our own lives and take care of each other.

I can only get angry; there is nothing more I can do.

Just let him go, Mom.

In the future, I don't know what will happen, but I will do my best to raise the family until they're grown up."

Mom just sat there absorbing it all. She was dazed in her own world. We both came to the final realization that he had decided he didn't want to be part of our life, and we could not count on him ever again.

Our life went on as usual. As for my involvement with the film project, by this time we had accumulated many hours of good footage. In the meantime, crises continued to occur in my life. In most cases whenever a family crisis occurred or there was any internal family issue, I had to coordinate with the filmmaking crew to make sure all of the drama that went on in my head, in my heart and in the family, was captured on film. This was not an easy task, but it was the kind of thing we did regularly. For almost every happy moment, sad moment, moment of conflict or moment of crisis, the camera was there. Since the film project didn't have any specific timeline or any extreme urgency to finish, the film had a life of its own. It became our child—that was why we had no other option but to continue to raise and take care of it with great love, great care and more passion as the years went by.

Despite all the obstacles—family crises and financial hardships -- I finally overcame them. In the summer of 1992 I graduated with a degree in electrical engineering. Because I had graduated during an economic crisis in America, I was unable to find a job in that field right away. So, I took the opportunity to continue working on the film project, with the hope that we could take the film to the next level toward our ultimate goal. This was when I really got serious and started spending more time teaching myself how to edit the film in the Steinbeck machine.

This was also a period of transition in the filmmaking—the transformation from linear to non-linear editing (non-linear editing was the computer-based digital video editing).

It was the most amazing time in the history of the filmmaking world, especially for someone like me who had just finished electrical engineering school. At the time, we were so serious about finishing the film that we even tried to give ourselves a deadline.

But something always happened, something related to either my life or my family situation that would spin out of control. As for me, I was holding two jumping fishes with two bare hands—on one hand I was working very hard with the team finishing up the film, but on the other hand I was chasing engineering jobs. By early 1993 I finally landed my first entry level engineering job with ID&TE out in Fort Jefferson, Long Island. I moved out of New York City to live with my mother, which was much closer to my job. Even though I was living out on Long Island at the time, every Friday after work I would commute back to New York City and work on the film project on Friday nights and weekends.

We did as much as we possibly could, so we could crawl toward the finish line. We continued doing this regularly for about two years. In the meantime I was working at my electrical engineering job. At first I was very pleased and really fascinated with what the engineering world was up to. As fascinating and as innovative as it was though, it wasn't very long before I became so discouraged by the corporate environment. My attitude toward my engineering career immediately began to deteriorate. I felt like I was becoming a robot. At the end of every day I felt as though I was doing nothing but following the orders and doing more or less the same thing over and over again. I began to feel like I was beginning to drift away from my true purpose in life.

I felt strongly that I needed to change careers, and pursue something that would satisfy my spiritual desires and bring me happiness. My inner voice told me that I must get back to filmmaking. This calling was getting louder and louder; the more I tried to resist it, the stronger it became. By this time I had a great desire to know more about my history and myself, and I was very eager to preserve the best part of my culture and tradition. This was beyond urgency; it became my obsession. It seemed that the calling of my destiny left me with no other option but to immediately accept and act upon this mission. This time, though, it had to be more prominent and more definite.

In April 1994, as I was having a very difficult time making the decision about what to do about my engineering career, I was laid off from ID&TE. Immediately after I was laid off, I was so desperate to get back to my love of filmmaking that I realized the engineering career was not something I wanted to pursue for the rest of my life. Carrying on with my filmmaking career was most suitable for me, but to reassure and back up my decision, I laid out all my abilities, skills, talents, passions and love of film. As I laid it all out I came to see clearly what I was really made of.

I said to myself: I have very strong technical and engineering knowledge. I love painting and illustration. I feel alive every time I play my guitar and sing; music had always been in my heart. Every time I volunteer to do anything for my community I feel as if I have accomplished something. I also have a strong interest in social work. I love talking and giving advice to people, young and old, men and women. I love to share honesty about my feelings as well as knowledge and wisdom about life and living. I have a great passion for Lao history, literature, poetry and politics. I came to realize that all of these were what I needed as basic principles and requirements for a filmmaking career. That's when I came to my senses, and knew for sure, exactly what I wanted to do for the rest of my life. I wanted to utilize all of my interests, passions and my love of filmmaking.

To move forward and take the film project to a much higher level, we definitely needed to go back to Laos, but for the longest time its doors were closed to the world. But now, again by coincidence, Laos was beginning to open its doors to tourism. With the help of some out-of-state friends I got a connection with a tour company that operated out of Elgin, Illinois and Las Vegas, Nevada. Through their touring company anyone could obtain a visa for touring Laos. This was the greatest news for me because my family had been blacklisted during the Lao revolution and I had lost contact with them all these years. We had not been able to communicate for the longest time. Every time we attempted to contact them by writing letters, they were inspected, opened and never delivered.

I was happy to know that there was a possibility that I could return to Laos to search for my two, long lost sisters whom my mother had left behind, and, of course, to embrace my beloved grandmother whom I missed terribly since the day that I stepped out of the womb of that motherland.

8

Personal Resolution

It was June 18, 1994, I was able to return to Laos with my two American friends, 16-mm film camera a video camera, and Sony TCD 5M cassette tape recorder as our low-key sound recording system. Of course, none of this equipment was legally allowed, but as filmmakers we planned to do whatever we had to do to capture the crucial moments. We also planned to search for all the images that we had been talking about for years back in the States—the images that would help the film reconstruct all of my childhood memories. By luck, one of the guides who was working for the tour company that we were with, was a Lao filmmaker who had graduated in Russia. As soon as we walked out of the plane our tour guide was right there to assist us, from carrying our luggage, filling out a customs form and going through the Lao customs system. As soon as we tried to explain to him what we had in our black bag he laughed, because he knew exactly what we had -- at least 35 rolls of film and a 16-mm film camera that we had disassembled, separated and put each piece into a different bag. He told us,

"Don't worry I will be taking care of this for you—all you have to do is just give me your passport, and I will get these through customs for you."

Because of him, we were able to just walk into Vientiane as if we were regular Lao citizens. After we went through customs smoothly, the tour guide told us that he was a member of the advisory board of the Lao National Archives. There, they were trying to preserve an archive of a couple thousand rolls of their old propaganda films that had been made by the Russian and Vietnamese for the PL government during the Lao civil and

Vietnam War era.

They also found two thousand rolls of film in the basement of the former Lao king's palace. These consisted of documentary film and some unedited, raw footage that had been made by the Royal Lao Army News and Media department, as well as some USAID film and uncut footage. So, in the first few days while we were in Vientiane, we spent all of our time at the Lao National Archives searching for some archival footage for our film project, and also looking to find a way to get to the city of Thakhek, so I could start searching for my sisters and visit the rest of my family. I wanted to visit my grandmother, all my great aunts, great uncles, aunts and uncles and all of the cousins I had never met.

At the Lao National Archives we found some good war footage in 16-mm. To be able to get all of the footage that we liked, the projectionist projected the footage onto the wall, and we shot it off the wall with our 16-mm film camera. After we got some decent archival footage it was time for us to get to my hometown, Thakhek. Finally, we found a car rental company that was run by the Australians; they also provided a personal driver for an additional cost.

Five days after we were hustling to get what we needed in Vientiane, we were in an old Land Rover, crawling over unpaved roads heading toward my hometown. We were struggling through the mud and zigzagging our way like crawling snakes with the speed of a snail to avoid the mud ponds, potholes and floods in the middle of road. In some parts we had to get out of the Land Rover and walk around the mud ponds and floods so the driver could maneuver the empty car without too much weight, otherwise it would have sunk into the mud pond. After twelve exhausting hours we finally arrived at Thakhek at dark.

The first night in my hometown I stayed in a hotel along with the crew. For the whole night I couldn't fall asleep. My mind was wandering with a thousand wonders and a million thoughts. I had been longing for this day for 17 years. I was finally here, and I had no words to describe my feelings—I was possessed by emotion. The next morning we were all geared up, the film cameras were reassembled and the magazines were loaded. The Sony TCD 5M batteries were renewed, new cassette tape were loaded. We were ready. I was emotionally prepared for my long day. We drove down the town's main road, passing downtown, toward my old neighborhood on the other side of town.

As the car stopped in front of my old house, a man walked up to me. I told him that I'm from America and I'm looking for my sister, Chayphet. He turned out to be my brother-in-law, whom I had never met. He said,

"Your sister is selling meat at the morning market; I will take you there right now. If you don't mind, please give me a few minutes to change my clothes."

I walked around the courtyard of my old house while I waited for my brother-in-law. There were so many childhood recollections that occurred; every footstep as I proceeded in that yard equaled a thousand of my happiest childhood memories. The very essence of that place was the soul of my existence. I am now a man who, as an innocent child, once ran around this courtyard, carefree from the troubled world. As I was caught up in my childhood memories, my thoughts were interrupted by one of my friends calling,

"Thavi! Thavi! Let's get going. Your brother-in-law is ready."

I hopped into the cramped Land Rover along with everyone else. There was a driver, two American friends, my brother-in-law, my niece, my nephew and me. Excitedly, we arrived at the morning market where the townspeople were buying, selling and hustling for their daily living. As soon as my sister spotted her husband and children with two Caucasian, she immediately knew that I was there to see her. She dropped everything and ran toward the car to greet me. She threw her arms around me and didn't let me go for a good half hour while we both were sobbing. Everyone in the market was sobbing along with us. At that moment there was no exchanging of words between us - only tears. The morning after we met I told my sister to take a day off from her work, so we went back to our old house, and she told me about my youngest sister—in her own words,

"Right after Mom and the rest of family were gone, on that day I was sad and felt so alone with a little two-and-a-half-year-old sister. At the time, the labor union rules and regulations were very strict. The authorities had control over every aspect of our lives: how we should live, how we should eat. The federal and local authorities organized our life for us. I was young; I had nothing except to work for the labor union to earn my food benefits.

"Keodouangchay was so small, and she needed someone to take care of her while I was assigned to work in the farms or wherever they assigned me. So the local authorities arranged for her to be with other Lao families that we had known in the past. That family moved up to live in Borpontiew (the old, small, former French mining town founded by the French during colonization). For the past six or seven years I haven't had a chance to see her, but we all can drive up there to find her."

So, we planned to drive out the next morning to Borpontiew to find my youngest sister. To get to Borpontiew it was a hell of a rollercoaster ride. After about three hours of again crawling through the muddy roads, floods, potholes, and mountain slopes, we arrived in the middle of nowhere. We found her in this tiny, little bitty town with a population of about a few thousand people. Again, it was another heartbreak for me to see my little sister living with and being raised by a family not related to us as if she were their own child. This tore me into a thousand pieces. I wished that I could just take her back to America with me, but life and politics in that tiny corner of the world are more complicated than they seem. I was standing there and staring at her with a flood of tears in my eyes, feeling so helpless.

After a few hours I asked the surrogate family if I could invite my little sister to spend time with me in Thakhek, while I went to visit the rest of the family including my grandmother, who I desperately needed to see, as well as tons of other relatives, and some young cousins whom I had never met. She was permitted by her surrogate family to tour along with me. We drove back to the city, and we spent the evening together at our old house, three of us finally together. We were reconnecting and tapping into each other's lives. It was a very emotional and heart-wrenching evening for me.

The next morning, after we had an intimate breakfast together, we geared ourselves up for another emotional rollercoaster event, visiting my ultimate favorite grandma. Only ten kilometers away from the city, we got to her village in no time. My grandmother and the rest of my relatives, along with the villagers, had no clue that their village was about to be bombarded by emotion, and entertained by a person from a different star.

That's what the Laotian word for foreigners is (especially white or caucasian) -- *Khon Tangdao*—exact translation: people of a different star. There I was, in the old, muddy Land Rover parking right in front of her hut. As the second of the cars came to a full stop I jumped out of the car; I couldn't waste a second that I planned to spend with her. As soon as she spotted me from the corner of her eye, I could tell from her reaction that she was in a very surreal state of mind. I knew that she couldn't believe what had just appeared in front of her eyes. I rushed to climb up the ladder of her house, and she just stood there, waiting for me to throw my arms around her. I squeezed her tightly in my arms and held her very close to my heart. I didn't let her go for a very good, long moment.

Here she was; I was holding her, embracing her, admiring her, feeling her strength and spiritual energy. Here she was, my super hero who gave me roots, who gave me my heritage, who gave me the essence of who I am. She was my past, but right at that moment she became my present. I felt as if I was in a time machine visiting my past. It was a moment of soul jubilation for me.

For almost an entire hour after my arrival my grandmother was still sobbing in my arms like a little child. On that day all of my relatives were constantly stopping by. I mean *all of them*—they had just stopped doing whatever they were doing. Some came to say hello, some just came to stare at me, and some came with many questions and much curiosity about life beyond the borders and barricades of their police state. My great uncle, my grandmother's oldest brother, who was 98-years-old at the time, came on his little, old scooter. I couldn't believe my eyes when I saw him pulling in; it was like watching a dinosaur riding a scooter. As soon as he came in he stared at me, and the first thing he said was, "I remember your teeth." He cracked me up real hard, right on the spot.

He was still the same old man I had always greatly respected. He was a former principal of my elementary school, and one of the craziest things was that he still remembered how to speak French. That was one of the oddest and most surreal moments for me, hearing the French words that came out of this old dinosaur. Anyway, all of my relatives (more or less half of that village) gathered together for a wonderful cookout. This was the greatest celebration of my homecoming; everyone was overjoyed.

It was very unfortunate, however, that I didn't have time to stay through the night and celebrate with the rest of my relatives. I had to get back to the hotel in the city as a safety precaution. Very early the next morning, however, my oldest and youngest sisters and I went back out to see my grandmother and the rest of my family. This was so I could properly say good-bye to her and everyone who was there. I spent all morning and all afternoon with her, and returned to Thakhek for dinner that same day.

I was emotionally exhausted and needed to recuperate after two days of an extremely emotional rollercoaster ride. I stopped by a little sidewalk soup shop along the edge of the Mekong River, where I used to roam as a child. This was my childhood territory. As I was waiting for my soup to be served, again my mind began to wander. There were so many things in that environment that provoked my childhood memories. A young girl was there who must have been in her late teens, and she asked me,

"Where did you come from brother?"

"I came from here; I mean I was born and raised here as a child."

The girl (with big surprise and wonder in her eyes): "How is that so!"

"Don't you believe me? I am from here; I used to swim in this river, around here (as I pointed it out for her), at least three times a day when I was a kid back in the '70s."

The girl just looked at me blankly, as if I were hallucinating with Crystal-Meth or some kind of hallucinogenic. I could totally understand her for perceiving me as I was high on Crystal-Meth, because at that time Laos was inundated with drugs, mainly Crystal-Meth. She kept persisting in her disbelief that I was Lao and a native of the town.

The girl: *"You said you were from here. Then why you don't phrase your sentences with the proper local slang and idiom?"*

At that moment, I felt so out of place. My hair stood on end with irritation from her honest comment on my Lao.

"What do you mean by not phrasing my sentences with proper local slang?" I asked.

Girl: *"You speak like a foreigner. You don't have a Thakhek accent!"*

"Yes, it is true. My Thakhek accent is questionable because my family moved around all the time. When I was between four and seven-years-old I was living in Vientiane, which is why I speak Lao with some Vientiane accent, but I know for sure that I don't speak like a foreigner, c'mon sister."

She gave me the most delicious bowl of soup, then she walked away with a soft giggling laugh and a disbelieving smile.

At first I thought that was awkward and kind of weird. But as I was eating and thinking about the deeper content and about what caused her to say what she had to say, I realized that she had said it in such a profound and honest way.

I came to realize something very special and most significant. It became one of the most extraordinary moments that I have ever experienced; I felt as if I was enlightened by coming to realize and accept the reality of what I had become.

Out of all these years of struggling, I found a better understanding and learned to accept the fact that I am a refugee living as an expatriate abroad.

I am a man without a land, and not a true citizen of any particular country. The national pride that I had for any nation I had been part of, was fading. Now, I am a citizen of the United States. I love America, and I am willing to sacrifice my life and die for the true principles that originally made it. However, the sense of truly belonging is always a question due to my differences in the United States.

Deep in my heart and with every essence of my existence, I always longed to and fought to hold on to my roots, my heritage, my Lao pride and Lao identity. I had been obsessing for my birthplace, Laos, which I couldn't even go back to visit for the longest time. Since the day that I left the womb of my motherland -- for all these years -- I was spiritually living in limbo. Crawling back to that womb and hearing such comments were a revelation to me.

What I had come to realize was that I am no longer a citizen of any particular country, nationality or ethnicity, but that I belong to a much greater entity. I am now a child of humanity and a citizen of the world. I am a part of all things and belong to every existing component of the universe's engine.

The next morning I left my hometown and headed to Vientiane, ready to return to the US. I was returning with a much greater understanding and acceptance of my life. Since then, I have been more at peace and able to resolve much stagnation that had clustered in my heart and soul from what had happened to me in my life. That was a big turning point.

Back in the US, I made the ultimate decision that I was definitely leaving the engineering career to be a professional filmmaker and to carry on with the hope of finishing the film. However, after we got back from Laos, it was very unfortunate that we ran out of money to sustain continuity in order to meet our deadline. Once again I was forced to go back and pursue my engineering career. I decided to move to Rochester, New York. While in Rochester I couldn't find any jobs in electrical engineering, so I worked for a temporary agency.

I worked in various odd jobs while I was waiting for luck to land me another job as an electrical engineer. As soon as I moved there, I began sinking into a deep depression because Rochester was cold and snowy, and there was not much going on, as there was in New York City. In New York City I had been physically and psychologically well established. New York City was the one and only place on earth, besides Laos, for which I felt so much love and attachment. Actually, by this time I had been having a love-hate relationship with New York City for almost two decades.

As each day went by in Rochester, my sadness accumulated until I became extremely depressed; even though I was surround by very good, dear friends who just loved me for who I am. But the feeling of loneliness inside me was indescribable. I needed a very specific kind of friend whom I could talk to about art, history, science, poetry and music. But, it was kind of rare in our Lao community in Rochester, at that time, to find some Lao friend with a strong passion and having ambition in arts.

One day I packed my backpack and told my supervisor at work that I was quitting the job. I said good-bye to all my friends, whom I dearly loved as if they were my own blood brothers and sisters. That was when I officially claimed that I was not just a filmmaker, but that I would be a professional filmmaker. I returned to filmmaking in 1997. Since then, despite the hardships in the independent filmmaking world, I've found my true self and true happiness. Everything I do has meaning for me. I feel that my life has real purpose, something to live and die for. I also have a goal in life. I am Thavisouk Phrasavath again, and I am alive and **happy**, as happy as my nickname is *"Souk,"* which means happy.

Ever since I came to the United States, I always dreamt and prayed for the wisdom and knowledge that someday I would have an ability to do something different for myself and my community. Since I stepped foot here I realized that the Lao community in Brooklyn lacked inspiration, and that there were no role models or someone we can look up to. We also needed leadership, definitely not the leaders who carried around their baggage full of the old mentality. We needed a leader who was well-informed, who acknowledged the usefulness of the knowledge and wisdom from the old country in the new country, the one who was comfortable to lead the community that lived in two different worlds, two different mentalities and two different human and family value systems.

We needed someone who could give us some vision, and dreams of a brighter future, where we would not be limited in our ability to create anything, be anything, and believe that there is no such dream that too big for the Lao. We also wanted Lao brothers and sisters from all ethnic descendants to be united into a community again. We wanted to be better prepared and more hopeful for our future generations, and have a sense of direction where we were traveling as a community.

179

I wanted to prove to myself and my Lao community in the area that all of these could be done, and also that our journey didn't end right after our resettlement, but it was just the starting point of our long-term process of building the foundation for our future generation. These are the kind of things that I was thinking so seriously about almost three decades ago. I wasn't only thinking about it, but I was working and being active and vocal about it at all times. This is one of the reasons that I needed to leave Rochester and get back to New York City to carry on my filmmaking and writing.

Despite all the knowledge, experience, passion and position that I already held in the filmmaking world for 14 years prior to this, for some reason during all those years I couldn't come to make a true and critical decision about becoming a professional filmmaker. Deep in my heart, however, I always knew that I had a great passion for it. Again, for me it was a love affair with art.

My family's finances were what had shaped my thinking and kept me from making a decision sooner. Each month my siblings and I had chipped in for the mortgage payment to maintain the house on Long Island. Then, because of my career decision, it became more burdensome for them, most of whom made very little money, to maintain the expensive mortgage. But, this work was urgent for me at the time. It was a calling—one that I couldn't delay any further, but had to reply to immediately—no questions asked. I knew it was my time to follow that path, so I did.

I became a starving artist. As for being a professional independent filmmaker, just like everyone else in the trade, I mostly worked for free or for very little money. I did what I did just for the love of the art. I was living from hand to mouth doing all the odd jobs I could. I did whatever I could to survive, as long as I could work toward finishing the long-term film project that I was evolving with my friend. I would do whatever it took to finish it, and to finish it the right way. I was willing to sacrifice at all costs.

Within this period I again became a refugee in the United States of America. I was moving around Manhattan Island, sleeping on old friends' couches and subletting apartment after apartment from friends. I lived in so many neighborhoods on Manhattan Island from the Lower East Side to Midtown, from the East Side to the West Side. I used to live on 2nd Street, 4th Street, 7th Street, 8th Street, Mott Street, Houston Street, 28th Street, 48th Street, Broadway, and back to my old beloved Brooklyn on Sheepshead Bay and Avenue J.

Within the first six years of my career change I moved around almost 20 times. That was one hell of a nomadic period for me. But regardless of how chaotic my life was, I really didn't mind it because every day was challenging. Every day I was growing; every day I was doing something that I was proud of. Every day I was productive and doing things that had meaning. I was so very proud of my nomadic struggling period, that I even named this episode of my life "Living On a Single Digit Budget," or more precisely, "Living on a Single Digit Budget in One of the Most Expensive Cities in the World." NYC was one hell of a ride, and I love to share this episode with everyone.

How did I survive on a single digit budget?

Before I share with you my single digit budget lifestyle, I would like to share my honest and very personal point of view on New York City. Again, this is personal speculation and one person's opinion.

This is my two-sided mirror of New York—one is actuality and the other is reputation or rumor. New York City had a very bad reputation for being a city full of mean, rude, indecorous, selfish people--the most heartless people on the planet. When I was first came to live in New York City, I believed all that was true, but I had simply misunderstood the culture of big city people. After so many years of living here, I developed a much better and deeper understanding. Most of the rumors about the attitude of the people and about city crime were just speculation based on coincidence or some unfortunate situation. They weren't based on the true experience of the New Yorker who actually lives here, or on accurate statistics and crime reports. It is true that New York City has a high crime rate—I am not denying that—but nowadays, city crime is everywhere on the entire planet.

The reality is—there are millions of the most kindhearted, honest, intellectual and peace-loving people living here in NYC. But, on the other hand—New Yorkers are some of the most brutally and extremely straightforward people; they have almost zero time to waste for no good reason. NYC is the home of dreamers, drama makers, the most ambitious and aggressive, self-motivated and artistic beings alive. New York City is chaotic, massive, messy, cluttered, crowded, uncertain and as confusing as its Interstate Highway 95, but whenever you manage to merge into one of its lanes, there you will find your own way to navigate through confusion and a comfortable speed to cruise along. You will also get in tune with its vibe and mentality.

I managed to survive on a single digit budget as an artist in New York City, not because of its toughness and roughness, but because of its kindness and generosity. Other very important factors were knowing where and when to buy cheap food, and how to sublet apartments for cheaper rent. Most of the New York City artists are world travelers and bi-coastal. New York City is the fuel that runs the Hollywood engine—most of the great filmmakers, great actors and actresses, writers, producers, directors, cinematographers, composers, editors, production designers, painters, musicians, you name it, have a residence in New York City and Los Angeles and elsewhere.

New York, which is home to16 million people, seems large, but the truth is, for the art community it has a very small and very tight kinship. When you tap into one little group, that group is connected to other groups; we are directly or indirectly connected to each other like a chain. Back in the mid-'80s I managed to tap into the New York City art community, and I've stayed in tune with the flow and resided within the colony up to this very day.

When I first connected with the art community I found the people were very much like me as far as the vibe, the pace and mentality. They more or less had the same philosophy and mentality. There were people who believed in giving, taking and sharing, like me. Because of the common ground that most New York City artists have, there is mutual trust and other components that bond and tie the entire art community together.

After I managed to build a bridge of trust and friendship with one artist, then, by word of mouth, favorable comments, and good recommendations, my reputation began to cycle around in the closed loop system. In the New York art colony news traveled fast. In 1997 when I tapped back into the New York City art colony, I was able to get hooked up almost right away. A friend of my dear friend, who got a job in San Francisco, was about to be away for seven months and she needed someone she trusted to sublet her apartment. Of course, I was the best candidate, so I moved in and settled down.

After I sublet an apartment from one good friend, that friend would recommend me to many other friends, and the word of mouth just kept growing. Usually, each cycle of rotating sublets for living space lasted between six months to two years. While subletting apartments from friends I never paid more than the price that they paid monthly. Most of the artist friends I knew had lived in New York City for the past 15 to 20 years, and most of them were living in rent-controlled apartments. The average I paid when I was subletting was between $350 and $650 per month. This was instead of the $1,000 to $1,300 per month or more for a studio apartment, which was New York's standard payment for rent in the late '90s.

Now, for the food. My soul food is mostly rice and vegetables, much less on meat and fish. Instead of buying food in regular supermarkets like Key Foods, ShopRite or Stop and Shop, I would go down to Chinatown to buy rice, vegetables, fish and beef. Almost everything in Chinatown is 50 to 60 times cheaper. One 25-pound bag of Jasmine rice sold for $12.99 to $15.00. For me, this bag of rice would last the whole month. For good quality vegetables, every day after 5 p.m. before the vegetable street vendors closed, they usually dropped their prices down another 35 percent to 50 percent. Any vegetable that was originally $.99 a pound, I could get three pounds for a dollar.

If I spent $5 to $8 for vegetables this was on average between 15 to 24 pounds, which would last me at least two weeks. Only, if I am a water buffalo then I would need a lot more than that. In summary, my living expenses averaged:

Rent and utility	$750 / month
Rice	$ 15 / month
Vegetables	$ 20 / month
Fish and Beef or Chicken	$ 50 / month
Cooking Ingredients	$ 10 / month

These were absolutely necessary for living, and the average of my total monthly expenses was between $850 to $1,000. If you are a starving artist, this is very manageable. You don't have to kill yourself from overwork and have no time to do your art and not be productive, get depressed, and end up on drugs or committing suicide.

I have eight basic principles for living happily:

I am living a simple life, which is the way to live long and real.

I don't own things that will own me.

I am only worried about what is necessary, not what I want.

I am happy with whatever I have, and admire others who have more than me. I do not compare myself to them or to anyone else who has a completely different philosophy and mentality than I do.

I let simplicity be the guide to achieving my true nature.

My life is not as complicated as I think it is. I just live and enjoy it while it's happening.

I am very flexible, but as firm as a bamboo tree. I do not uproot my principles just to accommodate other people's happiness.

Happiness is my first priority.

As far as my relationship with my dad and his family, it was kind of off and on. Unexpected things were constantly happening.

Early in the evening of October 13, 1998 I was trying to get ready to go out on a date. While I was shaving, I accidentally cut my face. I had never cut myself before, and I didn't know how in the world I had done it. I was bleeding quite heavily, and I couldn't stop it. I looked all around the apartment for bandages, but I had run out of them. So, I had to cover my face with a cloth and run out to buy bandages at the pharmacy around the corner.

After I cut myself, I didn't feel like going out on the date that evening. I almost cancelled my date, but to be polite I decided not to cancel. During the entire date I didn't feel well. I felt as if some bad spirit was possessing me; I don't know how to describe it; I just felt it in my stomach. My mind began to wander, and I worried that some weird thing might have happened or would happen. So, I said goodnight to my date somewhere around 10:30 p.m. and I decided to just go back to my place. I felt that I needed to be alone and get some rest.

I went back to my place and got myself a cold beer to help me sleep. For the longest time, from the mid-'80s through the mid-'90s, I suffered from a sleeping disorder. For years I was on nonprescription sleeping pills due to the effects of my childhood war trauma. I even went for sleep therapy. Every night, just as I was about to fall into my deep sleep, I had a recurring nightmare about this Communist Pathet Lao soldier with his green uniform, wearing his Mao Zedong cap, carrying his AK-47 assault rifle, and chasing me around.

Almost every time, just as I was falling asleep, this soldier was there waiting to chase me. After a while I was drawn to play a game of Catch 22 with my own nightmares. It was to the point where sometimes I was staying up for days. At that time I would do anything to either keep myself awake or make myself sleep as long as possible. In my case I was considered blessed, because it affected me only when I had just fallen asleep, so it didn't have much effect on my normal daily life and activities.

I was still able to function as normally as everybody else. Some of the catharsis of these childhood traumatic memories only occurred when I was under a lot of stress. Most of my recurring images were related to things that I had seen when I was a child growing up in the war torn country of Laos. I saw the horrible images of death and dying -- people getting blown away or being shot. A few times when I was really stressed, the recurring images seemed to be even more real and terribly raw. I was terrified by this puzzle—because I wasn't quite sure what state of mind I was in. Was I seeing this in my dream? Was I seeing it live? Was I experiencing the worst nightmare? Or was I hallucinating?

Very often I woke up in a cold sweat, shivering with my heart raging. After so many sessions of sleep therapy, the counselor told me it was very normal for children of war and war veterans to have these kinds of traumatic symptoms. From these words of comfort, and knowing my symptoms were common, I felt relief. I tried hard to be mentally and physically strong. I managed to recuperate and snap out of this severe condition. I still experienced the problem once in a great while, but it was not as bad as it had been. Beer always put me into a good sleep.

As I was lying in bed watching the local news channel while sipping my beer, the phone rang. It was my half-sister, Nui (Sinakhone), from St. Petersburg, Florida. As I tried to say hello, she cut me off.

Nui: "Here, big brother, Dad needs to talk to you!"

Right at that very moment I felt weird. That was really out of character for her. My half-sister is a sweetheart, just like all the rest of my sisters. Dad came on the phone; his voice was shaking and he was stuttering,

Dad: *"I just want to let you know—Ah! I am going to need your help."*

"What is going on over there? Is everything alright?" I asked.

Dad: *"Well, your little brother just got shot a few hours ago, and the doctor said he is in critical condition. I don't know if he is going to make it or not."*

As soon as my father delivered these words I began debating with myself. No! No! This can't be happening! My immediate reaction was frustration, confusion, denial and refusal to believe what had just happened.

"What can I do, Dad?" I replied.

Dad: *"I don't know, but in case he doesn't make it, then I am going to need you to be here."*

He paused for a moment—then continued,

185

"I will call you and let you know his condition."
I was speechless and in shock. I even forgot to ask how my half-brother had gotten shot.

Here I go—another sharp curve on my rollercoaster ride. As soon as I hung up the phone with dad, I immediately alerted the filmmaking team that we might have to fly down to St. Petersburg the next day or the day after. I finished making all the necessary phone calls at about midnight, then my phone rang again. I was almost too frightened to pick it up this time, but I knew it was urgent, so I had no other option but to pick it up. My half-sister was on the phone again,

"We just lost him."
She was sobbing non-stop. I asked her if I could talk to Dad. She said,
"He is too upset to talk right now. This is all I can say for now."
Before I hung up I promised her that I would get down there within a day or two. All that night I couldn't fall asleep. I was frustrated, angry and in disbelief about what had just happened. Even though I was not that very close to my father's family physically, but I loved them unconditionally. We were blood related, and we were family regardless. Although I was extremely upset and felt very sad when my father left for his new family, as I grew older over the years I had a better understanding of his situation. I still had great respect for him. He was my hero, and I loved him. It was not hard for me to just hop on a plane and be there for him. Two days after that phone call, I was in St. Petersburg, Florida. When I first arrived I tried to find out what had happened, and why my half-brother had been shot.

My half-brother was two weeks away from his 17th birthday. A member of his own gang, the Bloods, had shot him in the stomach. Back in 1987 we were filming some young Laotian teenagers who were associated with the Bloods in Stockton, California. I knew how serious this was then, but I didn't know how fast it had spread from California all the way down to St. Petersburg. I also did not know that my half-brother was already a part of it.

My father, stepmother, half-sister, the monks, and all of his gang member friends came to the funeral. Uniformed police and undercover police were there also to make sure there would be no drive-by shooting at the funeral procession. It was very sad to see the unopened monk's robe lying next to the coffin, waiting to be offered to the corpse of a young man who had just lost his life and would never have a chance to become a novice or pay respects to his ancestors.

On this day my father was more spiritual and culturally oriented than sentimental. He was making sure all of the traditions and Buddhist rituals were being properly conducted. Seeing the monks splashing the coconut juice over his face to purify his body and soul for his afterlife forced me to feel the pain and suffering of my father and stepmother. Above all, the entire ordeal reminded me of my own mother's pain and suffering that she had had to endure over the loss of her love.

Here I was looking at my stepmother, yet seeing the sorrow and pain of my own mother. Two broken hearts of two wonderful women who were innocently joined by the same man, weeping for the loss of their love. As I continued watching, all of the young Lao gang members were paying their final respects. They were filling the coffin with red roses wrapped in red rags. Red—the color that my half-brother and the rest of his gang were willing to die for. I came to realize how little a youth gang values life these days. Life to them is only worth a piece of cloth, their badge of honor for giving their life.

Most of the gang members who were attending the funeral didn't seem to have remorse. Instead they were proud of their gang identity and that some of them were paying the ultimate price for it -- glory. Most of the young gang members seemed to have lost their grip on their roots and heritage. Sad to say, they had really, truly lost their true sense and connection to humanity.

It was very painful for me to return from such a loss. We returned to New York City with some great footage. Three weeks after I returned from the funeral, we got the footage from the film lab, and it was ready to be edited into the main assembly. The way we dealt with this long-term film-making process was that we would shoot and edit along the way. For two and a half weeks, as I tried to edit the funeral scene, every time I sat in front of the editing machine looking at the raw footage, I couldn't get over the fact that the corpse lying in that coffin was actually someone I knew. This was someone who was blood related to me, who had just wasted his life for absolutely no good reason in a most undignified and meaningless way.

I couldn't get myself together to edit the scene. About three weeks later I decided to take a little tour around the neighborhood, and I was introduced by the owner of a local liquor store to a guy named "Jack Daniels." Several hours after that, I was editing the scene and I finished it within four hours.

Then again, due to the lack of financial support for the film, the team had to go their separate ways for a few months. Sometimes these hiatuses lasted a year or two.

I went on working as an editor for other people's films and music videos. In 1999 I was incorporated and had a little editing studio on Broadway between Franklin and White Streets in lower Manhattan. The independent film business was about to get better for me. Many people wanted to come and edit their film with me in my place. Again, though, the most unthinkable tragedy happened. This time was the worst, because it didn't cause only emotional or psychological effects, it affected the whole world's economy. This was September 11, 2001.

My little independent postproduction studio on Broadway in New York City was about a mile away from Ground Zero. I had no choice after that horrific event but to move back to sharing an apartment with my youngest brother, who was a Wall Street broker. Of course, right after September 11 all business in New York City was badly damaged, and his business was affected the most.

Later on that same year due to economic hardship we lost our home on Long Island then moved our mother and the rest of the family out of Long Island to Lyndhurst, New Jersey, where we could have easy access to each other. During the chaotic and disappointing time right after my father came and left, most of my younger brothers and sisters had decided to leave home. Now, however, they were moving back to New York City, the place they were familiar with. While all of this commotion was going on, we put the long-term film project aside and I had a chance to work on my own personal film project and music video. Besides that, I was editing other people's films, music videos, demo reels, trailers and short films.

At the time I was dating a Lao sweetheart named Mouky, who lived in Elgin, Illinois. I spent some time there over a period of three years before we tied the knot on July 4, 2004 in Elgin. Three months after we got married, Mouky moved to New York City to live with me. Right after things settled down, it was time to get back to finishing the damn long-term film project. I was afraid that after we had a baby this film project would never get a chance to be finished -- ever. So we pushed hard to make it happen.

By some luck and by being in the right place at the right time, things finally seemed to fall into place. In June 2006 we were selected to attend the Sundance Composers Lab at the Sundance Institute in Utah. There, every fellow must show the rough cut of their film for advice, criticism, and comments by top-notch filmmakers, fellow filmmakers and great composers. We worked very hard for about three weeks to get our rough cut in decent shape to show. The film was rather long; it was about 150 minutes. While we were showing the film, everyone seemed to be quiet and disengaged. I thought to myself, "oh no, everyone must hate it."

Right after the film was over, everyone was so quiet in the dark. The lights in the auditorium were slowly coming up, and I came to realize that most of people had been sobbing almost from the beginning through the end of the film. Everyone was more or less speechless. I was also speechless. I knew many questions would be asked regarding myself and my family situation, because that was what the core of the film was about. I took a deep breath and got ready to face reality. I was so curious to hear what everyone had to say about the film, because two films had been shown before ours, and all the advisors, composers and fellow filmmakers had so much to say about everything in those films, even though they seemed to be a much better rough cut with more polish than ours.

The moderator was up on the stage with a microphone asking if anyone had any questions to ask before we took a short break. After the break there would be a detailed group discussion. No one said a word, so the moderator made a quick announcement:

"After we finish our 15-minute short break we will all meet for a detailed discussion in the lounge in the front lobby."

At the discussion session all the advisors, fellow filmmakers, composers and everyone who had watched the film said they were touched by it. The film got love and support from everyone. We received great advice from the advisors and great comments from fellow filmmakers. That composers' lab boosted our confidence and gave us courage to believe that the film was right on track. The idea that we had had for years, and the way we liked to approach our storytelling was always out of the ordinary and unconventional. This proved to us that it indeed did make sense and was understood by people.

From that day on we saw light at the end of the tunnel. After 11 days of intense seminars, group discussions, and working with professional composers, I had accumulated more specific knowledge about how soundtracks and music have so much power and influence on images and motion pictures, and vice versa. We also saw how all the elements that create a soundtrack or music, and the elements that create images or motion pictures, have their own interrelation and contrast between each other.

As we all know, music score or soundtracks consist of melody, rhythm, tone, harmony, counterpoint and layer; while a motion picture or film is made of form, color, motion and the juxtaposition of moving images or still images. How the music score has a strong influence in film is fascinating. How each bit and piece of sound, musical notes and certain sounds of instruments find their way to compensate, counteract, contrast, give a voice and add a unique character or empowerment. When degrading or highlighting of images in moments of drama take place on screen they can suspend or create dramatic tension. How to achieve the compromise and empowerment between the music and the images is beyond common knowledge; it is a blessing and a talent. It requires wisdom, and that wisdom was well shared and transferred to us by those great master composers who were there at Sundance Institute.

Through those 11 days of intense and meditative concentration I began to see the images of sound and music. I also came to realize the power that sound and music have. The power of images that gave the evidence of the truth, and made believers out of the audience, made up only about 50 percent of what was called the movie. The music was also interpreting and defining all of those images into moods and feelings, and giving us direction in how we should pay attention to our emotions. This made up another 50 percent of the overall completion of the movie or motion picture.

I began to see and hear music as I never had before. Music began to make me think deeper, laugh harder and cry louder. Music began to speak to me in a way it had never done before. It allowed me to hear and see its uniqueness of inner voice and its visual scope. Since then, music has never been only the great composition of interesting musical notes, musical patterns and musical instruments, but rather deep from the heart, a deep inner thought of an expression of a very specific feeling. It is a special meaning that has a specific contrast or unique relationship or synchronicity with something very meaningful or metaphoric for something phenomenal.

On top of all this, I have come to have a greater admiration and greater respect for music composers, and I have learned a great deal about how to communicate with them in musical terms, musical metaphors and the certain specific language that composers use. I gained a great deal of experience in filmmaking that I never would have had an opportunity to learn otherwise. I could not afford to pay for even one class in filmmaking in my entire life. I learned so much vital musical knowledge that added to all of the other artistic knowledge that I had been accumulating over the years.

This gift of knowledge from the Sundance Institute helped me contribute more to the production team, and to have a deeper understanding of how to take our decent, rough-cut film to a much higher level. The higher level, in my personal understanding, meant the film would have an ability to communicate with an audience beyond narration, accompaniment of tempo music, factual statements, personal quotes, visual beauty and visual metaphors. The film would have to transcend the audience's intellect and emotions and deepen their understanding of the story. We also wanted the audience to have a deeper emotional connection with the subject in a more personal, yet universal realm, and in a spiritual space with the true essence of self revelation. We wanted the audience to experience the film as if they themselves were living the life of the subject and seeing the world from his point of view.

Everyone who was there the fellows, composers, lab staff and advisors are highly intellectual and spiritual group. They were all passionate about utilizing art to better our human condition and humanity. I felt so blessed to have such an opportunity to be one of the people absorbing the lifetime gift of wisdom. Every advisor and fellow whom I met and got a chance to work with gave very knowledgeable advice. All of them were compassionate, high-level artists, and their critiques were remarkable and profound.

Every piece of advice and knowledge that they gave me came from somewhere deep in their hearts, their kind spirits, their great intellects and their human compassion as great artists. I felt so spiritually connected and inspired by every one of them. They made me feel as if I had known them all my life. I was so appreciative of what the Sundance Institute had to give. They gave some things that all the money in the world can't buy. There was residual inspiration, confidence and affirmation of faith. Most important of all—the Sundance Institute gave the true essence of what was needed and what it took to be a great visual artist. The Sundance Institute was also reassuring that there was an existing place, the most remarkable place in our world, where true artists can be creative and productive—this is what the Sundance Institute is all about.

Back in New York after the Sundance Composers Lab, we set the deadline for finishing our long-term filmmaking marathon. We aimed to complete the film before my wife, Mouky, gave birth. At this time Mouky was already four months pregnant. Based on what we had, we were very confident that we would be able to complete the film on the schedule we had set. It was one of those intuitive things.

A month or two after Sundance the film was getting much better. We were restructuring it, trying out all the great new ideas, but every time we finished screening the film ourselves, we felt something very important was still missing. Something was needed to fulfill our emotional needs, but we couldn't figure it out immediately. I think it was about a month after we paid attention to a little voice in the back of our sub-conscious minds that one day, right after the end of the screening, my partner and I looked at each other, and we both realized what the missing puzzle piece was. It was an interview with my mother.

For some odd reason over two decades we had shot a lot of footage of my mother cinéma vérité, and had some brief interviews of her here and there about some particular subjects, but we had not sat down and let her tell her entire life story. This was the biggest puzzle piece that we had been missing for all of these years. This was the material we needed most to be able to give the best structure to the film. My mother was the star of the film. Finally, we managed to sit down and listen to her complete story from childhood to the present. She was a 72-year-old woman; she had been through many lives, and she had a lot to say. It took her two whole days to complete her story.

After the end of our second day of interviewing my mom, my partner and I looked straight at each other eyes and nodded our heads—we were in agreement—this was it. This was what we had needed for all of these years. As soon as the film was developed and we got the footage, I cut it into the rough cut, and after a few months of sculpting and polishing we almost had it ready for any festival.

Of course, my damn rollercoaster Journey of Life always surprised me and was action packed. This time it was something really good and really special -- one of the most precious things that I had been dreaming about for the longest time.

On Monday, November 27, 2006 at 3:37 p.m. our beautiful baby girl was born. She weighed 6 pounds, 7 ounces. It was an easy birth, and we named her Ahmeeta O. Phrasavath. Ahmeeta means enlightenment. Oraday, her middle name, was after my hero mother.

A few months after Ahmeeta was born, my mother's health began to deteriorate. Besides her open-heart surgery, diabetes, and arthritis, she was stricken by a very serious type of vertigo. This can be a very nasty disease. There are various causes for vertigo, but my mom's is the type that starts with an ear infection, then the eardrum bursts and the liquid that gives our nervous system a sense of balance dries out. Without that balance liquid, my mom suffered deafness and dizziness. She felt the sensation of spinning out of control all day, all night, all year round. She lost her sense of balance completely.

My mother's health situation became part of another setback for me. Now I had to worry more about my mother, and she needed additional help. I had to help my brothers and sisters take care of her 24 hours a day, 7 days a week. We didn't finish the film exactly on time, but at least we did finish two weeks before the 2007 Sundance Film Festival. We went to the festival with the completed and final edited film, but it was the temporary music version. We still couldn't find a composer for the film, and we didn't have enough money to hire one. After the Sundance Film Festival and the Berlin International Film Fest the POV (Point Of View) came to the rescue with the funds to finish. By the best of luck in the world Howard Shore came to rescue the film. With his musical vision, wisdom, musical genius and heart as kind as Buddha's, he breathed soul into the film. That's why "The Betrayal (Nerakhoon)" was such a soulful film.

After receiving the Grand Jury Prize nomination at the Sundance International Film Festival, the film was being officially selected at the Berlin International Film Festival. It went on contending as the underdog, but in high-level competitions got great nominations and won a number of prizes such as:

Cinema Eyes Honor Award Nominee, Full Frame Spectrum Award Winner, Ann Arbor Film Festival Grand Jury Award Winner, Cinereach Award /Human Rights Watch International Film Festival Winner, Fresno Independent Filmmaker Audience Award Winner and others.

Throughout the year 2008 the film was in festival circuits in North America, Europe and a few Asian countries—Hong Kong, China and Bangkok, Thailand. Finally, the film was blessed with a great recognition and honor. It received the 2008 Film Independent Spirit Award, Academy Award (Oscar) Nomination for the Best Documentary feature, and won the 2010 Creative Arts Primetime EMMY Award for Exceptional Merit for

Non-fiction Filmmaking.

From the sweat, hard work, devotion, dedication, passion and kindness of so many brilliant, artistic women and men who gave their souls and spirits and every essence of their being to this film, it became a monumental accomplishment and was beneficial to everyone who had been involved. If I had to list all of these men and women's names, I would definitely need to dedicate one chapter to the list. With all my love, my appreciation and my respect for each and every one of them—I believe they all know who they are -- I salute them, and from the bottom of my heart I thank them all.

For me this was destiny and the fulfillment of a mission towards deeper self-revelation, self-understanding and self-healing. The stories that my family shared with the world came from our honest, enthusiastic and deeply sincere hearts. It contributed to our motherland, Laos, to be able to rise once again with glory. Her name is now placed back on the world map where it belongs.

During 60 years under French Colonial rule Laos was already wiped off the world map. It was only known as a faction of Indochina. After 30 years of civil war and internal conflict Laos was obscured by confusion. The world was puzzling over identifying what was the head and what was the tail of the elephant. During the eight years of United States Covert War, Laos was just a secret logistic location, a hidden place and battle ground for the North Vietnamese Communist and US bomb dumping ground.

There is no monumental triumph that is achieved without intricate questions being asked. Following are the most asked questions from the audience who were so curious and eager to know more about the subject matter, and me as a subject of the film. I would like to take this opportunity to answer those questions to the best of my knowledge and honesty from my own point of view.

1. What was the most difficult and intricate challenge in being the subject as well as being the filmmaker?

Answer: It was very challenging for me that I was a filmmaker and also the subject. The toughest challenge was to be a self-critic and sensitive to issues that sometimes were too private to share. To know when to draw the line, or what is the right balance between sharing and exploiting, is sometimes difficult. I had to decide where to draw that line before the film became an invasion of my family's privacy and before it exploited them.

In my case the greatest thing was that I had some degree of control over the situation because I was also the editor. I had a certain degree of control over what to tell, how much to tell and how to tell it in the right way, because I was also the narrator and writer for the project. As far as in which direction the film was going—I was also one of the creators, so the navigation of the direction was a compromise. This was the journey of Laotian history, the Lao way of life that was being portrayed, the philosophy that was being used, the essence of our Lao ancestors captured and re-captured, and the voice of the Lao that we were hearing. This was a thousand years of visualizing the Lao point of view of the world and humanity. Recapturing, reconstructing and bringing back the true essence of the Lao world had to do with knowing Lao, being Lao, feeling Lao, living the Lao way of life and being part of Lao history.

But as far as being the subject and an editor of the film goes, I had an internal conflict between my worst self-criticism and my willingness to compromise for whatever would improve the story and better the film. It was difficult to overcome my self-criticism. Every day when I sat in front of either the Steinbeck machine, the D/Vision pro 2.2, the Avid Media Composer, the Final Cut Pro or the Avid Xpress Pro, I had to detach myself from being a subject of the film. I had to constantly remind myself that I was an editor and disregard how much I hated hearing my own voice, seeing how I carried myself on screen or how much I disliked my crooked teeth.

I had to rise above all of this personal idiocy and nonsense, and concentrate on the content. Whenever the content was right, and the delivery of the story was strong and came alive, I had to learn how to live with the moment that we captured—even if that meant my crooked teeth were being badly framed, I had mispronounced a word, lost my train of thought in the middle of a talking head interview or whatever. I was my own worst enemy; for over two decades I was constantly having an internal conversation, self-debate and monologue with myself. I had to disregard my self-criticism and self-hatred so the on screen Thavi could have his opportunity to tell the story and be himself freely without interruption from the off screen Thavi.

Questions 2 and 3 are usually asked by Lao and other Asian audience around the country. I think these two questions have been asked the most because they have something to do with Asian culture, tradition and Asian mentality. This is in contrast to the nature of cinema, which might trigger them or intrigue them mentally to ask these questions in particular.

2. How did the film "The Betrayal (Nerakhoon)" get to be so intimate?

Answer: The film was able to achieve a high degree of intimacy and managed to go deep into the core emotions of the character for the reasons being the film is about my own mother and father and the rest of the characters are my own family members, neighbors, friends and relatives. These are the essence of the true relationships full of trust between blood related people. Intimacy was revealed in relationships between mother and son, father and son, brothers and sisters, neighbors, friends and relatives. The other advantage was knowing the language and understanding the rules of Lao culture and traditions, which we used during the process of capturing the moment or trying to re-capture the essence of past events.

As a matter of fact, the main subject of the film (my mother) didn't understand a word of English. She only knew how to speak and understand Lao. I am very fortunate that I speak, read and write Lao. I can't imagine being the filmmaker and not being able to do these things. How in the world would I have been able to have an intimate communication with my mother? How could I get someone like my mother to talk about her emotional pain, spiritual suffering, relationships with her children, childhood upbringing, her hopes and dreams and to whom she lost her virginity?

It had to do with the capability of communicating in the right language, the proper way of utilizing the culture and, in my case, knowing and having a deep understanding of my own family history, my Lao culture, roots, heritage, faith and Lao values. Knowing how to read, write and speak Lao is the key to all of these doors. Imagine if I didn't speak Lao and wasn't a member of the family. Would a Laotian family be that open to me? Perhaps one in a million would be that open to a stranger.

One thing that people have to understand about the Laotian is that we have a very high sense of pride. Exposing family failures, dysfunctions or internal conflicts between siblings, love affairs, financial debt—these are taboo subjects. These are subjects that we don't normally speak freely about or even share with our close friends. Culturally, this is considered tarnishing the image and is embarrassing to the family and clan. Exposing such matters usually causes the family's bond and kinship to break.

I dared to break away from the traditional ways of defining communication, and to heal our wounds by communicating and sharing our pains and hardship with others—friends, neighbors, relatives, the public and strangers.

I didn't do this in order for us to be known or to get personal recognition, but rather for the purpose of exposing the subject that mattered the most to our Laotian history and the history of the relationship between Laos and the United States. This had directly affected our family and my own personal life. I personally believed that there is a deep wound that still infected both nations' souls.

It was time to expose the truth that caused the Laotian crisis and circumstance. Being a child of two motherlands, one that had given me my birthplace and the other that gave me liberty, I was growing up in a generation that was seeking remedies for healing the wounds and scars. I wanted to restore the greater relationship between the two motherlands. I felt like a child caught in a custody battle.

I had the urge at the time to jump on whatever train was available that would take me to a place where I would be able to achieve this goal. This goal was driven by an inspiration to preserve my family's story. What happened in Laos during the Vietnam War was something that my family and I did not want to let pass by without letting the world know. We felt that it was our duty and responsibility to share with American public and a new generation of Laotian-Americans about our Lao history and the role that we served in the U.S. covert war. We wanted to properly address and acknowledge Laotian history, Laotian refugee issues, conditions and crises, and explain the long-term effect on the family that is caused by war. Furthermore, we wanted to share the Laotians wisdom, prophecy and how it shaped our personal view of the world and human history.

All of these issues were so close to our hearts that we allowed ourselves to be vulnerable, and to open our heart and our spirit, because we—the Phrasavath family -- understood the necessity.

3. How did the film "The Betrayal (Nerakhoon)" get to be such an emotional attention-grabber?

Answer: *"The Betrayal (Nerakhoon)"* is a deeply personal, human story; that is what makes it so emotionally gripping. It's a story of ordinary people trying to find a way to live their life, overcome their obstacles and achieve their ultimate goals -- goals of staying alive and escaping the nightmare of an American ghetto. This is the story of every American immigrant at one time or another. It's the kind of story that anyone can relate to. Also, the story has to do with the intimate relationship between the subject and his/her passion to keep the family in harmony and protect its values.

Furthermore, the individual characters in the film seemed to be unconscious of the presence of the camera, and they appeared to be seamlessly natural on screen. This helped the audience to easily suspend their conscious minds, so that they could move into the mind space, heart space and spiritual space of the Phrasavath family. While the audience watched the Phrasavath family, in their sub-conscious mind they were watching their own life and the unfolding saga and drama of their own family.

Also, the feeling of intimacy in the relationships between different individuals on screen transcended into the audience's own personal relationships. This had a lot to do with how we, the filmmakers, universalize the Phrasavath family. So, the Phrasavaths became the mirror that reflected and intrigued the audience to raise questions regarding their own relationships with their own families. The Phrasavath family became a classic example representing millions of other Asian families out there in the world. That was why whatever happened to the Phrasavath family on screen became everyone's concern.

As previously mentioned, Laotians and many other Asians keep their family life and personal matters private. What goes on behind our closed doors and closed community gates is nobody else's business but ours. It took a lot for my family to be able to open up, allow themselves to be exposed and be intimate in front of a camera; but physiologically they didn't see me and the rest of the team as filmmakers. They saw me as their older brother and his group of friends. My mother and father, especially, saw me only as their son.

I was the son who was trying to find a way to heal the family's wounds and scars, and also to work through the causes and effects of the war and the atrocities that we had been through. A lot had to do with my being the head of the family, and no one in my family daring to ask any questions regarding the trust issue of documenting and archiving the family or my involvement and relationship with the project. My family was always supportive, and they acknowledged the difficulty of the process.

My family was also well aware that I'd been trapped in a situation where there was no point of return or walking away from the project.

We kept hanging on and working our heart out, giving all that we humanly possible can. Every one who came along each gave their heart and soul to the project.

Because the film was so intricately woven in multi-layers of evident and hidden betrayal, and was so complex due to the nature of the subject matter, it literally took us over two decades to unwind all the layers.

Who said no one is betrayed in the history of "The Betrayal?" There are layers of betrayal; there is always somebody being betrayed. This is the essence that creates suspense, grips us emotionally and grabs the audience's attention.

9

I Am

Being a Lao refugee and also being an artist living in the US for almost three decades, I came to realize that America did not always seem to be what we hoped and expected it to be. As we all know, America is a country that consists of many cultures and religions, multi-ethnicities, multi-races, heritages and traditions. Based upon all of these separate entities that reside in each state, and because each state is so vast and functions and operates by many of its own separate laws, each state is almost like a separate country. America is already a country that consists of non-homogeneous societies. Because each of these non-homogeneous elements or components makes up America, it is a mosaic, a truly beautiful masterpiece. If I may use a metaphor from the food category, to me America is a Gigantic Wok of Stir Fry not a melting pot.

As for me, the first generation, like many other first generations of many immigrant descendents, I was longing for or still believed in the old ideology of the American melting pot. Due to the suppression and pressure of the environment that I resided, I was ready to give up my past, living in the present, assimilating and chasing after the American Dream. I used to believe that was the fastest way to success and would guarantee future security. In my case, this smooth road to accomplish the dream almost ended with a nightmare. At the beginning of my 29-year journey deep into the American wilderness, I totally believed that was the way to go. But the further I traveled that road, the more I personally came to realize it was the smoothest passage to spiritual death, depression, a lost sense of my own true self and my true identity.

Money, social status, name brands, high profile social clubs and guilds are great, social-cosmetic materials that could help me to conceal my true self and identity and easily help me blend in to the society. If I am lucky enough to be able to accumulate all of the above I will be more accepted into the society as a respectable individual. But then I came to realize, as I was trying to be part of a so-called respectable society, I was creating an artificial character out of my true self. It was so wrong how I was approaching it. I taught myself to apply my own cosmetic—coat my words with sugar and honey, get myself into social functions, masking myself with a lot of smiles regardless and naïvely believing that I am now almost a perfect "American"

As I was trying hard to be what I believe is a so-called "American," I came to much larger and bigger questions. I often ask and debate with myself, what is an American? Does the word "American" really exist in this day and age?

From my own internal debate I have concluded that to me there is no pure definition of the word "American." If there is, then why do we call the native and indigenous Americans "American Indians," why not just "Americans?" This is what made me believe that from the birth of this land and continent before it became America, its destiny was to be a motherland that will give birth to multi-races, multi-heritages. To be an American without any attachment is more like a tree without roots.

Look at America as if it were a gigantic mosaic wall. For this wall to be the most beautiful masterpiece, every small piece of glass must maintain itself, be individually self sufficient as its own separate entity, as part of a multiple unity consisting of one gigantic piece.

But for the gigantic piece to achieve a level of mastery, each of those small elements must maintain their own maximum quality and stay true to what they are made of. This is why knowing who we are and what we are is very crucial. Regardless of whoever we are, whatever our roots, heritage and every essence of our ancestors that comprise us, we have to learn to have pride in our own race and to adore, cherish and respect every other person who is different from us. We must also be happy with whatever we are and whatever we have, adore whatever we are not, and admire whatever we don't have.

Humanity only exists if all of the components that make it are counted as if fully part of a great entity.

As for me, I have to once again ask myself what it really means to be Lao-American and living in America, as well as being one ethnicity, a citizen of the world and a child of the universe. I personally believe that to be able to talk about such an issue I first need to have some deeper understanding regarding the following:

★Basic principles of America.
★The old phenomena of the American melting pot.
★Roots and heritage.

★Understanding the basic principles of America is very crucial. To understand the law of the land and know your rights gives you a better sense of direction and helps you to move forward without political or legal complications.

★Why is understanding the old ideology of the American melting pot critical in our early stage of development or preparation for becoming American?

As we all know, America is the nation of global immigration, the land of multi-culture, multi-religion, multi-races and multi-ethnicities. This is key to recognizing your own existence.

Again, to me the American melting pot was more or less an illusion, a beautiful American term that was used for political correctness in illustrating that the American Dream was not the American reality. To me, America is not a big melting pot. It never has been. If it did exist then I personally never existed. If I had fallen into that melting pot, I would be melted down or resolved to a solution.

Let's look back at the time when this land was conceived. All ethnicities of the indigenous people were fighting each other for their own separate territories. They were willing to go to war and die to protect their territory and their identity as people of the tribe. Each of these indigenous people want to preserve their own culture, traditions, religion, law, rules and ways of conduct according to what each tribe believed to be the right way to live their lives in peace, harmony and serenity with their own adapted environments.

The indigenous fathers of this land, who set the pattern of the mosaic for many generations to come, made a masterpiece out of it. The fortunate thing that we, the new American generation inherited is the existing pattern of the original design. Since the day I stood in front of the court being sworn in to be a citizen of this great nation, I knew I had a responsibility as a citizen of America toward my new, beloved country, where I would live and for which I would be willing to die.

One of my responsibilities as a citizen of this great nation was to be a part of and to help fulfill the masterpiece of that original mosaic set forth by our indigenous fathers and mothers of this land.

In my personal, firm conviction, roots and heritage are the keys to it all—value, beauty, quality and the strength that has the potential power that holds and ties everything together. The roots and heritage of each individual, ethnicity, nationality, race or color are all elements that will add to the magnificent beauty of the American masterpiece mosaic—the coexisting of individual pieces as part of the whole. All pieces need to be dignified.

For me to be able to fully function as a productive member of the American community and society, I need all of these basic foundations and principles. As a first generation Lao-American I can't just be melted away. I came to plant my roots and to benefit this country, not to take its profits away. I came to this country to share, cherish and contribute. I came to this country with a piece of American history at hand. I came to be a great American, and significant other in America's gigantic mosaic.

I am a proud Laotian-American. My thousands-years-old traditions, culture, heritage, knowledge of life, human history and wisdom of humanity that I inherited and will pass on to my next generation, should be counted as a token of my appreciation to the nation that was the surrogate home to me and Laotian-Americans for some generations past and will be for many more generations to come.

All the things I brought with me to this country, whatever treasures that I have, I intend to use to strengthen and beautify this great country, to make it an even greater nation, enriched by significant moral values and humanity, as well as racial and ethnic beauty. A nation where a future society will adore, admire and celebrate their differences. It is a gigantic American mosaic where each piece and each color, shape and size are all complementary to enlighten each other's beauty and noteworthiness.

America is the arena of will—I have to always be ready to challenge. To be able to survive in this arena I need a great weapon. This arena can be very brutal and unforgiving, a place that takes no prisoners. Only winners and accomplishers are respected and welcomed with big rewards and honors. In my opinion, to make it through the challenge in the arena of will, I need the greatest weapons of all. It is my personal belief that the three most vital weapons are:

1. Roots and Heritage
2. Knowledge
3. Wisdom

I'll illustrate this as a metaphor about a swordsman who has a double-edged sword.

*Roots and Heritage are the components that make every essence of a swordsman. These are his geometric proportions, his natural postures and movements, his awareness and sensitivity, his unity of attack and defense, his constant motion, his control of centerline, his alternation of circle and line, his predominance of the mind, his spirit, his bravery, his devotion to maintain his legacy and swordsmanship, his pride and his strategy. We can't walk into this arena of will without all of these essences of the warrior. This is our armor and our shields that will protect us from direct blows.

*Knowledge is one side of the double-edged sword.

Knowledge is the most necessary principle that the swordsman has to learn from his teacher and master, but knowledge and tactics alone don't cover all of the angles of attack by his opponent either in the offensive or the defensive. The swordsman with all the knowledge of swordsmanship isn't necessarily a sword warrior. He is a fool for not knowing and not see-ing a difference between knowledge and wisdom.

For us the commoner, the common knowledge is what we can learn from schools, seminars, institutions, books, the library and the Internet. You can find great knowledge from all of these available resources. Many people are very knowledgeable, and receive high degrees in specific or a variety of areas in the form of bachelor's and master's degrees all the way up to PhDs.

Whatever degree we have, don't let it fool us or let it make us become conceited from all the knowledge that we have learned. If we believe that all we need to be able to fully function in our life and world are degrees, that might be detriment to ourselves.

To me, the more things that I know, the more I feel like I know almost nothing. So every day I have to remind myself that I am not a full-cup mind or a sword with one edge, when I have the capability to strive to be a sword with two edges. I must always remain as a humble student of life and keep an open mind to the world and universe out there in the open. I keep my mind as if it were an empty cup, so I can always receive and absorb new things.

★**Wisdom** is the most powerful weapon of the three because wisdom is a composition of three components: the roots, heritage and knowledge. Wisdom is a living experience including all knowledge, as well as being part of the roots and heritage. Real life experience is practicing and utilizing all principles of knowledge I have learned and accumulated by the power of the minds with a strong foundation of my roots and heritage. This will still give me enough of what I personally call internal wisdom. Internal wisdom is something that I earned from my inner self. Internal wisdom is not something that I can just learn and search for without living its experience.

Compared to a swordsman, this is another side of his sword's edges with an intensive practice and training of all his principles and tactics of how to combat and execute his opponent.

There is also another kind of wisdom that I call external wisdom. This I usually can receive from the men or women who have gone before me, who have been living and experiencing their life before me. This can be anyone who has experience in practicing and utilizing their principles, knowledge and accomplishments. It can be my mothers, fathers, grandparents and great grandparents. They are the well of my external wisdom. That's why in Lao culture and Lao tradition, the children are respectful of their elders and they always ask their elders for their guidance and blessing.

Compared to a swordsman, this is the other side of his sword's edge with the experience of multiple combat and executing all of his opponents and now he earns his dignified place as being a true sword warrior.

To be American. America is not demanding that I must give up my roots and my heritage. America needs my roots, heritage, ethnicity, culture and beautiful traditions. I came to America not to take, but to give. The best gift to give to America is my own precious self. But the gift would not be precious if I didn't have any attachments or components of a greater essence such as culture, tradition, roots, heritage, knowledge, wisdom, inspiration and determination.

America needs intelligence and we are intelligent.

America needs love; that is what we give, love.

America needs true history. Guess what?

We are the living American history.

America needs hopes and dreams. That is what we are, the hope and the dream as well as the future of this great nation. Either we like it or not. America is now our new home country, so love it and give it to America. Give the hope and the dream that our new motherland needs.

America also needs a visionary, and we, the Laotian and Laotian-Americans, are visionary people in our own right. We came here less than four decades ago, but we have already accomplished as much as many other ethnic minorities in this country have accomplished by comparison. We should be proud to be Lao-American; we should be as proud of what we have given back to this great nation as what this great nation has given to us.

We must dream and envision what we can do for America, what we can do for ourselves and what we can do for our beloved Lao brothers, sisters and all other fellow human beings in our community and our society.

Give for the pleasure of giving.

There is no gift that when given from the heart is considered to be too small or too little. It is worth all the same in weight and value of human compassion.

Take for the pleasure of whatever we really need.

Giving is never considered losing but gaining.

So, dream!

Dream before you go to sleep.

Don't wait until you fall asleep to dream and please don't fall asleep while you are dreaming.

Don't forget, the benefits from all the good deeds that we have done for others are what we have done for ourselves. My mother and my father always taught me to give with no strings attached to your gift, without expecting any favors in. To be able to give is always the greatest blessing. That is why in the Lao culture, we like to give and share everything we have, even something as small as a cup of water when we greet our guests and welcome them to our homes. That is already a measurement of the depth of our gratitude.

To me, being Lao-American means being equal to everyone else. Disregard race and ethnicity. We are as good, we are equal, we are as capable as everyone else. America is the land of opportunity, but don't forget that an opportunity is what we must create for ourselves with our own will, our own inspiration, our own knowledge and wisdom.

One basic principle of Theravada Buddhism that I inherited and used as my inspiration for daily living is:

"Ahta hi Ahta no Na tho."

"Mself is the only one true self that I can depend upon."

So, I am myself, not selfish

So, I accept myself as I am.

So, I am proud of what I am made of.

If you can't be proud of who you are, then it is time for you to dig deep into your roots and find the many essences that make you what you are. I'll bet if you start to pay attention to all the details you will find a lot more than you think.

So, be ourselves and be proud of whoever we are, but also be counted as part of the main entity - don't be left out and fall behind. Use your pride and inspiration to ignite your roots and heritage's engine. Keep your knowledge and wisdom nurtured and productive.

I am what I am today because I used all of the weapons that I had. I am what I am today because I was fortunate enough to be able to attend university to gain my knowledge and have a respected elder who gave me some great external wisdom, and I was experiencing life, which earned me internal wisdom.

I am what I am today because I was humble enough to recognize the difference between knowledge and wisdom, and I was ambitious enough to earn myself a sword with two edges instead of one. I was also very fortunate to acknowledge every person with whom I ever crossed paths. I treated all of them as if they were my teachers, so I could learn whatever they had to offer.

In the past I lived many lives, and during different periods of these lives I crossed the paths of a variety of people from all kinds of backgrounds and pasts; from criminals to high priests, from the homeless to the wealthiest. Regardless of whomever I met, I stood my ground and maintained my true self, so I could be a good student and learn whatever I was searching for. Each master has his or her own bag of tricks about life and living. These bits and pieces of tricks, knowledge and wisdom, that I accumulated over the years, became my most vital weapons.

Without these vital weapons I wouldn't have stood a chance in fighting to survive in the unforgiving arena of will. I am humble. I am open-minded. I am a good student in the university of life. I believe only the best students can achieve a masterhood and achieve to the enlightened level of understanding their own internal selves. I also believe that before I can understand our world and our universe, I must first know myself. One of my grandfather's favorite sayings:

"Everything is started within ones internal self."

I have a deep internal desire in my heart, as well as a strong will and determination with confidence and most important, humbleness. I was humble enough to recognize my internal calling to be a servant, a messenger, and a mouthpiece to speak the truth about the history of my motherland, Laos, and to pass on the philosophy of our ancient Lao wisdom and knowledge about life and humanity with the world beyond the boundary and a womb of our motherland.

As far as my filmmaking career, and especially my involvement in the making of "The Betrayal (Nerakhoon)," for many fans and audiences who were interested in knowing more and had many questions regarding it— how was all the writing to come about?

Besides my own personal statements in the talking head interviews the rest of the other writings had mostly (or more likely all of them had) come from the old Lao Buddhist manuscripts, old Lao literature, Lao poetry, Lao proverbs, and bit and pieces of Lao oral history that had been taught by my parents and grandparents.

All of the prophecies that were used in the film were from the ancient Lao manuscript called *"5000 Years Prediction."* Most of the parts that contained the history and comments about the faith, rituals and traditions were adapted from Lao oral history and folklore stories. For example, I got the eagle story from my own personal political view after translating the poetry called "Nok Ten Ziew," that I remembered from my second grade class.

These are good examples of how to utilize what I have inherited from the old country, combining ancient wisdom with modern living to bridge the gap of human history and universalize the Laotian life and the Laotian philosophy and experience. This was just as important as the rest of the great history that was written in the history books. Every essence and every bit, piece and neuron of Lao history, folklore stories, poetry, proverbs, literature and ancient Lao manuscripts are the elements that spice up my family's and my rollercoaster journey and years of waiting around to see the story unfold.

Out of my own personal concerns and frustrations 20 some years ago came the initial spark of inspiration that encouraged me to choose the specific path to this achievement. My biggest achievement was to let the world know that I loved my motherland and all Lao (68 ethnicities), and was proud to be Lao and now Lao-American. Our forgotten history, our human dignity and our contribution to this great nation are beginning to be noted.

Many or all of our fathers who served as warriors in the Vietnam War in Southeast Asian countries of Laos, Vietnam and Cambodia are at least now out in public, and part of the most important and critical point of our history. They are helping to restore and correct the history books. New pages containing critical and truthful points, which were intentionally omitted in the past 35 years are now being written by, not a philosopher, not a historian or elite educator or expert outsider, but by ordinary people who lived the life of that war, survived that war and represent a living history of that war.

As for being a filmmaker and a writer, I am very hopeful for a better future in the way we communicate visually and verbally. I believe making films and writing stories to share, to communicate, and to express our internal self is the greatest method for a better understanding about our self and deeper understanding of the differences between our culture, history, faith and political points of view. This is one of the best tools for expanding world peace, human rights justice, social, education and the human condition.

One of the reasons that I wanted to be a filmmaker was because I wanted to share my point of view on life and to share my Lao history with the world. Having been the victim of war, writing was one of my very best and most honest friends, and was also the beginning of my personal therapy and self-healing.

Twenty-six years ago was my beginning, the beginning of my soul's spiritual healing and self-therapy. It was also 26 years of preparation, progression, development, regaining strength, and dissolving the effects of the trauma and war atrocities I witnessed.

Whether I was ready or not I had to be able to step out of the womb of comfort, love and kindness, and be part of and function in a world full of

pain, hate, selfishness, greed, ego, arrogance, unjustness and all sophisti-
cated human challenges. There was no choice given to me. When I was 13
years old, I was forced to step out of that womb. Since then, it has become
my destiny. It personally took me a long period of time going down the
loneliest road of my life before I came to acknowledge my own responsibility.

After acknowledgement, came my responsibility for my own destiny. I
personally came to realize that destiny can only be fulfilled in a proper
manner if, and only if, my spirit, soul, and physical health are free from
pain, wounds, suppression of the environment and oppressive authority.
I was fully aware of my calling to serve, and my serving was to be part of
the fuel for the internal engine of humanity. As young as I was when I was
injected into that combustion chamber, the only choice I had was to break
down into molecules and be ready to be used. From going through the
process, I transcended into an inspiration and potential energy that held
many broken and wandering pieces of elements and components together.

Now that I am looking back on my journey and living my life with peace,
I am happy with what I have and all my accomplishments. Even though
I had once stepped far away from one loving womb, I had now entered
another greater and much bigger womb. Now I am truly a child of the
universe, living in the home deep within my own heart, comforted in my
own invented zone, satisfied with only everything I really need, not necessarily with all of what I want. I am an existence that resettled in the womb
of humanity under the roof of the universe. I am.

As for all of us being the descendants of the earth's ethnicity and citizens
of the universe, we have a great responsibility to teach, preserve and be-
queath our humanity to our future generation.

As for all the Lao of all ethnicities and the Lao-Americans, we have an
important responsibility to teach our children, grandchildren and many
generations to come, to know the wisdom of our Lao's view of humanity.
Our duty is not only to teach them how to say the word:

"*Sabaidee*" (How are you? in Lao.)

We must teach them that we are SOMEBODY.

We have to teach our children, grandchildren and great grandchildren to
know the true meaning of who we really are. And we ourselves also should
never forget the true meaning of our extraordinary journey to America.
The struggle and hardship that we long endured to build our life and home

away from home. The endeavor of turning our desperation into a hopeful future for our children and the generations to come. The monumental achievement of conquest and triumph overcame our trauma. Our beyond-extraordinary will power, courage and strength self-healed our hurt, wound and fear of war. This is our determination to live in peace freedom and liberty in the nation whose prevailing moral principle is to value the integrity of humanity, and never to lower or degrade that principle.

As for the present time, my love and relationship with my blood related family couldn't be any better. My respect and honor for my father have been fully restored. Being a father to a precious child of my own, I have a much greater understanding about unconditional love.

Through the absence and abandonment of my father, he made a strong man out of me. I am stronger because I am a survivor. I am better as a human being, because I have been through life and hardship. I have emerged because I was drowned; life became much more meaningful when I knew the true meaning of life and death. There was nothing that I could afford to take for granted. When I said my father was my hero, my warrior and my everything in life, indeed I meant every word from the bottom of my heart. Through his absence and abandonment he gave me the best gift any man can imagine, that is the power to forgive, and a divine power to have a heart full of unconditional love—not just understanding the meaning of the words, but living them, experiencing them, and feeling them from the core of my soul.

As for my hero mother,

Through her broken heart and disappointment—

I inherited the courage of the ultimate warrior.

Through her pain and suffering—I inherited residual inspiration.

Through her sweat, anxiousness and apprehension of being a single mother, and through the tears of her enduring the tasks of men's hardships struggling to raise her ten children with bare hands, I became a man who has seen the world through the eyes of a woman.

Dream before you go to sleep.
Don't wait until you fall asleep to dream.
Don't fall asleep while you are dreaming.